A SINGULAR MAN

In an age of millionaire candidates
and slick public relations techniques,
Senator Hubert Humphrey stands
almost unique on the American political scene.

Without large financial resources,
often all too blunt-spoken, this self-
made statesman has grown in stature
over the years until now, in the vital
election year of 1964, his remarkable
record and personality is of para-
mount importance for every American voter to understand.

Here is the first full-length portrait
of the man who soon may be a heartbeat away from the Presidency. . .

About the Author

Noted Washington writer, *MICHAEL AMRINE*, is the author of the recently published *THIS AWESOME CHALLENGE:* The Hundred Days of Lyndon Johnson.

Mr. Amrine also wrote *THE GREAT DECISION*, a study of the Truman decision to drop the A-Bomb, which was chosen by the American Library Association as one of the most notable books of 1959.

THIS
IS
HUMPHREY

By **MICHAEL AMRINE**

Foreword by
LYNDON B. JOHNSON

POPULAR LIBRARY · NEW YORK

POPULAR LIBRARY EDITION

Dedication:
For three pioneers:
Milton and Mabel Amrine, and Bryna Brickman . . .

Contents

Foreword

A Note From President Lyndon B. Johnson

Hubert Humphrey and I came to the Senate in the same year—1948—and have already seen a lot of history together.

In recommending to the Democratic National Convention a running mate for the 1964 campaign, I talked to people from all parts of the country. I had one overriding purpose—to find the man best qualified to assume the office of President if that should ever be necessary. Hubert Humphrey was that man.

His story is a very American story. I hope that reading it will give you a better understanding of this remarkable man.

Lyndon B. Johnson

PART I

The Towns

"I learned more about economics from one South Dakota dust storm than I did in all my years in college."

HUBERT H. HUMPHREY

CHAPTER I

Among the Few

One day in August 1935 a bright young man of twenty-four was sitting in the gallery of the United States Senate. This tourist had come by bus all the way from Huron, South Dakota, for a first look at the big and important city of Washington. He was nearly broke and was traveling on borrowed money. But he had badly needed a vacation from the drugstore where he and his father and brother had worked so desperately to keep afloat in the depression.

On this August day, as he sat in the gallery and watched the apparent aimlessness of a routine Senate afternoon, some expansive fantasies danced through Hubert Horatio Humphrey, Jr.'s head. He had very little formal education, though he had a great thirst for knowledge. Forced by the depression to leave the university, he had been trying to accustom himself to the idea of working as a pharmacist for the rest of his life.

He had taken a short course in pharmacy college—on borrowed money—and he loved meeting people in the drugstore, selling, wisecracking, and even arguing—about politics or anything else worth an argument. But the business was hard on the feet, and the depression had been hard on the stomach—and the nerves.

At this stage of his life, Hubert was a skinny young man who impressed everybody with his energy and vitality. Contemporaries said that something in his looks and his cocky expression reminded them of James Cagney, then at the top of his fame. (Today his own sons look at photographs of their father as a young man and say, "He looked like Pat Boone.")

From his seat in the visitors' gallery he saw through the desultory Senate ritual to the drama of democracy. Here was an exciting business; running a government looked a whole lot more exciting than running a drugstore.

That night he talked late with his uncle Harry, who had

made this Washington trip possible. Hubert had a standing invitation to stay at his home in suburban Cabin John, Maryland. Dr. Harry Humphrey had always been an inspiration to his nephew. An old Washingtonian and long-time government employee—he was chief of plant pathology for the Department of Agriculture—nevertheless he had not become disillusioned about the importance of good government. They said of him out West, "He went East to school and became a big success back there."

To Uncle Harry, his nephew had long "looked like a comer." He had often told Hubert that if he studied and worked hard he could go right on up "the ladder of life." That night in Cabin John Uncle Harry gave him both barrels: "Others have done it and you can do it too, with hard work, study, and the right principles."

That very night Hubert wrote home to Muriel Buck, his fiancée:

Dear Bucky,
    This trip has impressed one thing on my mind. . . . I need to do more reading, more writing and more thinking if I ever want to fulfill my dream of being someone in this world. Maybe I seem foolish to have such vain hopes and plans, but, Bucky, I can see how someday, if you and I just apply ourselves and make up our minds to work for bigger things, we can live here in Washington and probably be in government politics or service. I set my aim at Congress. Don't laugh at me. Maybe it does sound rather egotistical and beyond reason, but, Muriel, I do know others have succeeded.

It would be dramatic to say that from that moment young Hubert concentrated on going to Washington but it wouldn't be true. He would make several U-turns on this road. Still, it is remarkable that he went so fast.

Thirteen years after that letter to Bucky, Hubert H. Humphrey, Jr., was a United States senator.

Bucky listened to him talk about these ambitions for years, but it was not until 1948 that the nation was aware of his alliterative name.

That year, in Philadelphia, a Mayor Humphrey of Minneapolis leaped into national fame in one jump. As a delegate to the Democratic convention, Mayor Humphrey had

11

decided that the party platform must carry a civil rights plank, phrased in no uncertain terms. This would support the program for which Harry S. Truman had fought as President, and so it would support Truman, the nominee—but the convention was scared to death of the issue.

Most of the convention leaders were seeking a moderate measure, some evasion or compromise, which would promise the Negroes something but would not cause delegates from Southern states to walk out. Mayor Humphrey, who struck most people as an aggressive liberal, thought no such compromise was possible. And he thought, and said out loud, that it was a moral issue. Finally, in a dramatic speech that won over the convention, he cried out, "The time has arrived for the Democratic party to get out of the shadows of States' Rights and walk forthrightly in the bright sunshine of human rights."

On the roll call the amendment carried by 69 votes and no delegate was prouder than Dad Humphrey. Also a delegate to the convention, Mr. Humphrey, Sr., was privileged personally to announce that South Dakota would cast 8 votes for the amendment.

Years later a speaker introducing Senator Humphrey at a national convention of the NAACP would say that Humphrey had been "the John the Baptist of civil rights, a voice in the wilderness, before the rest of the country woke up. . . ." When Humphrey walked to the podium after that introduction he brought down the house by saying, "Well, I guess you all know what happened to John the Baptist."

Long after the Philadelphia convention many politicians still thought that perhaps Humphrey had cut off his own head, instead of waiting for someone to do it for him. It was said that (a) the Southern delegates could never support him for President and (b) no Democrat could hope to be the nominee of his party with Southern delegates solidly against him. In politics one can never be sure even of premises like these. But to some they are unquestioned facts of political life.

In 1948 it was thought that Hubert Humphrey with his civil rights fight had struck a mortal blow at the candidacy of President Harry S. Truman. Southern delegates dramatically walked out on the convention. Later the Dixiecrats ran their own presidential candidate, and that made 1948 hopeless, the politicians said—that closed out a hopeless year for Harry Truman because he already had to contend with the defection of Henry A. Wallace. The Progressive party did scoop up 1,000,000 votes that year—nearly all of them taken away from the Democrats, and hundreds of thousands of Southern votes taken away by Humphrey's civil rights plank.

To Humphrey and his supporters, however, it was a moral issue. They had carried forth the fight, even though Truman supporters themselves, at the convention, hung back on the platform plank that supported the President's program.

After the election, politicians said that without the civil rights plank Harry Truman could not have won his surprise victory, for he took away from Thomas E. Dewey certain Northern industrial states and cities, through the help of the Negro vote.

Humphrey went home in 1948 and ran for the Senate against Joseph Ball. He won by 250,000 votes, the first Democratic senator ever elected in Minnesota.

When he entered the Senate, to be sworn in by the stately old Republican, Senator Arthur Vandenberg, Humphrey sneaked a look at the gallery, to be sure that his family was sitting to the right of the clock.

As he was sworn in his father leaned forward, hoping to see everything, but his eyes misted over, and he dabbed them with a handkerchief as the great moment occurred. He prophesied a great future for his son. "He's going to be a great senator. . . . Maybe he is going to be something else too."

Maybe, said Washington observers, as they took notice that *Time* magazine put the young senator's face on their cover. By this time hundreds of thousands agreed with Uncle Harry: "Here is a comer." But as for going beyond the Senate, they said, *maybe*, but a very large maybe indeed.

The *Time* story said some people thought him "too cocky, too slick, too shallow, too ambitious . . . clever without being wise." But *Time* also said, as Humphrey was starting his Senate career, that he "proved himself an honest and able public servant, with quick, retentive mind, inexhaustible vigor and considerable political courage."

Today many Americans, particularly those who have listened to Humphrey—on the Senate floor or on television— have an impression of a man who has changed a good deal since his brash and cocky days as a new senator.

In Washington he has become one of the men who lead the Senate. His most partisan opponents there will freely grant that he has an extraordinary mind, a real and inventive

13

talent for government, and a skill in committee questioning and Senate debate that are unsurpassed in the present Senate.

Many conservative commentators—and senators—will concede that one part of Dad Humphrey's prophecy has come true—his son has indeed become a great senator. The closer one gets to him in the Senate the larger he seems, for he works hard on legislation. He is consulted, he leads, he introduces major bills and key amendments.

This reputation for maturity does not extend far beyond those who have heard and seen Humphrey in action. For all his skill as an orator, say his friends, the "real Humphrey" is not appreciated until one has had a chance to see him in action—in debate or campaigning, or in private and public discussion.

His voting record is impressive; it is considered "almost perfect" by many farm and labor groups—and by small businessmen.

Although literally hundreds of audiences have heard the mature Humphrey, he is still not very well known to the average newspaper reader "out where the voters live."

What would "the voters out there" see if they could come to Washington for a close-up of the senator? What would they see and hear as they approached that office in the new Senate Office Building where Senator Humphrey works ten, twelve, or fifteen hours a day?

Who is Humphrey? What is he like? What is the work that he is doing at such a furious pace? What does he really *say?*

Those who know him only slightly, will tell you, "He's a talker." But his staff say that he's a worker. And most of the time he enjoys his work.

No one who knows the Senate will deny that Humphrey is one of its hardest-working members—one of the steadiest workers in all Senate history, for that matter.

They have seen him arrive in his own 1955 Cadillac at the new Senate Office Building at nine or nine-thirty in the morning. A person trying to understand him saw him driving his Cadillac impressively through the traffic and was told, "He's got to have a big car, that's the small town in him." But once he was hurried to the White House in a car belonging to one of his assistants. The assistant drives a Volkswagen. "Those great White House gates looked down solemnly while our little beetle went through, and when we stopped,

14

the senator rolled out and unfolded to his height of six feet. It was an impressive sight."

Formerly addicted to flashy socks and bright pin stripes, the senator is now one of the best-dressed men in the capital. He has even adopted "the diplomatic homburg," but it doesn't seem to bother the home folks when he walks down Main Street. Humphrey has a way of saying hello to everybody, including the filling-station men, the section hands, and the "retired gentry" standing in front of the bank, whittling. His hello speaks louder than his homburg, it would seem.

Most of the staff members have been in the office since eight-thirty and will not leave until sometime after six—or seven—or eight.

The senator, who isn't going to leave the office until nine, ten, or midnight, arrives full of energy and—usually—good will. He sweeps in, walking fast, with his chin up, his eyes twinkling, and his coattails flying. It is a little like a magician's stage entrance—"I know you have been waiting for me—now let's see what I can do that will be interesting and amazing." The fact is that people's spirits usually lift when Humphrey enters a room.

Once inside his office, he works with incredible concentration, applying himself to paper work, telephone calls, staff conferences, and visitors. In spare moments he picks up the dictating machine and rattles off several messages. He may do this in the middle of a phone call, when the other party is away from the line. Generally he likes to have someone with him while he works—a secretary, an assistant, or someone working on another project.

As a Minnesota senator he is considered—even by hard-shell Twin Cities businessmen—to be a "man who gets things done for us." And by all the groups and associations interested in foreign policy he is considered one of the main voices in the Senate.

For many reasons, including his experience as a delegate to the United Nations, Humphrey is a particular point of contact for ambassadors from all over the world.

What are Humphrey's special interests? Who are his special friends, what groups are backing him?

He is interested in foreign affairs, and farm policy, and a fair deal for labor—and he is also interested in just about everything else under the sun: Israel, India, and Pakistan, civil defense, conservation, nuclear fallout, small business, "policy-making machinery," and countless other subjects.

As to what groups are backing him, if one means by that who is putting up large sums of money, the answer is, no one. And there are no groups of backers, no certain blocs, solid for Humphrey in the sense that there are for some other prominent political figures. From the start of his career Humphrey has taken care never to be controlled by any segment of society—he has never been labor's mayor or the farmers' senator. The farm and labor newspapers and journals all point to his record as the kind they like to see in Washington. But it is not a hard and fast connection.

Many agree with Eleanor Roosevelt who said he had a "spark of greatness." His close associates readily compare him to Franklin Roosevelt and often to Theodore Roosevelt—because of his energy, wit, and imagination.

Reinhold Niebuhr has said: "The senator knows more about foreign policy than any of the other 'front runners.'"

Max Lerner, the New York *Post* columnist, put it this way: "He has all along been one of the four major contenders among the Democrats . . . of the four, he is the one who strikes me as having, to the highest degree, the requisite qualities to make a good President, perhaps a great one. There is no one on the horizon who can . match him in his courage and his commitment to a liberal democracy, along with experience, ability, and a remarkable growth in maturity."

David Demarest Lloyd, writing in the *Reporter*, has said Humphrey is "personally bright, witty and charming . . . has the common touch . . . the party's most accomplished extemporaneous speaker. . . ." Rowland Evans, Jr., in the *Herald Tribune*, has said, "Humphrey's mind is endlessly flexible and absorbent, his knowledge of affairs is little short of staggering and his approach to the great unsolved political questions is on the whole original and imaginative." *Newsweek* says, "To the handful of top-ranking officials in Washington who make the real decisions of foreign policy, few voices in the U. S. Senate carry greater authority. . . . Humphrey is a member of the select inner group that really runs the Senate. . . ." Douglass Cater in the *Reporter* writes, "The extemporaneous Humphrey reveals awesome mental faculties. He shows a real mastery over the vast masses of technical information that enshroud most problems ranging from farm parity to foreign policy." These remarks indicate how far he has come since his first days in the Senate, when Rufus Jarman, in the *Saturday Evening Post*, summed him up as "brassy, bouncy and irrepressible."

You may hear that he talks too much or too glibly, that he is ambitious, a one-man band, and not a team player. Sometimes a person who is favorably impressed by his energy and originality will say with a shake of the head, "But he isn't an administrator, and that's what you need in the big white house."

From the Right you may hear that "he has slowed down some, but he is still liable to go off by his lonesome on a liberal tangent—a dangerous man to have in the presidency." From the liberals' left end you may hear that "he used to be a real fighting liberal, but he has settled down, a lot like all the rest of them."

From his admirers one hears that he is now a mature liberal, and from a liberal leader in Washington this writer heard: "I know what his convictions are, and I know he can usually win if he says he can. There are some other liberal senators who are fine at losing—but if a thing is possible with some power behind it, I know that Humphrey can get it through. If it can be done, he can do it."

His admirers never compare him to anyone mediocre. They say he is mostly like himself, a new flavor. They say he is an original, and not a copy of anyone else, living or dead. And they say he has learned and adapted and matured from experience. They also compare him to former American leaders.

Mainly, they say, he is spiritually akin to the Middle Western liberalism that produced the elder La Follette, George W. Norris, William Allen White, and many others.

They say he has the basic liberalism and human sympathy of Franklin D. Roosevelt. His political ideas and methods, and certain mercurial personal qualities, often remind people of F.D.R.—people who used to work very closely with the late President. Some consider that he even has some of F.D.R.'s faults: such as liking to give every caller the impression that he is not only listened to but agreed with, and having a certain lofty absentness when it comes to tedious details of organization.

But one observer considers that F.D.R. was far more calculating and conscious about everything he did. Humphrey, it is said, goes from one event to another and from one phase of thinking to another, without having a program in the back of his mind, as Roosevelt was said to have. Friends and foes of F.D.R. agreed that he loved to calculate and manipulate people. Humphrey has sudden inspirations about how to deal with some problem or conflicting groups of persons, but he does not spend weeks or months deciding precisely how everyone must be manipulated. One lifelong friend of Humphrey assured the writer: "Perhaps sometimes he should be, but he is never calculating."

Humphrey has been compared to the late Fiorello La-Guardia, the short, fiery, great mayor of New York City. Like LaGuardia, Humphrey as mayor loved to race around his city, and he took an interest in everything from the hospitals to the libraries to the zoning laws. It has taken him years to acquire some sense of dignity, and sometimes he appears to be somewhat of a clown. However, both men spent years of their lives studying government. There is nothing amateurish in their mayoralty records: they were professionals from the day they started. Their admirers say that only the greatest practitioners can be skillful enough to laugh a little at what they are doing. And millions of voters have felt comfortable with such people, because they are not stuffed shirts.

Some people think he is like William Jennings Bryan, and not merely on the grounds of oratory. Both had the same broad strain of prairie progressivism and reform. But there is a large difference in their ways of approaching the world's store of knowledge. Bryan, particularly in his latter days, at the time of the Scopes trial, was positively resistant to science and learning. He did not really understand the fiscal system and would not listen to those who did. Humphrey, perhaps more than any man in the Senate, has a positive enthusiasm for scholars, researchers, professors, and experts of all kinds —so long as they know what they are talking about. Sometimes Humphrey tells an audience, "I learned economics in the Dust Bowl during the depression," and this means a great deal to him. But Humphrey has also studied economics in universities and spent many hours with the subject in the Senate. He almost became an economist instead of a political scientist.

It is more than twenty years since a newspaperman in Minneapolis wrote some paragraphs about the young man he had just met—a professor of political science who was running for mayor.

He seems to be a wonderful and meteoric young man . . . bouncy and gay, built on springs, with a clear-cut fierce face and a pleasant young grin. He puts firecrackers under everything.

He is a strange combination of good sense, political erudition, imagination and enthusiasm. A lot of people are afraid of it, but I always vote, kerplunk, for enthusiasm. I mean *true* enthusiasm . . . there is a lot of bogus enthusiasm in political campaigners. . . .

Mr. Humphrey's enthusiasm is real and springs from true power.

Friends of Senator Humphrey believe this is an accurate description of the man today, and while they think his enthusiasm has been moderated by maturity, they think he still believes that Americans and the democratic system can find a way to overcome almost any obstacle.

"He doesn't have to describe the American dream, although he can do so in the best tradition of the Fourth of July," says one admirer. "He *is* the American dream, he has lived it."

If Hollywood were inventing an all-American candidate, said another, he would be like Humphrey of South Dakota and Minnesota: a big man (nearly six feet), with a good speaking voice, and a fair-sized family (three boys and a girl) . . . a small-town background (make it the Middle West) . . . but a good education (Phi Beta Kappa) . . . a good background near the soil . . . and an ability to get along with labor and with business. Naturally you give him an eloquence that can sway a crowd—or even stampede a convention. . . .

But this scenario doesn't quite explain how a pharmacist, rolling pills and dishing up bowls of chili in his dad's drugstore in Huron, South Dakota, became in two years a teacher of political science . . . and in another two years mayor of one of the dozen largest American cities.

All the standard ingredients still don't explain what in this all-American voice so intrigued Mr. Krushchev in the Kremlin. How did the star debater of Doland, South Dakota, population 500, come to be matching wits with the "tsar" of all the Russias?

19

Every biographer, like every psychologist, and like every mother who knows her children are not alike, must admit we are fundamentally ignorant of basic causes and effects in the mystery of personality.

There is more here than the all-American theme.

CHAPTER II

Doland—One Horse and Two Banks

Where did Hubert Humphrey come from? To many, he has represented Minnesota for enough years that he somehow seems to personify Minnesota.

But he was born and brought up in a neighboring state, and there is quite a difference between these neighbors. He was born May 27, 1911, in Wallace, South Dakota. His infancy and all the years through high school were spent in another small town. Certainly anyone who wants to understand Humphrey should understand Doland. And the first thing to know is that it is not in Minnesota but in South Dakota.

We should be careful about summing up so many square miles of territory. We should not picture all of one state as a green and pleasant land while we put its next-door neighbor into what the furriners used to call "the great American desert." Today, South Dakota has modern water conservation developments, has made the Badlands into a tourist attraction, and the Black Hills are considered real vacation country. In Mount Rushmore and in its own Passion Play, produced in an American Oberammergau, it shows an interest in art that springs from a popular vitality if not from a sophisticated literacy. But there is still more distance than you see on the map between Minneapolis, and its rivers and wheat and factories, and the territory around Spink and Beadle counties.

And let us remember that, in South Dakota, when Hubert was growing up, life for most people was a great deal different than it is today.

One day the senator was talking to the writer about old Doland friends—Alfred Paine and sons Dick and Art—and the Ewing boys, Ronald and Donald, right across the street —and Joe and Evelyn Wilkins, and their mother, Patience Wilkins. And the senator said, "Their house was real close— you just walked in one door and out the other when you

21

wanted to save steps . . . that's the kind of folks they were to us. . . ."

Humphrey's characterization not only tells a lot about such a family . . . but about such a town.

Doland claims a population of five hundred persons. You can drive around every block and past every house in Doland in ten minutes—and if you do, you will wonder where those five hundred people are. The answer is, of course, that the figure includes those on outlying farms.

"Downtown" Doland is one block long, and the street seems to be a block wide from curb to curb. But this fine wide street is not paved.

There is a tiny railroad station, in which most days there is no ticket agent. The station really exists only for a little business in connection with the shipment of grain or stock. The dominating features of the Doland sky line are the grain elevators. Just as steel dominates Pittsburgh, and lobster pots give the flavor of a Maine fishing village, so the existence of Doland is summarized in the elevators and in the grain bins just outside town. Old-timers will still call such a place "a settlement." This place exists because a few people settled here, and so far as the world is concerned, here are a few people who have the mission of growing, grading, storing, or shipping grain.

You reach Doland by extremely straight roads, as straight as taut wires, stretched across a map. In such flat prairie, when you are planning a road you don't have to allow for much variation in terrain. You don't have to fill in many low spots or cut through hills. In the real dry country you never even make a bend or a bridge for a river. You draw a line and build your road.

Driving north toward Doland, you turn right at a lonely intersection, miles from anywhere. Only one farmhouse is visible. However, you can see that other human beings have erected road signs. Men have been here. You flash straight as a string toward the east. The chances are, at midday, that you may meet one other car. In a few minutes, at a perfectly safe seventy miles an hour, you are there.

You pass a few houses and you come to the railroad tracks.

There is the grain elevator, and the black letters on aluminum that identify the Peavey Elevators of Doland, South Dakota. You also see the name on the Chicago & Northwestern Railroad's depot. Then there is the water tower (a survival tower for this settlement), and on the tower there are other black letters to tell the birds of the air that here is Doland.

But a visitor may still have the feeling that they left something out. Where are the five hundred people? There are only a couple of Tom Sawyers walking down the street—and in a moment they are on the horizon, and out of town. There is another human being, a man, just loading a sack of feed onto a pickup truck. Otherwise there is a dog, asleep—and a few dragonflies that are only pretending to be busy.

The town stretches two block from edge to edge one way, and four blocks the other way. The elevators loom, not really very large, like blocky soldiers against the sky. The twin ribbons of the railroad run in silver lines from you to the horizon—and die out, like music far away. At almost any place in town one can stand on a front porch and in the sharp and brilliant light scan with perfect clarity the open country. The horizon lies around the town, very close and very far, like a circle drawn by time in the dust of the earth. The horizon and the sky seem to say: Here you are, what will you do about it?

The big questions seem very close in this small place.

Doland people remember Hubert Humphrey and his brother Ralph as pretty typical Doland boys, who went barefoot in summer and wore long underwear in winter, like anybody else. Their home was comfortable and though they never had any spending money jingling in their pockets, perhaps they enjoyed a good deal more ice cream than most boys, because they could get it so easily at their dad's store. Legend has it that Hubert always kept his friends supplied with plenty of ice cream, whether his dad was aware of it or not. Others say this is not too likely a story, because it seems that whenever anyone thought of a businessman who might give something to somebody, they thought first of Dad Humphrey.

The boys had two younger sisters, Fern and Frances. Fern Gosch, whose husband was killed in the war, lives in Huron, South Dakota, and works in the family business. Mrs. Gosch has two children, Diane and Ralph. Frances married a Public Health surgeon, Dr. I. Ray Howard, from whom she is now divorced. She and a son and daughter live in Baltimore.

Like American kids everywhere, the Humphrey brothers worked and played and squabbled on occasion. Young Hubert had a paper route from the time he was seven until he was

23

sixteen. When he was ten he opened a checking account in one of Doland's two banks. "I used to write checks for twenty-five cents and drive the banker nuts."

While still under twelve he found time to practice the piano every day for an hour for about a year. He wasn't very fond of practicing and he says that he had no particular musical talent. But Dad Humphrey gave him a phonograph as a reward for his diligence. It disappeared one day when Ralph was building a homemade radio and a couple of tubes burned out. In this emergency Ralph traded the phonograph for a couple of tubes, thinking he would square it later with Hubert. Solomon himself couldn't find out now whether it ever was "squared." Hubert still claims that he never really got full payment for his phonograph. Ralph has some other items he would like to settle. Then as now they behaved like brothers.

Young Ralph's was the first radio in Doland. He and Hubert would snuggle under the covers at night wearing earphones, and when their mother poked her head in to see if they were asleep they would appear to be lost in dreamland. Actually they were shaking with silent giggles as they listened to broadcasts from stations as far away as Kansas City, St. Joe, Missouri, and Minneapolis. One day Dad took the boys on a fast trip to Minneapolis. That afternoon was the only time Hubert ever saw a city until he went to college at the age of eighteen.

Another pleasant feature of the Humphrey boys' young lives was the annual trips to Mother Humphrey's home neighborhood around Webster and Wallace, South Dakota, not far from the Minnesota line. Mrs. Humphrey's father, Grandfather Sannes, was a favorite with the Humphrey children, although he was most strict and preached a doctrine in which work was about the equal of life and life meant work.

Like many other independent-minded farmers, he never charged anything, always saved something, and repaired everything so long as it could be made to work. Grandfather Sannes always had a little machine shed for every single piece of his farm machinery. At his death he had an inventory of 7000 bushels of wheat.

Humphrey has always visited many relatives still living there, such as Uncles Torval and Tollef and Aunts Andrine (Mrs. Grimes) and Helen (Mrs. Hougen).

While still a boy, Hubert had a very serious time with pneumonia. This illness is almost forgotten now, but it was once a prime killer. In the flat Northern prairie country the old wives used to look up at the first really gray skies and announce that there was "a smell of snow in the air." They knew that blizzard time was pneumonia time.

Hubert ran a fantastically high fever—"he was like a stove to the touch." The whole town knew he was about gone. Dad Humphrey had heard of some new "miracle drugs" that might be used in such a case. He got on the phone to his wholesale druggist and finally got a small supply of a new and at that time radically experimental drug. It seemed as if there wasn't much to lose by trying it. Hubert is alive today only because his father and the family physician in Doland took a chance—and because the drugs were known and available to his father as a druggist. As it turned out, he was left with some lung damage, sometimes called "calcification." This has not slowed him down but it turned up surprisingly, as we shall see later, when he was examined by army physicians.

This illness was one of the great dramatic trials of the Humphrey family. Young Hubert knew that he had had a close call—the whole town told him so, while they welcomed him back to daily life.

Later he was touched by tragedy in the death from pneumonia of two of his friends. The Twiss family was (and is) close to the Humphreys, and one of their boys, Woodrow Twiss, died while a high school freshman; Hubert wrote a note for the newspaper in which he said that "the school was much grieved and shocked." Later the town and the high school in particular was shocked again when Edward Johnson (often mentioned as a Humphrey debating partner) died toward the end of the school term.

The school created prizes in memory of both boys. Inscribed on the award cup that honors Edward Johnson, the first name—from the graduation class of 1929—is Hubert H. Humphrey, Jr. On the cup now there are other names of which Doland is quite proud. There are the McNickle twins —both of those boys became generals.

Humphrey is still proud about this cup. He also thinks about the luck and fate—and drugs—that kept him alive when other boys like him did not make it. In the short time since Hubert and Ed Johnson and Woodrow Twiss were boys, medical science has advanced so that rarely does anyone in the United States die of pneumonia, and science could make this true in any country anywhere.

25

Once again a very large fact could be seen very plainly in a small place. And it is not irrelevant to many policy matters which reach the desks of senators in Washington, who may turn in ten minutes from the problems of America's towns to the problems of towns half a world away, towns in India or Africa where we would like to have healthy friends.

There is a startling dramatic scene in Noel Coward's motion picture *Cavalcade*, when the young lovers are seen on a ship, looking out over the moonlit water. They play out a scene in this romantic and idyllic background. Then they move away from the ship's rail. The camera lingers just a moment on the life preserver by which they have been standing and there is the name of the ship: S.S. *Titanic*.

There is something of the same kind of shiver hidden in the high school news notes of the Doland *Times-Record*; this is the chirpy column that "wrote up" the enthusiastic activities of Hubert Humphrey's high school class.

The name of this column, for reasons unknown, was "Hi-Sco-Pep." Hubert Humphrey remembers this strange assortment of syllables today as if he were still writing weekly notes for it. But all the news that is recorded there about Hubert and his friends, about football, basketball, debates, plays, and parties, now has a note of irony. These notes all speak of "the class of '29."

At the time they were written no one knew that the unsinkable bull market was soon to hit an iceberg. None of these classmates knew they would be marked for life because they were "children of the depression."

When the reader now turns the yellow pages of '26, '27, and '28, it is with a strange, fateful feeling that he reads that Edward Johnson and Myrtle Drayer and Hubert Humphrey did well in debate work. It is interesting to see that Edward Johnson, Lewis Terpstra, and Hubert Humphrey received letters in football. The same three were members of the basketball team in 1928. In oratory Hubert Humphrey and Lewis Terpstra were entered and strangely enough they won only second place. Later Humphrey obtained a place on the tournament team that won the district debate contest and went to the state tournament.

Humphrey and Terpstra and Dick Paine and Robert Fryer are recorded as having made a good showing in track.

One note ends like this: "The class of 1929 has always been at the top in scholarship. We're out to win!"

We don't know that our subject wrote these words. But it is not stretching things to say that two phrases of three words give a lot of the story of young Hubert Humphrey as he left Doland for a somewhat wider world—"Out to win! Class of '29!"

Humphrey was graduated in the spring of 1929 with very little idea of what was going to happen in Wall Street, in London, and in the entire economic network of the world, after that certain black Friday in October 1929. But today he, like many other veterans of the depression, feels the depression was a plague that tested all of them and the American way of life. To some young Americans, the depression is part of history, like the sinking of the *Titanic*. But to Humphrey, as to many who faced bitter years after the crash, this was a major experience—not just of the pocketbook but of the heart.

"Out to win" is a slogan that any associate of the senator might think of in connection with him. His office assistants, his immediate family, and his critics emphasize the fact that "he just loves to win." And it is a recurrent theme when old neighbors of the Humphrey family discuss Hubert as he was then. "That boy always gave it everything he had, no matter what he was doing. . . . I wouldn't say he was egotistical . . . but he seemed to take it naturally when he had the lead in the play or the operetta. . . . Couldn't sing, but he tried. . . . Pretty thin, but he played football. . . ."

Young Hubert was always interested in athletics, particularly competitive sports, and to the present day he remains passionately interested in all kinds of games. He is an enthusiastic fan at spectator sports, and friends say the way he watches them can scarcely be called "passive participation."

He pursues no particular sport and no regular program of exercise, but he still radiates the energy and vitality of an athlete. All descriptions of him and his early-day photographs agree that, in the words of one Doland woman, "he wasn't slender, he was skinny." He clearly regrets that he could not have been a football star but his physique was better adapted to track. There is a note in the "Hi-Sco-Pep" column about the high school track team that went over to Aberdeen one Saturday. A couple of the boys won first and second in their fields, but there is also this whistling-in-the-dark item:

Our distance men made a very good showing, they are Hubert Humphrey, Alvin Hahn and Emery Bell. Hubert placed fifth in the half-mile run. These men are all beginners and the ability they have will be sure to develop.

It may seem surprising that one boy could go out for track, baseball, basketball, and football and meanwhile be a star of the debating team. But in a high school as small as Doland's —there were less than a score in the senior class—the students had to take a lot of different parts if they hoped to have any kind of school activities. People who knew him in Doland, like those who have known him elsewhere, say that Hubert enjoyed practically all school activities and always looked on a new activity as a challenge.

However, it gradually became clear that his deepest interests were in scholarship, debating, and politics. Yes, even when he was in high school he was interested in politics. An unsigned note in the *Times-Record* gives a clue to the spirit of the Doland debating team in defeat. The team in April 1928 included Hubert, his buddy Julian Hartt, and another classmate, Earl Hanson. They went over to Vermillion for the state tournament after they had won their district championship. Hubert's team had the affirmative side of a question concerning the McNary-Haugen farm relief proposals. They lost, "eliminated by the team from Madison." Whoever wrote the note for the Doland paper said further, "The strength of the Madison squad is indicated by the fact that Madison had but recently defeated Watertown, Aberdeen and Sioux Falls. Holding the Madison speakers to a two to one decision is evidence of the Doland boys' ability. Doland high school looks to the new year with full expectations of maintaining, if not surpassing, the past enviable record in debate. This record includes three district championships during the past five years." We shall run across this never-say-die spirit in some other debates—and some other defeats —years later.

Life in Doland High School was quite competitive, scholastically as well as athletically—there were many prizes, awards, and plaques. Intellectual activities were related directly to the life around them. When the teen-agers debated things like the McNary-Haugen farm bill they were pursuing, perhaps more immaturely but no doubt in a more orderly way, the same arguments their fathers were pursuing on the street corners of Doland—particularly in the drugstore.

In grade school and high school Hubert was also active in school theatricals, and had the lead in the senior play, *Captain Applejack*. As Ambrose Applejack he portrayed "as mild a man as ever scuttled a cup of coffee" who "changed into a bold, bad buccaneer of the Spanish main, cussing his crew, calling for his grog, dragging forth a comely wench, sticking his knife into a treacherous dog, and finally putting down a mutiny by cutting cards with its leader."

He was considered good-looking and a good dancer. But in those days high school boys and girls were thought "too young" for real dates.

When the high school year came to an end the four students who had placed highest in the four years of scholarship were three girls and one boy. The valedictorian was Hubert Humphrey and at the graduation ceremony he "spoke the farewells of the class" in a "sincere and convincing manner."

Everyone connected with Hubert Humphrey knows that his late father was and in fact remains a major influence in his life. Even today he will speak of his father and his views as a living and present force in his judgment of affairs.

Dad Humphrey was a big man, jolly and outgoing, who loved all kinds of people. He was fond of children and dogs and horses, and in general interested in all human motives and all forms in which life expresses itself. When he laughed, he would shake all over. People remember that he shook the furniture when he was really amused. He had a tremendous curiosity, was a great reader of newspapers and books, and was always ready for a friendly or perhaps a heated discussion. An earnest and keen student of politics, he developed firm convictions and had a cogent way of putting his facts and his conclusions together. He was not bitter on many subjects but he loved a lively dispute.

Several South Dakotans describe Dad Humphrey as "the greatest talker I ever knew," a description which would amuse many Washingtonians who know his son. Some reporters, who refer to Congress as the "cave of the winds," feel that Dad Humphrey's son is the greatest talker *they* ever knew. It must have been like two Niagara Falls to hear them together. People in Doland say that Hubert didn't learn debating at school—he *taught* it. There was always a debate at the dinner table at the Humphreys'.

Dad Humphrey read as voluminously as he spoke. He read and taught his sons to read the papers and messages of the Presidents. They read Ben Franklin, Tom Paine, and Thomas Jefferson. They also read volume after volume of Elbert Hubbard, and they liked Edgar Guest, but they found more to chew on in *Bryce's American Commonwealth*. Their particular favorites were books about Woodrow Wilson. Over and over again they read the life of Wilson written by Joseph Tumulty, his secretary, and *The Intimate Papers of Colonel House*, the shadowy figure who was to Wilson what Harry Hopkins was to President Franklin Roosevelt. Ralph and Hubert used to give Dad Humphrey the latest book about Woodrow Wilson for Christmas and they would take turns reading aloud on winter nights.

They still talk in Doland about the great fight those days over the question of selling the municipally owned power and light company. In those days many villages and cities built their own light companies. After World War I they were greatly astonished to find that some people had learned to call this "socialism." No one then or later ever thought of Dad Humphrey as a socialist, but he was passionately in favor of Doland's owning its own utility.

A large private firm proposed to buy the Doland power and light company from the town. The company promised that service would be cheaper, greatly improved, and in addition a new and superior system of street lighting would be installed throughout the length and breadth of Doland.

This was a subject of many town meetings. Dad Humphrey was a central figure among those who thought not only that this would be a poor idea as a business proposition but that it was a sin and a shame to take the town's own facility, bought and paid for by the community, and turn it over to a soulless corporation. Doland people can still remember that Dad Humphrey, usually a jovial wisecracker, a promoter, and an original and enterprising businessman, could turn into a flaming advocate and defender of what he believed was right. He could be a great castigator of the "forces of evil," and in the biblical phrases that come easily to the tongue in South Dakota he would "smite the enemy hip and thigh" when he went into battle.

Hubert recalls that as a boy of twelve he heard the great

rumble of thunder from this grown-up battle over the power plant. When the city council met and his father went as a citizen to fight and make speeches, young Hubert would be permitted to go along and sit in the hall or perhaps by an outside window. Half asleep in the balmy summer air, he would crouch there far into the night. As the argument grew heated he would wake up to see his father as a champion of the forces of good doing battle with the forces of evil.

In Doland thirty-five years later one citizen said, "We all had affection for the Humphrey family and we greatly respected Dad Humphrey—and I'll say that although I could also find him very stubborn and I certainly disagreed with him sometimes." The author asked if this citizen had been on the other side from Mr. Humphrey in the great fight over the power plant. Back came an instant and decisive answer: "I certainly was against Dad Humphrey, and I was right."

And Dad's son, the senator, said in 1959, "Dad fought them to a standstill and he lost, but he was right, and the power company did come in and take over the plant, and they never did make good on their promises and the fancy street lights are not there to this day."

Thus Hubert Humphrey learned and remembered views about public power issues long before he sat in the Senate and heard of Hell's Canyon and Dixon and Yates.

The dramatic power plant fight was not the prime event of the Humphrey family story in those days.

A fundamental part of Dad Humphrey's political attitudes was the belief (shared by many political leaders in the Middle West) that the banking system was useful to financiers but was often parasitic and actually harmful to the productive economy of the country. As Doland put it, Dad Humphrey was afraid of banks.

In general he hated and feared bankers. He felt that bankers and their friends in government worked out arrangements to their advantage, charging high interest rates that made them fat but choked off the farmer and the small businessman.

The social historian might trace some of the ideas of Humphrey, Sr., and others like him to the agrarian reformers of the latter part of the nineteenth century. Spiritually he was a descendant of the Populists. His generation had also been exposed to Henry George's single-tax theories and his thesis that all interest was "unearned increment" and therefore

31

sinister. William Jennings Bryan, from the neighboring state of Nebraska, had campaigned three times for the presidency with promises to revamp the country's currency and its financial system. One might say that, geographically and spiritually, Bryan and Dad Humphrey had grown up not too far apart.

In any case Dad Humphrey had an "interest in civic affairs"—what was called in the thirties "a social conscience." In his own way of life, as a hard-working and enterprising small businessman, he had seen some of the same things that the miners saw in West Virginia and the Okies in Oklahoma. The American system did not always work perfectly, and something more than individual pluck and luck might be needed to make it work better. To Dad Humphrey this seemed self-evident.

He conceived of community resources and government as mechanisms to be used to help out citizens when through circumstances not of their own making they needed help. As a druggist selling veterinary supplies, he also developed a keen sense of the waste involved when a man lacked proper medicine to cure or prevent costly losses. It offended the pioneer's sense of saving precious material if human effort or valuable livestock were lost because cash or credit was not available for trustworthy people at the right time. Waste is a sin—that's a statement ministers don't even have to preach in Doland.

There was another major theme in Humphrey, Sr.'s thinking. He developed a keen interest in international affairs and came to think of Woodrow Wilson as one of America's greatest Presidents. It was a personal shock to Dad Humphrey when the country rejected the League of Nations. It was a personal sorrow that Wilson had lived out his declining years seeing his great dreams come to nothing. Then in the twenties and thirties, as on the home front he saw the economic system of the world going smash, he saw the world once again preparing for the insanity of a great war. He felt, as have many scholars of history, that the Nazis might never have come to power if we and the rest of the world had backed the League of Nations.

All these things he talked over as naturally as breathing. He went over the day's news with his growing sons, sounding out ideas, testing their facts and logic. Constantly he talked about the president of Princeton University, and later of the United States, the martyred political scientist who had dreamed of a parliament of man.

And time and again Dad Humphrey harked back to the thesis that in a country that was basically rich men by their own labor should be able to make a decent living. Therefore America should have a financial system—beyond mere profit and percentages on a banker's statement—that would give men a feeling of pride and dignity. Man should be able to pour his energy and his wits into something of his own that would take care of his own. Dad Humphrey was never a socialist, he was always a businessman, and he loved the sign on the drugstore that told the world this enterprise was "Humphrey's." The father wanted the very opposite of centralized control from far away: he wanted all the Humphreys of the country—on the farm, in labor, or in small business—to be able to stand up proudly and independently. H. H. Humphrey, Sr., may not have had a complete and uncontradictory dream of a system—but in the person of Dad Humphrey it was an attractive philosophy. His ideas rested foursquare upon his politics, his religion, his business, and his own personality and character. He was learning all his life, trying hard to understand the world and to get ahead in it.

And when he thought something was good he went to work to sell it, whether it was a new radio or a new political theory.

His sons are chips off the old block, but one leans toward business and the other toward politics.

CHAPTER III

Family Business

In the Doland years the whole family worked together in Humphrey's Drugstore. Hubert sold hog vaccine and radios and Eskimo pies and large economy-size bottles of aspirin, cascara, rubbing alcohol, and a thousand other items. One of his father's own preparations, called "Humphrey's chest oil," achieved a local reputation as being marvelous for chest colds.

Hubert and Ralph learned at a tender age to distinguish between the "wets" and the "drys." Such standard drugstore items as castor oil, cascara, essence of wintergreen, et cetera, were called wets. Others, like sodium bicarbonate or sulphur or tannic acid, were known as drys.

At the same time they heard Dad Humphrey's criticisms of Calvin Coolidge and Herbert Hoover. If the tape recorder had only been invented Humphrey's would certainly have sold it and perhaps we should have a recording of how they talked in the drugstore—one moment about oil of wintergreen, the next about the President.

How did it happen that Humphrey, Sr.—"a businessman" —was such a critic of things as they are? This is one answer he used to give: "I heard William Jennings Bryan and became a Democrat."

What kind of a businessman was Dad Humphrey? A quick look at the record indicates that he wasn't too successful. Several times he was on the edge of bankruptcy. But a quick look doesn't tell the whole story. He was operating in the state of South Dakota in a period of war and drought and depression. His story is matched by thousands of small businessmen who found it difficult and sometimes impossible to keep their doors open. Considering the total record, one might conclude that Dad Humphrey was an exceptional businessman, for he did keep the store and the Humphrey business name alive through thick and thin. He lived to see Humphrey's become a thriving business.

Dad Humphrey started business in Wallace, South Dakota, and lived, as many businessmen did in those days, in an apartment over the store. It is hard for those who have known Hubert Humphrey as a politician for over twenty years to realize that for the first twenty-five years of his life he was nearly always in the family drugstore or close to it. He was born over it, he was brought up as a child in it, he worked in it at such an early age that his father had a special ramp built for him so that he could walk up behind the counter and serve the customers without having to stand on tiptoe. Through his high school days he worked constantly in the drugstore. A couple of times he had to be called home from college to help his father keep the store going. Later he and his brother slept in the drugstore basement. He courted his wife in the drugstore. He supported himself at college by working in a couple of drugstores. To this day he still thinks of life in the store as a pleasant way to live.

Dad Humphrey loved his drugstore and, like many American businessmen, was proud to be in business for himself. He went through many vicissitudes. Once his store was burned out and he was just about broke. Once he opened a store that was really about fifteen square feet in the middle of another man's grocery store. In Doland he nearly went completely bankrupt. But he was always enterprising, always trying something new.

No one says that he had any particular drive to make money, but it seems clear that he just loved meeting people in the store and being in the center of things. He was determined to make a living for his family out of his own business and not by working for another man. He was obviously something of a supersalesman. So far as his opportunities permitted he was what would be known on Madison Avenue as "a terrific promotion man." He firmly believed that when a man walks into a store he likes to be able to call the owner by name and that it helps identify a store or restaurant if it is called Joe's or Brown's or Humphrey's. So he told his sons always to remember people's names—and to see that people remembered theirs. At times he would try to build up the lunch counter side of the business. Once he had tables and booths for fifty people. In the depths of the depression Humphrey's was serving a solid meal, including dessert, for twenty-nine cents. "Regardless of what the main dish or the dessert was, the whole thing was always sold for twenty-nine cents," says Senator Humphrey today.

In the twenties and thirties drugstores began to undergo the change that eventually transformed them into a species of department store. But in Dad Humphrey's time it was quite a novelty for South Dakotans to walk into the drugstore and find radios and phonographs on sale. Hubert used to install radio aerials, first as a helper and later on his own. He enjoyed scampering like a monkey on somebody's roof in his tennis shoes to stretch the copper wire. In those days you had to have a long aerial before you could bring in the voice of Calvin Coolidge or Al Smith, to whom the new invention was known as "the raddio."

One year Dad Humphrey had what proved to be a home run of an idea. He decided to go in heavily for selling medicines, serums, vaccines, and other preparations in the veterinarian line. Here he had hit on something that was extremely useful to the farmers of the community. The customers came into the drugstore to get their sheep dip or their dehorners, and to get advice on what to do with animals suffering from "croup" or "the heaves." And once there was a threatened epidemic of anthrax, a most contagious and sinister disease of cattle. Humphrey's, far ahead of other stores in the region, helped avert a catastrophe—and it also made money.

Dad and the Humphrey boys read every bit of literature on how to treat animals that the veterinarian houses published. They often arranged Saturday afternoon demonstrations of some new item. And they were never loath to try out something new, in the process assisting at the birth of a calf or getting rid of worms in a dog. So it happened that Hubert had vaccinated hundreds of hogs before he graduated from high school. There is no question that this work gave him an earthy knowledge of the farm and of farmers. They still laugh, over the border in Minnesota, about the time when Hubert was debating with an opponent on some farm issue and made the boast, "I'll bet you I've vaccinated more hogs than any man in this audience." He was a little perplexed when several people tittered and burst into giggles and finally into an uproar. The town veterinarian was sitting in the front row and the young orator had just overreached himself somewhat—he was hogging too much credit, you might say.

Meeting people in his store or on their land, Dad Humphrey was a natural to figure in practical politics as well as in discussion of great issues and great men. The trouble was that in Doland it was not too practical for a Democrat to be interested in practical politics. In the twenties there were only three other Democrats in town. Once he ran for the legislature but was defeated. Later he was elected mayor of Doland. The mayoralty, of course, was not a political job —in fact it wasn't much of any kind of job. But his election shows that, in spite of being a town rebel in a way, he was a very popular citizen. (After the family had moved to Huron he ran again for the legislature and made it by a whacking majority.)

Throughout boyhood days Hubert had the nickname of "Pinky" or "Pink." "This had nothing to do with my political complexion, thank goodness," the senator says today. The name disappeared sometime after he went to Minneapolis. No one, including the senator, knows exactly how it originated. Some say that he sunburned quite easily. In any case it is a common nickname in the West. He turns warmly toward anyone who greets him as Pinky, for he knows it will be someone who has known him many years.

In 1952 all of Doland turned out to honor Pinky. It was the seventieth anniversary of the town on October 9, and it was also a homecoming for Spink County's favorite son. His speech to his Doland "family" may be of particular interest.

In part he said, "I remember such Doland families as the Sherwoods, the Labrie family, the Garthwaites, the Shults, the Riskes, and many others.

"I was privileged to grow up in a town that had the finest of characters, the finest of people, people who lived in a small town but had a great perspective and a vision, people that understood what was going on in the world and understood something about human relationships." The senator spoke quite earnestly to his friends and this speech, far away from Washington, to the people who had known him best, perhaps gives direct clues to some of his main motivations.

He said, "[I] promised my mother that I would not mention politics in my speech today. She takes a dim view of some of my political activities." The main part of his speech, however, was about world affairs and he sounded a theme that Dad Humphrey would have been most proud to hear.

"The faults and problems of today are not due to any one man or political party or any one set of circumstances.

"World War I was the beginning of a great change on the face of this earth.

"One of the greatest men America has ever produced was Woodrow Wilson. He challenged America to grow up. He told the parents at the close of World War I that unless they did something, their sons and daughters would be the cannon fodder, would be the soldiers, would be the wounded and maimed of another generation.

"But we closed our eyes; we closed our ears; we closed our minds—and lived in a fool's paradise.

"When we rejected his League of Nations, when we set aside our opportunity to be our brother's keeper, when we refused to take on world leadership, during that fool's paradise, we got a Hitler, a Mussolini, the military leaders of Japan, the Bolshevism and Stalinism of Russia.

"Americans closed their eyes to the festering sore that was to be found in this world, a malignant growth of totalitarian dictatorial brutality.

"I say this because there are parents in the audience with their children. Unless you make this greater determination to bind up the wounds following World War II—as should have been done after World War I—you can just kiss these boys and girls good-by."

He also touched on his favorite theme—working for peace by sharing America's wealth with the world—and concluded with this peroration: "What worries me today is that people were perfectly willing to spend $450,000,000,000 to kill, to win a war; and yet I hear people complaining about spending a few billion dollars to try to win a peace.

"Our government has been trying to create a world order and a world situation in which we could have the opportunity to create conditions conducive to peace. . . . Our government has been trying to prevent mankind from being engulfed by a horrible, vicious philosophy.

"All over the world people are suffering. And the longer they suffer, the more bitter they become. The more bitter they become, the more jealous they become of us, the greater is their desire to destroy us.

"The best defense of this nation is to share, to be a share giver. The best kind of defense for America is not that of rattling the saber but that of opening the heart.

"If any mother or father were to ask me today, 'What can I do to make sure there will be a future for my children?' I would say: Be of good heart, good spirit and compassion and generosity. Be willing to give your time or your

38

service or your goods. Be willing to sacrifice and to share —and quit complaining."

He said that "we need people just as devoted to democratic and Christian principles as the Communists are to the sinister principles they embrace."

In defending the European aid program he said, "I was taught in church that it was right to feed the starving; it is right to heal the sick; it is right to lead the blind; and it is right to teach the illiterate. This is what the Americans have been doing with their dollars abroad."

This theme, in which America's riches, her desire for peace, and the moral imperative are woven together, is echoed in many speeches over the years. His associates say that his churchgoing and his biblical references are very far from being put on for political purposes. One friend from college days said recently that it always somewhat surprised him "that a liberal intellectual thinker like Hubert would get up on a Sunday morning and go off to church, but he seemed to get a great deal out of it." This occasions no surprise in Spink County.

Around Doland it was taken for granted that Pinky Humphrey would be religious. He was baptized as a Lutheran in Wallace, South Dakota, and later attended Methodist church, where his father was a leader. In Washington he attends the Chevy Chase Methodist Church.

A religious outlook is taken for granted out there, where people say without any self-consciousness, "She was a good Christian woman." They use the word "Christian" as an ordinary adjective. It means respectable and charitable, and can be and sometimes is applied to people who technically aren't Christians. There was one Jewish family in Doland. One might wonder how they got there, but they were part of what a man would unconsciously call "a Christian community." You see, "It wouldn't be Christian not to invite them over."

It is sometimes said, "It is too bad that Pinky didn't become a minister. What a mighty force he would have been in the Church!"

The story of the ultimate decline of the Doland drugstore goes back to the days after World War I when the big wheat market and the big inflation had burst and the Middle West went through one economic shock after another. For most people in the United States, the depression really arrived with a bang in October 1929. But all through the central West there was a great wave of bank failures in the early twenties. As Hubert says now, "Many bankers went to prison and many committed suicide. It was a tragic era." The first cruel blow hit Dad Humphrey in 1927.

At that time the drugstore seemed to have a bright future. The Humphreys lived in a house about as nice as any in town. It is a big blocky white frame house with a big basement, a big upstairs, two bathrooms, and a double garage. Even today Senator Humphrey recalls proudly that it also had a concrete driveway. That was a real distinction in a town where there were very few sidewalks. A special feature was their own gasoline pump. Mrs. Humphrey's pride was the hardwood floors. The whole family enjoyed the fine shade trees and the large peach and cherry orchard.

One day, after many rumors, the Security State Bank closed. Dad Humphrey was hit hard; he was practically at the end of his rope. But he was able to borrow money and get additional credit, and he moved what assets he had over to the other bank in Doland. Yes, they had two banks there. It seems strange now, but many such tiny towns used to have two or three banks and the countryside really could not support them. This, as it turned out, was the cruel case in Doland. Within thirty days the second bank, the State Bank of Doland, failed, and Dad Humphrey was just about as broke as he could be.

Hubert was sixteen years old at the time, just finding himself as a debater in high school. He remembers that he came home from school and as he rounded the corner he saw his mother standing under a tree in front of the house crying. His father was talking to two men whom Hubert did not know.

His mother, weeping as though her heart would break, told him that Dad had had to sell the house. They got six thousand dollars for it, an enormous price for those days. When the men had gone Dad Humphrey also broke down and wept.

"To us this had been much more than just a house, this was our wonderful home and our whole world," says Hubert. The Humphrey family had to move to a much smaller house and though it was clean and comfortable it was part of a shattering experience.

This was the first time Hubert ever saw his father weep.

He believes his mother was really heartbroken, and it was frightening to the children to see their father redouble his efforts to make the drugstore a going concern. Eventually, like many other neighborly businessmen of the twenties and thirties, he just threw away account books which showed that he had thousands of dollars "coming to him." He knew it wasn't coming, so it was no use keeping the books. What would happen to them if the drugstore crashed like the banks? What did it mean, that a part of Doland "crashed"? How could this happen?

Millions of adults as well as children would soon be asking these questions and those days are still remembered by many people. And particularly by our subject. Yet when he speaks of Doland his face always lights up.

CHAPTER IV

Huron's Leading Druggist

In the fall of 1929 Hubert went off to the University of Minnesota and Ralph stayed home to help in the drugstore. Ralph wanted to study law, but there wasn't enough money to send both boys to school at once, so he and Hubert took turns going to a university. Always more interested in business than Hubert, Ralph became the manager of the Humphrey drugstore.

Uncle Harry Humphrey sent Hubert fifty dollars and he got a job that would provide board and room in return for such housekeeping duties as making beds, firing the furnace, helping out in the kitchen, and so on. He also worked in Swoboda's Drugstore. There was never a time when he had money in the bank to guarantee the next semester.

In the middle of his sophomore year Dad Humphrey called him long distance and said the family was going to have to leave Doland and try their fortune in the larger town of Huron, fifty miles away. He had already located the building where he thought he could put in a more modern drugstore. He said, "At least they won't be able to say of me that I went broke in a one-horse town." Dad Humphrey did not mean this in a derogatory way. He had lived in and loved Doland for seventeen years. But it was more serious to go broke in Doland than to try again and perhaps go broke somewhere else. There simply wasn't anything else for him, as a druggist, to do in Doland. If he went broke in Huron, or in some other larger town, he might at least be able to get a salaried job as a pharmacist in someone else's store.

Actually no one really knew what would happen if the Humphreys wound up completely stony broke, but they were very close to it in this year 1931. Millions of other Americans were in the same fix.

Dad Humphrey went over to Minneapolis to visit with Hubert on the Huron move. They held a brief excited conference over the counter at Swoboda's. The rules were strict and the job was valuable, so Hubert couldn't possibly take a couple of hours off. After work they held a soul-searching conference at the Radisson Hotel. Dad Humphrey said they just had to move "to protect the little we still have."

To the father, the whole question was "whether we can get credit to carry us a little while. We have to get five thousand dollars in credit. We just have to have it." He said, "I need your help. Otherwise I believe I've got to get out of business."

Dad and Hubert went to a wholesale drug house in Minneapolis to see a partner in the firm named Henry Doerr (the firm is now merged with McKesson & Robbins). Henry Doerr saw their situation and took a chance on a family and a drugstore that he had known for many years. He gave them five thousand dollars' worth of merchandise on credit in the next few weeks, and that enabled the Humphreys to open their store. The night before they opened Dad Humphrey reiterated, "Boys, we've got to make this go, this is our last chance." But with the Humphrey promotional arts they beat the drums for a "gala opening." And on that day they gave each lady visitor a single, beautiful rose.

Dad Humphrey had hated to take Hubert out of school and he tried to ease the leave-taking as much as he could. He gave him a small amount of cash and urged him to go to Minneapolis and spend it foolishly! And for that last two weeks he let Hubert take the Model A Ford so he could tear around town and have a good time, "and go out in a blaze of glory."

Hubert dreamed of getting back to college but he realistically thought this would be the last he would ever see of the campus he had learned to love. In the back of his mind was the thought that perhaps at some time he might be able to go away to pharmacy school and get to be a pharmacist at least. Both his parents, and later his friends the Dewey Van Dykes, and of course others, were always stressing the necessity of an education if one wanted to make the most of one's talents and learn about the great world that existed outside of Beadle County.

Dewey and Hazel Van Dyke were like a second mother and father to Hubert, and even to this day the senator listens closely to Dewey and values his counsel. He thinks of Van Dyke as a man who knows quite a bit about the world and just about everything about Humphrey.

Dewey and Hubert were active in scouting together and often went on camping trips, and Hazel and Muriel also enjoyed the outdoors and the company of a couple of dozen "young Indians."

Before his marriage, and even to some extent afterward, young Hubert gravitated to the Van Dykes and the relaxation and philosophical conversation around their kitchen table. The Humphrey family was a close-knit one, and the advice Dad Humphrey gave his son was respected and his son attempts to apply it to current life today. At the same time the Humphrey family life was centered on the drugstore, and there seems to have been some special understanding, or perhaps a more easygoing approach to life, that attracted young Hubert to the Van Dykes. He needed a place where he could really talk without the pressure of the store coming in sooner or later.

It is hard to put into words the kind of inspiration provided by persons with the Van Dyke temperament. But there is something about them—this is often the case with teachers in small Midwestern towns—which recognizes talent and gives confidence to their protégés. Today the senator has his wife and family and many admirers to give him confidence, but it would seem that in his youth he needed an extra portion of insight and inspiration, and the Van Dykes helped him.

Dewey Van Dyke was not a teacher, and he had retired from the job he held for years in the Huron post office. But he still had an eye for talent, and when the senator recently visited his home town Dewey was insistent that Humphrey talk to a young boy whom Dewey was trying to persuade to go to college to study political science. The meeting was arranged in the crowded schedule, and it was plain to see that the Van Dykes thought that once again they had located a young man with the authentic spark. A member of the senator's party said, "As long as America continues to produce people like the Van Dykes the American dream will be a faith strong enough to move mountains."

The Humphrey drugstore in Huron opened in 1931 at the bottom of the depression. There were already five other drugstores in Huron and it is putting it mildly to say that these stores and other businesses did not welcome the family who had fled from Doland.

Dad Humphrey told his sons that they would have to redouble their hard work, their salesmanship, and their pro-

44

motional ideas. On all the main roads leading into Huron they put up signs advertising Humphrey's drugstore.

In time Dad Humphrey succeeded in getting the Walgreen agency. He and his sons had often discussed what the rise of big chains had done to the independent small businessman. They felt it was better for the small businessman and no doubt for the community if he ran his own place not as a manager but as an owner. Yet there were advantages to buying in quantity as a Walgreen's agent.

They went in for veterinarian products more heavily than ever.

Over their drugstore sign they hung another one that a farm products company (Anchor Serum) gave them. This was nothing but a representation of a pig, life size and very homely. Years later when the store front was modernized the boys thought they were a little too sophisticated to hang out the old pig again. But in the first two or three weeks so many customers objected that they put the old pig back up and there it remains to this day. The story of the sign that wouldn't stay down is told and retold in Huron.

In a town the size of Huron there may be two or three men's clothing stores, five or six drugstores. One of each is likely to be known as "the farmers' store" or "that country place." One clothing store will be a little more likely to have sheepskin jackets and gum boots, and the clerks will know their way around the farm—and they themselves will work unabashedly in shirt sleeves. (Of course anyone—except maybe a banker—will work in his shirt sleeves on a hot day —but the country store people are just a little more folksy.) Such a clothing store is less likely to have wall-to-wall carpeting, soft lighting, and the genteel manner that might discourage the farmer who comes into town on Saturday afternoon, maybe with a little manure on his boots.

So far as drugstores are concerned, there is no question in Huron that Humphrey's was the farmers' drugstore. This was where farmers felt at home, where they learned things, too, about veterinarian products, which could be a matter of life or death for the livestock. No doubt when the farmers saw Humphrey's shiny new glass store front they wanted to be reassured by the old pig sign that this was still their store. Hubert learned something when he hung the pig back over the doorway of "Huron's Leading Druggist." The ghost of the sign may still be seen on a door in the new Senate Office Building.

In the winter of 1932-33 (as Franklin D. Roosevelt studied the affairs of government between his election and his inauguration) Dad Humphrey was able to scrape together two hundred dollars to send Hubert to a pharmacy college in Denver, Colorado.

Hubert had been helping his father and he was officially listed as an apprentice, but he would have to go to an accredited pharmacy college before taking the state board examinations that would make him a registered pharmacist.

So he went to Denver to a school that started at 7:30 A.M. and finished at 10:00 P.M., with classes on Saturday until two-thirty in the afternoon. "We had to do our studying and work out our chemistry problems and so forth after those hours and on weekends."

Today the senator says, "That was a wonderful school and they had a wonderful head of it who was very good to me personally. I never learned so much before or since in my life. I was about twenty-one or twenty-two and I drank it in and was either being lectured or studying, night and day."

He started in January and finished in May of 1933. He says that he has always enjoyed a scientific subject and he never missed a chemistry problem. "There is something about science that is so satisfying. When you know it in science you really know it, and there isn't anything doubtful or indecisive about it."

But he adds that Denver was "real cram learning." He says, "that is about the only way I have ever learned anything— I have never had the opportunity to take my time and learn things in a leisurely and reflective way."

Back home, Hubert enjoyed being a young man about town in Huron.

Dad Humphrey had been appearing from time to time on the radio, broadcasting news and reading poetry and otherwise furnishing the material for a program advertising Humphrey's drugstore. The elder Humphrey had also gotten to teaching a Sunday school class that had eighty members, which was tremendous for that size town. So sometimes he read inspirational material on his program; at other times he would read from an American history book, saying, "People ought to know about these things and somebody ought to read them to them."

Young Hubert also took to the microphone as a duck takes to water. His ability to win an audience, which he had demonstrated in Doland High School, was evidenced on the radio, at meetings of the Young Democrats, and in occasional invitations to make a speech. He had been a Boy Scout in Doland. Now as a young man he became intensely interested in the Scouts and later became scoutmaster of the Methodist church troop. In that connection he was asked to make a speech at a businessmen's luncheon and service club. His topic was something like "The Meaning of Scouting," but those who heard it still talk about it. Even then, at the age of twenty-two, he was eloquent, already speaking two hundred and fifty words a minute, and he held them spellbound in the Marvin Hughitt Hotel. He could make them laugh and almost cry over "The Meaning of Scouting."

Now that he was a registered pharmacist, Hubert felt that he would probably stay in the drugstore business, but he continued to take enormous interest in politics. There seems also to have been a stubborn thought that he might still complete a regular college education. But these were very tough years.

The November of 1929 was still a black memory when there came a November that meant even worse news for the dry West.

The summer of 1933 had been extremely dry, and crops were virtually a total loss. Then one November day the residents of Beadle County, like the rest of South Dakota, saw the sky cloud over in a peculiar way. It turned a sickly off-color yellow—they were to learn that it always foretold the coming of a strange storm. That day the sun turned pink and then red, and what little green vegetation was left after the drought turned yellowish green, then gray. Then the sun turned gray and the dust came. A black cloud of very fine grit rolled over the town of Huron. People put handkerchiefs over their mouths and squinted through slits in their fingers on their way down the street.

That year there were ninety such dust blackouts. At one time dust was an inch and a half deep on the window sills. Then came the grasshoppers and locusts, like plagues out of the Old Testament. It almost seemed that the insects were moving in as the cattlemen and farmers moved out.

Dad Humphrey got into his battered Ford with the pig serum and hit the road as a salesman, trying to keep his family going. In the next three years, as Hubert worked behind the counter or went with his dad on trips to demonstrate or sell veterinarian medicine he heard many a tragic story of hard-working Dakota farmers come down from

47

minimal standards to poverty, through no fault of their own. In town he saw merchants come to the same pass. He saw sheriff's auctions. He saw one small business after another close its doors.

Later, as Franklin Roosevelt's New Deal took hold, the Humphreys felt, as did thousands of others in hard-hit South Dakota, that relief checks had saved the town. There was no doubt these checks saved the family business too.

Ralph Humphrey went to work as a supervisor for a government agency. Many who worked with this agency now just refer to it as "the federal government," but it was the Works Progress Administration, known as the WPA. People saw many of their neighbors working with them. And today many "prominent businessmen" could, if they tried, remember the days when they worked on the WPA.

Whether or not the present-day businessmen and comfortable farmers of South Dakota can remember when they worked for "the federal government," their economic lives, and perhaps their physical lives, were saved by the WPA. At a somewhat later period Hubert Humphrey himself was a regional director of education for the WPA in Minnesota.

It is these years that Humphrey has in mind when he says, with poetic half-truth, "I learned more about economics from one South Dakota dust storm than I did in all my years in college."

It was these years he had in mind one day in the Senate when he grew disgusted with pompous talk about bankers. Other senators were both shocked and amused when Humphrey said, "I remember when bankers were falling from windows thicker than pheasants in a Dakota cornfield."

One should not read too much into an incident or elaborate too much on family memories, but certain themes seem to emerge from what we know about the Humphrey life in Doland and Huron.

Struggle. This was a hard and hazardous life. People in the Middle West and particularly in what may be called the "dry states"—Kansas, Oklahoma, and the Dakotas—are naturally touchy about the question of just how well suited that country is to human habitation. If you laugh at Boston, you may not even be heard, but if you laugh at Deadwood, South Dakota, you are sure to hurt someone's feelings. And if you "wonder how people can live there," be warned: they live with a fierce pride in where they live; they have fought and they love what has been dearly won.

48

James A. Farley made one of the few boners of his career when he spoke in a derogatory way about Governor "Alf" Landon's home state of Kansas as a "typical prairie state." These states don't see themselves as typical; each is unique— and also blessed. The masthead of the Huron *Plainsman* says that in the Dakotas "live the most fortunate one percent of the nation."

To an outsider, however, the fact seems clear: some parts of the world seem to flow with milk and honey, and some don't. When the dust storms and the depression hit the Dakotas, conditions were really severe and American citizens were hungry. These times were tough for the farmer and tough for the businessman, and even Dad Humphrey might agree that they were also tough for the bankers. Even in good years, when people meet on the street in Doland or Huron, they constantly discuss water. "We just need a little moisture, we'll be all right."

It cannot be said of South Dakota that the livin' is easy. The economic outlook of its towns cannot be compared with similar towns nor the countryside with the black earth in Iowa or rich Wisconsin, or the more favored natural resources of their neighbor, Minnesota. All in all, this is a tough country, in which it takes great endurance and persistence to build a civilized community. That has been done in this unlikely soil, but it has not been easy. Around these towns the horizon is a ring of fate; on the flat earth the highest mounds are the graves.

Competition. This was a competitive life. Dad Humphrey was always competing. He was a small businessman, keeping alive and being competitive. There was not just the simple competition of one drugstore with another or with the "chains" and the "mail-order house." There was competition with the elements, with the economic system, and with all the other places a farmer might spend his dollar when he had it.

Hubert saw this "in real life" and in the endless round of school sports and debates and scholarship competition. By the time he was in high school Hubert had a well-developed competitive temperament.

Democracy. In many ways there was pure democracy in these towns. When there are so few people in a community they all know each other very well—sometimes too well, as Sinclair Lewis demonstrated when he wrote of similar communities not far away in Minnesota. There were no truly rich and not many who were considered poor. Several nationalities and religions were represented. As Senator Humphrey puts it today, "Even the *prejudice*, where there was prejudice, was out in the open. We knew what everybody was and what they thought."

The facts of life—childbirth, courtship, marriage, death—were close to the surface. They were seen in a harsh reality, but when disaster struck people were warmly close. There wasn't much veneer, or entertainment, or civilization, or art, which could long divert anyone from the elemental struggle. Work was the cardinal necessity and prime virtue. It was essential—to get enough food and to produce enough food surplus for the "cash money" that was needed to buy medical care and drugs for people and farm animals.

In Doland or Huron it isn't possible for a businessman to be very far removed from the farmer to whom he is selling something. How distant can two men be when both are wrestling a hog? Dad Humphrey and Hubert often showed farmers how to give a hog the needle that would save its life—despite its fighting, squealing protest. Everyone in these towns had to work, to keep himself alive and to keep the towns alive. There is a democracy in work as there is in the polling booth.

Religion. Religion in this section of the country is part of daily life but it is not assumed that everyone should believe the same thing.

Doland, for instance, had three churches: the Redeemer Lutheran church, which the Humphreys used to attend at times, the Methodist church, which became their main church, and the Catholic church. In the rural area south of Doland were two more, the Ebenezer church and the Emmanuel Mennonite church. Between Doland and Huron is a neighborhood known locally as the "Hutterite colony." They are Mennonites, and there are many of them in the area, with their unusual combination of mysticism and practicality. In Hubert's time there was one Jewish family. So it cannot be said that everyone belonged to predominantly familiar denominations of Protestantism.

The Mennonite philosophy, like that of the Society of Friends (or Quakers), is completely pacifist. A strong vein of pacifism, or at least anti-militarism, runs through many of the religious and political beliefs of the central West. It is sometimes forgotten that wave after wave of immigration from Europe brought to America precisely those people who wished to escape the militarism and "old quarrels" of Europe. Thousands of these men wished to avoid conscription on the European plan and to get out of a European atmosphere of national rivalry. They came to a new country, America, with hopes for a peaceful future, leading an international movement for a world in which uniforms and cannon would be only a memory. There was a time, after the Civil War and before 1914, when men envisioned a world of scientific progress in which mankind stood on the brink, not of chaos, but of a fruitful Golden Age. Dad Humphrey had seen this vision; he felt it could have blossomed again if governments would follow Christian principles and if Woodrow Wilson's idealism had triumphed.

Optimism. There is another basic theme of the Middle West, of Doland and Huron, and perhaps it is part of the "American temperament"—pure, joyful optimism. If old New England or the poor South sometimes cannot share this trait, the West still tries to believe in the great tomorrow.

Many visitors to America have been struck by this paradox: the fullest and most ebullient optimism of the American temperament is not found in the older and richer parts of the country. It is found on the margins, on the frontier, where it might be expected that life would be grim and people would be pessimistic.

But there is something in the frontier and in the temperament of the men and women who go there with dreams of making raw country into settled country, and settled country into populous country, and then of course into prosperous country. This dream runs from the stony marginal farms of New England to the driest mesas of New Mexico and California. And the strange thing is that in the wake of the railroads and the gold and oil strikes, in water power and in uranium finds, this dream has often been fulfilled.

Some small towns realize that their tomorrow has already come—and gone. All over the West are small towns that once expected to grow into small cities and then into large cities.

In the early days there was great competition among towns hoping to be chosen as the county seat. In many counties there were three or four towns in the battle that only one could win.

Doland, like innumerable other new towns, had an "Opera House." The townspeople produced their own music festivals, but they fully expected that someday elaborately cos-

51

tumed opera companies with professional singers would stop there on tour.

Dad Humphrey once spent much time—and money—trying to keep a hotel alive in Doland. "But of course it failed," says his son today.

Why shouldn't Doland have a hotel?

Men of vision and talents might stop there and see what a place this could be!

Well, what could it be?

It could be twice the size! Or ten times!

Much of pioneering seemed to involve lifting yourself by your own bootstraps. In our rich country this sometimes seemed to work. But often the law of gravity won.

Still, in America, anything can happen. If.

If we get a little rain. These were the dreams—and fears —one heard discussed in the forum—and the drugstore was the forum. In this Athenian community where everyone was a citizen, including the children and the dogs, there was one place where everyone was welcome—even on a Sunday. This was a social center in a lonely place. In towns like Doland and Huron people have to make their own entertainment, they have to work at providing a social life—so they can have a little fun or get a little education. They must "do it themselves" if they are to rise above the raw struggle with the crops and the stock and the illnesses.

In such towns the drugstore is a great social center. The drugstore cowboy standing in front of the store, chewing matches and spitting into the street, represents a social life that at the moment isn't working for him. But the social life flows here in a constant stream—at least in decent times. This is where businessmen and farmers have a cup of coffee, this is where the mother takes the kids for an ice cream cone in the afternoon. There may be a weekly newspaper—but the drugstore is a *daily* newspaper.

"I think I'll go down and see if they've heard any more about the Smith boys."

"Why, what happened?"

"You didn't know? I heard it from Charley—in Humphrey's this morning—seems the Smith kids were wrestling in a haymow, both of them rolled right out the window. One has a busted collarbone, but the other maybe has a fractured skull."

The drugstore is where the young people of the town go on dates to have a Coke or a fudge sundae.

52

Hubert Humphrey grew up in a small town in a hard time in a competitive world. He heard the dreams and experienced the tragedies of the people from a front-row seat—at the drugstore counter, the weekday social center.

Surely we could say that Hubert Humphrey very early saw life as a community process. In a way his family included his entire town. He spent his childhood and adolescence at the center of his world.

Today Senator Humphrey dives into a crowd and swims through it like a fish in water, splashing with energy. He enjoys himself with crowds and seems to be as natural and unself-conscious as most people can be only around the kitchen table.

We are not going very far if we assume that his early life in Doland and Huron had a lot to do with his family feeling for crowds of people. He was brought up that way, and it made him different.

CHAPTER V

Muriel

It was in the winter of 1934-35 that a Huron girl named Muriel Fay Buck was talking to a girl friend who asked her if she had recently been into Humphrey's drugstore. It might be fun to go down there and have a Coke and meet the good-looking Hubert Humphrey.

Muriel's father had been the owner of one of the main industries in town, the produce company, which had a big plant up by the railroad tracks. His plant was about the largest building in town, but he, like Hubert's father, "lost out" in the depression and had to sell his business at a tragic sacrifice.

As the daughter of one of the town's leading businessmen, Muriel did not often go into "the farmers' drugstore." But she had met Hubert in 1933 and often saw him around Huron.

She went and had a Coke. This proved to be a turning point in the lives of Hubert and Muriel, and therefore in the lives of countless others. We can't be exactly sure how it happened, but it would seem that if Hubert hadn't mixed a Coke for Muriel Buck that day he might be mixing them still, as Huron's leading druggist.

Muriel's father was Andrew Eshleman Buck and her mother was Jessie Pierce. They came of English, Pennsylvania Dutch, and Holland Dutch ancestry. Mr. Buck, like Dad Humphrey, had a wide reputation for being generous and kind but was also known for his firm character and convictions. Also like Hubert's father, he had not been much interested in the church in early life, but when Muriel was a child he joined the Presbyterian church. Eventually he was elected an elder and was a faithful supporter of church activities.

Muriel was born in Huron, went through the high school there, and was graduated in 1930 as an excellent student. She also studied piano at Huron College for several years and was considered a poised performer in concerts before an audience. When Hubert went into politics, she was nervous about making speeches but has since learned to take them in her stride. She has an older brother, Merle Frederick and a younger brother, Gordon. They are both keen on flying and are both private pilots. The whole family loved outdoor life and in good times took extended camping trips. A couple of times they went to Yellowstone and to Colorado, accompanied by their pastor, the Rev. Hubert Kitelle. Mr. and Mrs. Buck also enjoyed hunting ducks and pheasants, which are spectacularly plentiful in South Dakota, and both mother and father were good shots.

With her brothers Muriel played a great many boys' games as a youngster and was a bit of a tomboy. She was interested in hunting and fishing and loved the out of doors. While still a child she achieved some local fame by swimming across Bigstone Lake, where her family owned some property. The lake is 155 miles north of Huron, and the Bucks spent summers there, taking their chickens, ducks, dogs, and cats. They raised turkeys but really didn't make a cent on them.

Muriel says she was somewhat spoiled by being "Daddy's favorite." In her teens she worked with her father as a bookkeeper, trying to keep his books straightened, and got to be rather good at it. She earned the sum of ten dollars per week. When he lost out in the depression and had to sell his business, she says, "it was a real blow."

After Mr. Buck's retirement from the produce business he opened up tourist cabins on Bigstone Lake and it is now a prosperous resort place although the Buck family is no longer involved in its management. Mr. Buck died in April 1944, before Humphrey was elected to his first office, so he did not live to see his son-in-law's political successes, but he had always predicted that Hubert would have an outstanding career.

When Muriel met Hubert she thought him quite attractive and pleasant-looking, though not handsome in the conventional sense. She felt he had a magnetic personality—not that she believed in "love at first sight." Many Huron girls thought he was "cute," an expression that may now sound square but was then perfectly legal and tender for describing someone attractive to the opposite sex.

Muriel and Hubert had several dates and pretty soon were considered by the town to be going steady although they had not themselves decided exactly how they felt. She found

55

Hubert quite restless, and though outwardly he seemed set on staying in the drugstore business, inwardly he was undecided and discouraged. It did not seem he was "settled down," ready to plan his life for years ahead.

From the couple of years that they went together, they both remember frequent trips to a place called Lampe's Pavilion, which held dances every Wednesday and Saturday. Muriel and Hubert always loved to dance together. Apparently he has always been a talented dancer. Years later former Senator John Sherman Cooper said, "He is easily the best dancer among the presidential candidates." No matter what else happens to him, Senator Cooper's tribute will be unmatched.

The young couple were in love but they weren't sure about their future. The depression was a dominant delaying factor. South Dakota was getting along somewhat better in the late thirties but there had not been a really good crop year in a decade. It was still a tough country and hard times. Hubert's brother went with his intended for three years before they felt they could be married.

Hubert seems to have taken his own good time to make the final decision to be married. He himself says it appeared to him a very risky step, since he had so little money and practically no prospects. Muriel hints—as his assistants have said —that when it comes to personal decisions Humphrey often takes a long time. She says he never really proposed to her. And they both say they do not have a definite picture of how they arrived at the final decision. They say that, in real life, such decisions are not made the way they are on television. This particular thought amuses Mrs. Humphrey, who says, "We don't know exactly how it was decided that he would run for mayor or the Senate. You know, things have a way of happening; you talk about them quite a bit and then, without talking, events begin to happen and they seem to have been decided." At any rate, September 3, 1936, was the date they settled on.

The wedding wasn't to be a large affair but it wasn't just for a dozen friends either. Muriel thinks that one advantage of a small town is that you can plan such an event the way you want it. It was to be at eight o'clock in the morning so that everyone from the drugstore could go. Muriel got her wedding dress, a blue velvet sheath with three-quarter-length sleeves, which she topped off with a Juliet cap, in Watertown. Hubert, in a brand-new suit, arrived ten minutes late and in the voice that can fill a hall he filled that particular hall with the statement, "Great guns, I'm late."

However, this unpunctuality couldn't be blamed entirely on Hubert. Later the town learned what he was waiting for —his sister Frances couldn't find a garter.

After that beginning the affair went off without incident, both bride and groom being in good voice. The historian can only regret that they decided against having a wedding photograph, and they themselves have regretted it ever since. They left the church in a shower of rice and started off on their honeymoon—to Minneapolis and Duluth—with sixty-five dollars in their pockets. (The latter statistic helps answer the unspoken question about why there were no wedding photos.)

They were driving Dad Humphrey's Ford and on the way home they had an auto accident in broad daylight, thirty miles from Huron. The happy couple came around a corner at the same time that a cow started across the road. They killed the cow but were not hurt themselves. The car was damaged and after they had settled with the farmer, apologizing profusely and promising to pay (which Dad Humphrey did), a repair car went out to pick them up. So they returned somewhat ignominiously to Huron, pulled into town in their limping car.

The newlyweds used to talk about taking a trip to Italy on a tramp steamer if they could get a little money together. Hubert had always dreamed of traveling to far places. It was conversations with Muriel, sometimes rehashed with his father or the Van Dykes, that led Hubert to take the steps that got him out from behind the drugstore counter. He made up his mind to return to the University of Minnesota. One gets the clear impression from interviews with the main parties, and their friends, that the newlyweds were interested not only in education and in getting away from the endless routine of the drugstore but also in seeing what the great world might be like. Even when Hubert went to Minneapolis he continued to work part time in a drugstore, and to this day he remains surprisingly involved in the business management of Humphrey's Drugstore.

Today they can be nostalgic about the escapades and hard times they went through, but it still means a great deal to them that they endured together and have come up the scale together. Although he is seldom home in the evening and frequently is away on weekends, Humphrey still gets tremendous support for his work and his energy from his family. He often says he could not work as he does without the firm support of his family. A friend has written, "Humphrey is too sophisticated to say a thing like that unless he really meant it." He would never say this as a political line, nor repeat it as a cliché.

Some persons in recent years have expressed surprise that Muriel does not know more about all the ins and outs of current political battles. Others have expressed surprise at the opposite—they are amazed at how much she knows about current politics considering the very active life she has lived as mother, chef, travel agent, and general foreman for a busy senator and three boys and a girl.

She has supported her husband in all his major efforts—sometimes financially. She was so anxious for Hubert to get his university degree and his master's that she shared with him the duties of breadwinner. In Minneapolis and in Louisiana, where he did graduate work, she could always find some kind of office job. She knows what it is to feel shoe soles wear thin walking from one employment office to another.

At the time Hubert was studying for his bachelor's degree she was expecting their first child, Nancy.

In those early years she almost never had any household help. (A college student named Orville Freeman sometimes "baby sat" to give the young couple a chance to go to the movies.) By the time Hubert was running for mayor for the first time, Hubert, Jr., called Skipper, had been added. Although they wanted to name him for his father and grandfather, Muriel and Hubert agreed that Skipper was *never* to be called Junior, so they started referring to him as Skipper even before he came home from the hospital, and the nickname has stuck. Robert was born in 1944 and Douglas in 1948, years that were milestones in more than one way for the Humphreys.

Even as a harried young mother, Muriel was in on most of Hubert's political discussions. As often noted, Humphrey does not compartmentalize his life. "Right from the beginning Hubert included me in all discussions with his political friends and we were able to grow up into our public life together," Mrs. Humphrey says. "Of course our early political plans were made in the living room and kitchen of the Humphrey apartment."

She has a philosophical attitude about politics and the ups

and downs of campaign fortunes. She is interested and she works at campaigning with her husband. But she avoids looking on politics as the absolute key to existence. Both of them try to avoid taking things so seriously as to sacrifice the emotional health of their family.

Muriel thinks that one of the cruel things about politics is that it is so personal. Often her husband or her friends are involved in political situations that necessitate choosing among old friends, all of whom may have been close to the family for years. Yet when party leaders work for a nomination for some office, various factors (including friendship) must enter in.

Like Hubert, Muriel still remembers vividly how broke they were after their first election defeat. She is familiar with the emotional pinwheels of a campaign. "You give it everything you have because you wouldn't be in it if you didn't think you had a good chance to win." She says that her attitude might be different if they had a lot of resources or a fortune that might be lost. It helps her to think, "We don't have much to lose." She knows, however, that "there are friends of ours who have sacrificed much more than we have." As for herself she has often supported herself and helped to support her family, and was not too dismayed when they had to live on a very tight budget during the depression. She has a rock-bottom fatalistic attitude which she sums up by saying, "I have always figured I can take in washing."

Today she is often able to appear for her husband on those rare occasions when he decides he can't be two places at once. (Yes, he does decide the other way—often.) She says, "I wouldn't try to make a political speech, but I have learned to understand a little about the people in this enormous country—that makes it easier for me to visit with them."

All of the Humphreys' time in Washington has been spent in the same home, a comfortable and unpretentious two-story frame house in an unrestricted "family-type" area. It is a forty-minute drive in traffic to the new Senate Office Building. The senatorial staff claims that that travel time makes life harder for them. Humphrey hits the office with forty ideas that have come to him in the forty minutes of silence in the car.

For years Humphrey made it a practice to get up quite early in the morning so that he could have a play period and social breakfast time with his children. More often than not he would be working late at the office or going to a dinner to make a speech or to a city council meeting, so these mornings were his family time.

Their home near Chevy Chase, they believe, provides a perfectly normal suburban atmosphere. The street is a curving drive that amounts to a dead end, so there is no great flow of traffic. William Simms, who for many years was Humphrey's first assistant, used to live on the same street. Next door is Congressman George McGovern, an old friend who now represents the Huron-Doland district of South Dakota in Congress.

Congressman McGovern says that Humphrey is the best friend he has in Washington. They have many midnight sessions in the Humphrey kitchen. Sometimes they sit there and drink milk shakes. It just happens that the onetime druggist thinks he can make a particularly delicious milk shake. On other occasions they may drink something a little stronger. But always they are pretty apt to be talking politics every minute they are together. Another neighbor is Senator Russell Long of Louisiana. Social life for the man of this family doesn't differ much from his working life. That doesn't mean he doesn't like it.

Mrs. Humphrey, on the surface at least, seems to be far more relaxed and easygoing than her dynamic husband. But she finds the Washington pace makes her tense. When Humphrey wishes to, he relaxes almost completely and he can take a nap almost any time. He will take forty winks, if he feels like it, even in an automobile that is whisking him from one engagement to another. But some of his friends feel that even when he is playing games—even at home, playing ping-pong with Skipper or Bobby—he drives pretty hard to win, laughing and joking incessantly and excitedly. He has never been introduced to a game that he didn't like. Muriel says that after a couple days' trial he is surprisingly good at most any game. Then he plays hard, and some observers say that not very often is he truly relaxed.

He has never taken much interest in such intellectual games as chess or bridge as played by experts. Of course, according to many of its proponents, poker is an intellectual game, and he has been known to play poker with old friends but not really often enough to consider it a regular recreation. No one in the Capitol building has ever picked up a ringing telephone and had Hubert Humphrey ask him to an evening of poker—and very few have ever heard him propose *any* other kind of relaxation or holiday.

Mrs. Humphrey loves to sew and is an acknowledged expert. Making her own clothes was a great way to save money in the days when they really had to count the pennies. She is always making something new for her daytime wardrobe, and she loves to show visitors various drapes and slipcovers and other difficult jobs that she has accomplished herself.

She honestly loves the work and planning that go into making a home comfortable and charming. She supervised the building of their new Minnesota home on Waverly Lake, an hour's drive from Minneapolis. In a way she contributed greatly to its design: she stipulated that it was to have work areas and play areas and no space that wasn't used for one or the other. It is exceptionally attractive inside and out and has a magnificent though small living room dominated by a floor-to-ceiling window looking out on their private water frontage. She relaxes much more in Minnesota than she does in Washington and loves swimming and water skiing. When the boys were puddling around barefooted in the mud, building a nest for their pet ducks, their mother, also barefooted in the mud, would be alongside them. On the other hand, she is no gamine, but a capable hostess.

She completely landscaped the grounds and keeps the home filled with her own floral arrangements. And by and large the responsibilities of budget and maintenance are on her shoulders.

It is not easy to characterize Mrs. Humphrey. She certainly is not solely an unassuming and non-aggressive woman who sees herself as "just a homemaker"—she is these things, but that would imply that she is non-political. It would be a mistake to suppose that she couldn't be expected to understand national politics and world affairs. She is somewhat unprofessional as far as politics are concerned but she has sometimes made as many as a score of appearances in one week, at "campaign coffees" in election years. In recent years she has taken an active part in campaigns, making speeches that are not oratorical or argumentative but more in the nature of greetings from the senator or from party headquarters.

She is not a driving person who enjoys the limelight and doesn't yearn for higher status. She does not drive her husband but neither does she pull back to slow down his drive. There is no doubt that she stands behind her husband and her importance to his career cannot be minimized.

PART II

The City

"The time has arrived in America for the Democratic party to get out of the shadows of States' Rights and walk forthrightly into the bright sunshine of human rights. . . . In these times of world economic, political and spiritual—above all, spiritual—crisis, we cannot, and we must not, turn from the paths so plainly before us."

HUBERT H. HUMPHREY

CHAPTER VI

The School of Politics

Hubert Humphrey loves politics. He seems to look on the Senate as his home—he certainly spends more time there than at home. But there may be a place he loves even more, according to some of his friends—and that is his university.

When Humphrey first saw what a university was, he says, it opened his eyes to the whole world. He and his family had talked and read politics for years. But it was not until he got into the university that he realized how many books there were—and that there were students and professors who were professionals at trying to understand government.

So far as ideas are concerned, he says, "I had known there were such things as hamburgers, but I didn't realize there was T-bone steak." This metaphor seems to indicate that Humphrey was hungry for education, and no one should doubt it.

When the young Humphreys went to Minneapolis in 1937 so that Hubert could finish his university education, six years had elapsed since his abruptly terminated sophomore year.

As a student, Hubert threw himself into every subject in the same way that he attacked everything else. When he looked over the catalogue and saw all the courses he would like to take he put up a fight to carry twenty-one credit hours. The powers that be told him he should take only sixteen or eighteen. He insisted that he had the money—just barely—and claimed that in his drugstore, if somebody wanted five bottles of aspirin and had the money, no one would think of saying they could only have three. College courses weren't like aspirin, replied the management, and Humphrey lost the argument.

That didn't keep him from taking books out of the library and carrying them home in basketloads. His method of studying, then as now, was to throw himself on a subject, through the printed word and through listening and talking to every person he met. It may not be true that Humphrey was born talking, but the writer will testify that persons from every period of his life will say that Humphrey was a great talker. This is what Doland people thought. This is what they thought in Huron and what they frequently said at the university. But at the university people could see that Humphrey's desire to be with a crowd, forever socializing and talking, was one way of seeking out new knowledge. His conversations were *not* monologues; even when he made a statement it was often really a means of asking a question. He must have been listening and reading *some* of the time; you don't get a Phi Beta Kappa key, as he did, simply by being the best talker at the Saturday night bull sessions.

And it happens that the Humphreys' apartment became the storm center of what were surely some of the most re-markable—and long-continued—conversations in the history of political science. These conversations—with many of the same participants—lasted for decades.

No one really thinks *political science* is a science. No one seems quite sure what it is. It deals in literature and biog-raphy, sociology and psychology—and history. Its leaders would like for it to be objective sometimes like a science, but it can't quite get society into its test tube.

Yet there is a subject *called* political science, whatever that may be. And the people who study it—and teach it—do produce a high proportion of people like the subject of the present book: men who are successful in politics. Some say this is something of a coincidence. They say what happens is that the boys who are going to be good politicians naturally gravitate to political science—and what they learn there doesn't hurt them but doesn't really help them either. There's a school of thought that says politics is an art, and artists aren't taught, they are born and teach themselves.

In any case, the University of Minnesota had about the best school of political science in the country when Hum-phrey was studying for his B.A. Dr. William Anderson, now retired, was head of the department and nationally known. It would be impossible to calculate how much administration and legislation have been influenced by his students—and *their* students. Another favorite teacher was Ben Lippincott, a professor with an active interest in history as it is made day by day in the real world. These teachers, now elder statesmen, were the spiritual or intellectual godfathers of many men who have made recent history. Few teachers can count so many of their "boys" in the United States Senate. Besides Minnesota's Humphrey and Eugene McCarthy, a lad named Gale McGee became a senator from Colorado, and another young fellow, Wayne L. Morse, who was an assistant professor at the university from 1924 to 1928, is now a senator from Oregon. Morse and Humphrey shared honors in 1959 when the University of Minnesota presented them with its highest honorary award, the Outstanding Achievement Award.

A younger man on the faculty, also a well-known scholar and theoretician, was Professor Evron M. Kirkpatrick. Though he was about the same age as our young druggist from Huron, it is sometimes said that Kirkpatrick "helped to invent Hubert Humphrey." His educational background and familiarity with history greatly impressed the young South Dakotan. Like many others in the political science orbit, Kirkpatrick had long had an interest in practical politics. As things developed, he was able, alongside Humphrey, to study American politics from the inside to a degree few professors have ever surpassed. For many years a Humphrey adviser and campaign helper, Kirkpatrick is now executive director of the American Political Science Association, which has offices in Washington. This leads him away from partisan politics . . . but not out of sight. He is still in touch with Humphrey and is constantly consulted on campaign work.

The political science professors and students who sat drinking root beer, eating popcorn, and talking on Saturday nights at the Humphreys' apartment were the nucleus of a group with whom Humphrey is still connected.

One of the young students in this bunch was Orville L. Freeman. In some ways the future governor of Minnesota has been Hubert's closest personal and political companion. When Freeman showed up at the university he really had no interest in political science, but he and Hubert fell in together and Hubert more or less talked him into a political career. Unlike Humphrey's family, Freeman's took no interest in politics. Hubert was thin, Orville was a football player, and looked it. In temperament they are quite unlike each other. Their friends criticize Orville for being blunt and undiplomatic, they criticize Humphrey for trying to please everybody. They have been told, "One would never pick you two to be buddies," and they smile broadly. But they will talk the whole night through when they have the chance. In many ways they behave like close brothers. And that means they are "friendly" competitors; sometimes the competition becomes quite sharp. If they should ever split they would be angry like brothers!

Orville is younger than Hubert, but because Hubert's education was delayed they were in college together. Then Orville's political career was interrupted by military service. When he came home Humphrey, then mayor of Minneapolis, put him in charge of veterans' affairs, and in later years he has been campaign manager for Hubert. They have constantly advised each other on policy and tactics, and they still work together very closely in Minnesota political affairs. But Orville is now serving out his third term as governor and because of the nature of political structure and loyalties there is ordinarily some friction between the camp of a governor and the camp of a senator. To some extent this is true here. There are differences between "Freeman followers" and "Humphrey followers," but by and large they have maintained a remarkable degree of closeness. This does not mean that Freeman is "Humphrey's man" in the statehouse, as Orville or Hubert will be the first to tell you.

Dr. William Kubicek, as a young man and a student, became a friend of the Humphreys in the early days. He and another medical research man, Frederic (Fritz) Kottke, argued and talked politics with the political science bunch and shared their general outlook on civic affairs. "It was geography," says Humphrey. "He lived next door. If Kubie had lived six blocks away there is no question he would have had a completely quiet life in the laboratory." Dr. Kubicek is still one of Freeman's closest political advisers and is in frequent touch with Humphrey. At this writing he is state secretary of the party, and so can be considered a professional.

In the give-and-take of the weekly discussions and in the classroom Humphrey was learning a great deal of history and political theory. When he visited Rome a few years ago a friend who went with him to the ruins of the Roman Forum was really dazzled by Humphrey's discourse on the Roman Senate and the decline of the Roman Empire. Political scientists, of course, study their Plato and Aristotle, and students of oratory study their Cicero, even more minutely than political commentators in Washington study their Lyndon Johnson, or their Robert Tafts. But it startled the friend, who had never had occasion to see Humphrey loosen up a little of his book learning, to hear Humphrey take off on Roman history, with some Greek comparisons.

The more standard or old-fashioned type of professional politician is inclined to think there is something incorrigibly amateur about almost all of Humphrey's advisers. What other senator goes into laboratories for advice and pulls professors into the hurly-burly of campaigns?

Certainly few university departments have had so many students and professors with such an active interest in politics. In Washington many senators and other figures have pipe lines to their old universities or to universities that specialize in a subject with which they are concerned—such as economics or foreign affairs. But there is something about the political scientists (or the scientific politicians) who for many years have followed Humphrey that sets them apart. This group found ideas—and dreams of power—intoxicating. Thousands of voters have since then heard the echoes of those Saturday night sessions.

Graduating in 1939, Phi Beta Kappa and *magna cum laude*, and with just a few dollars in his pocket, Hubert took off in the fall for a teaching fellowship at Louisiana State University at Baton Rouge. Kirkpatrick and others at the University of Minneapolis had helped him to get this job, which would enable him, if all went well, to get his master's degree.

Louisiana politics at that time was a seething mass of corruption and comedy, following in the wake of the breakup of the Huey Long machine. Scores of Louisiana politicians had been indicted by parish grand juries, city grand juries, and federal grand juries. The latter were led by crusading O. John Rogge, then with the Department of Justice.

The day Hubert arrived in Louisiana the state police had been called out to quell some labor trouble. He saw them at various points in the state capital with their motorcycles, helmets, and machine guns, trying to keep the lid on "threatened rioting" at an oil refinery in Baton Rouge. "I wondered if I were in the U.S.A. or in a Latin-American revolution," he says. The incident gave him occasion to think about fair play in labor strife.

The president of Louisiana State University, an appointee of the assassinated Huey Long, had recently tried to run away to Canada, been nabbed by the police and brought back, and was now "moving from the state university to the state penitentiary." Morale at the university wasn't high, but it was coming up because there seemed to be no place to go but up, after the regime of James Monroe Smith.

In the political science department Humphrey found some first-class minds. Among them was Charles Hyneman, who had offered him the job and afterward took a personal interest in the lanky young man. It was some time later that Hyneman was asked, "Didn't Hubert talk too much?" Hyneman replied, "Yes, but you have to remember he learns so much while he is talking."

Muriel came down to join him and they quickly made friends there, as they have everywhere they ever lived. Hubert and another student were particularly attracted to each other. This was a young man whose father had been a senator and whose uncle was now governor of the state, a post he was to hold off and on for many years. This was Russell Long, son of Huey and the nephew of Governor Earl K. Long. As the son of a senator he would have had a certain attraction for Humphrey anyway. But Russell, who was quite a contrast to his late father, was something of the same kind of mixture of studiousness, pragmatism, and the common touch that Humphrey is. It is quite interesting that both of them, coming from entirely different types of constituencies, were rated very highly by their fellow senators and by the capital press corps as capable, knowledgeable, and hard-working representatives of their states. For years they were close neighbors and friends in Washington.

When he was being examined on his master's thesis, written on "The Philosophy of the New Deal," Humphrey was thoroughly ribbed by Hyneman, Bob Harris, and another favorite professor, A. B. Daspit. Just as Kirkpatrick and Anderson and Lippincott had in Minnesota, Hyneman and Company in Louisiana felt that Hubert should go into politics. "If we let you go through with this master's thesis and thus certify the work you've done," said Hyneman, "you will be a great loss to politics.

"If you get this degree, particularly with honors, you'll just go out and be a teacher and eventually you'll be a professor. Then you'll teach other students, and political scientists will think you are a great scholar, but nothing will ever happen to you."

For a couple of hours they rode Humphrey, sometimes pretending to be serious, to keep him on the anxious seat. "It is a moral duty to flunk you, Hubert," Hyneman would say. "I owe it to the voters up there in Minnesota, or South Dakota, or wherever you are disappearing to. You could amount to something in politics, but I don't know if you ever would be a good teacher. But if you get this degree in your hand you're just going to run away like all the rest of us and disappear into an ivory tower."

They might also have been critical of the content of young Hubert's thesis. It was not really a comprehensive survey and distillation of the rationale or philosophy of Roosevelt's domestic policy. It attempted to cover that water front but, as Humphrey will now confess if pushed, it amounted to the political philosophy of young Hubert Humphrey. Very likely that philosophy was identical with that of the more idealistic and liberal members of Roosevelt's entourage, but the point is that it was written from Humphrey's inside to the outside, and was a lyric or a sermon—not a scholarly survey.

Years later Henry A. Wallace, when he was friendly with Humphrey, read the thesis and autographed it facetiously, but with respect, "Dear Hubert, you get an A."

Perhaps this would make a neater story if it were not necessary to add that only six years after he wrote this thesis Humphrey decided that Henry Wallace had gone off the rails and "become irresponsible." So the student of the New Deal eventually gave bad marks to the man who had once given him an A. He still feels Wallace personally is a fine man—but that politically he was led astray.

Since then Humphrey has changed somewhat in his social philosophy and would not subscribe 100 per cent to everything that he wrote in the thesis. However, it is of some interest to take a look and let the words of the young man speak for themselves.

The main theme was that "the New Deal gave America a revitalization of democracy. The new administration opened its political ears to the multitudinous demands of the people." (Even in a formal thesis Humphrey's style was oratorical.)

"Prior to the New Deal . . . persons in places of responsibility . . . were disciples of the theory of 'what's good for business is good for you.'" Humphrey said that the political leaders of the twenties went further and adopted a complete laissez-faire attitude of "what's good for business is to let business do as it pleases."

The pre-depression trend was summarized thus: "Democratic processes were not functioning . . . government was listening to the voice of finance and industry: agriculture and labor dissipated their energies in dissension and political apathy." This has been a keystone of Humphrey's view of the nation; he did not see anything wrong with our government—but plain people had not mobilized (before the New Deal) to make it meet their needs.

In his youthful view the American economy had been for a hundred years "essentially speculative" and the ideal had been to get rich "as quickly as possible." As Humphrey saw it the New Deal had sought to change this national ideal, "to preserve the capitalistic system, with no desire to destroy individual liberty, but rather to adjust personal freedom with the social good." Young Humphrey's theory was that the New Deal was attempting to change America's outlook from pure individualism to individualism within a social framework. This ideal still means a great deal to him—initiative he regards as one of the great qualities of any man; encouraging initiative he considers one of the prime characteristics of American society.

Humphrey thought that Roosevelt had been trying to build up a system of checks and balances within the economic structure, but without direct control of industry, labor, and agriculture.

He felt that the New Deal was seeking to establish further basic rights in addition to the traditional rights of personal liberty: political participation and self-government. To his mind there was a whole series of new rights, primarily economic. Perhaps most of these would be accepted as part of the New Deal's goals by the authors of the New Deal. However, one must not forget the years of conversation between

Humphrey and his father or the combination drugstore and town hall they managed.

There is no doubt that Humphrey's father subscribed to these human rights as Humphrey did when he listed them as basic concepts of the New Deal:

(1) The "right to creative work, to profitable and useful employment."
(2) The right to an adequate standard of living.
(3) The right of collective bargaining . . . and the right of the worker in a substantial share in management of the industry to which he has devoted his . . . life.
(4) The right to security against unemployment, accident, illness, old age.
(5) The maintenance of health.
(6) The right to leisure and its effective use.

Humphrey placed the New Deal in the direct line of developments from Jefferson through Jackson to Populism, Progressivism, and Wilson's "New Freedom."

He also made it quite clear that he believed the New Deal had not tried to manage or direct the American economy and that probably we had a system "too complex and delicate" to be planned in all its details. He felt, as he thinks now, that government should regulate excesses, set up checks and balances, and take a pragmatic approach to help out here and slow down there, but that in the present state of knowledge of economics it is not possible to go very far toward managing and directing so complex an economic organism as the United States system.

This was perhaps a distinguishing feature of his thesis. Another was his concept of the worker as having some kind of property right and some kind of human right in the management of his job and even of his industry. Another concept, which the New Deal did not emphasize as much as Humphrey did, was that of extending democracy and greater economic opportunity to international affairs. At that early date he was most insistent that our expanding democracy should give economic aid to other countries. And he specifically praised the reciprocal trade agreements developed by Cordell Hull as Secretary of State.

Thus, at the age of twenty-nine, he was expressing in a reasonably mature and sophisticated way one of the dominant themes of his career, a note that he was to sound over and over again—that America's productive factories and farms should be developed in a democratic fashion and her products used as a power for peace and security throughout the world.

Humphrey has sometimes said that the real liberal New Deal period ended in 1938 and that America has not had a truly liberal outlook on domestic and world affairs since then. Many other liberals in 1940 and the war period shared this attitude and resented the preoccupation with international affairs that had caused the glorious crusade of the New Deal to come to a halt. In fact some outstanding liberals turned isolationist because of a combination of attitudes: deploring war, wanting to keep out of Europe's quarrels, and wanting to concentrate on domestic policy to further "economic democracy." It is interesting to note that Humphrey never flirted with isolationism, just as he never flirted with Communism. We may assume he learned internationalism as he learned to polish bottles in Huron's Leading Drugstore.

Certainly it was there that he learned another major concept which he attributed to the New Deal but which certainly came right out of the Humphrey family—namely, that a human being has a "right" to the maintenance of health. In trying to determine what Humphrey meant by that we read in other speeches of his a general theme. He believes the economic and political system must not permit human beings to suffer from needless disease or malnutrition or medical deficiencies, which could be met by a proper organization of resources, including using all employable persons' talents in productive work.

There is a firm moralistic tone in this thesis on the New Deal, as there is in many of Humphrey's major efforts to define his philosophy. No one who knows him, including opponents who have watched him for years, doubts that he is sincerely religious. And there is no question that he considers it not merely wasteful to let a man be unemployed or a family be unnecessarily sick in a land of plenty; he considers this a *sin*. Similarly, he not only considers it shortsighted of the United States if it does not use its wealth to help underprivileged countries, he considers it wrong for America to be glutted with surpluses while other people are underfed or even starving. He believes the Founding

73

Fathers at Philadelphia were enunciating moral principles, he believes F.D.R. did the same for his time, and he believes America should do so—in action—for the whole world to see today.

In his own phrase of 1959, "Today the world does not need massive retaliation, but massive doses of health, and food, and education."

In a real sense, this is part of Humphrey's religion.

CHAPTER VII

Defeated—and Famous

What else might Hubert Humphrey have been?

In his undergraduate days he had sometimes thought he might become an economist and he is still interested in the subject. At various times he dreamed of being a lawyer and today when he speaks of the subject there is a note of regret in his voice. He says, "I really never knew how long I was going to be in school, but it didn't seem to me that I would ever be able to make it and get a law degree." He also thought of going into public relations or of being a radio commentator.

Immediately after he got his master's from Louisiana State he returned to the University of Minnesota as an assistant instructor in political science. He applied to various places for various kinds of jobs, but always he was interested in politics.

At one point he made out an application to the National Labor Relations Board. He also wrote once to Jonathan Daniels, afterward famous as a White House assistant, when Daniels was an assistant director for the Office of Civilian Defense.

In his letter of application Humphrey said, "I am interested primarily in work dealing with public relations or community organization. A good deal of my experience centers around public speaking and organizational activities." He also said that he had "considerable experience in the field of publicity and information services."

In 1941 he went to the WPA, first as a supervisor of teaching in the Workers Education Service and then as director of war production training and re-employment. It was in this job that he first had a chance to become acquainted with union labor. Next, in 1943, he went to the War Manpower Commission, of which he became assistant regional director. Many of the jobs for which he applied might have altered the course of his career. For example, a civil defense job might have led him away from Minneapolis and into the Washington bureaucracy. It was at this time that he studied civil defense—and he never throws anything away. He is still interested in the issues of civil defense and is one of the few American national leaders who takes it seriously.

From 1933 until 1945 Hubert was getting his education and holding a variety of jobs, but in retrospect it seems that all of them, like the interest in civil defense, contributed to his later career as a senator. In particular he got administrative experience.

The important political facts on the official record of this period are that he made his first try for political office—and was defeated for mayor of Minneapolis in 1943, and then came back to win in 1945.

But not so visible, at least in retrospect, are the facts that during this period he really became the leader of Minnesota liberals and that he performed the astonishing feat of welding together Minnesota's two liberal parties—the Farmer-Labor party and the Democrats.

The circle of political scientists or scientific politicians was still buzzing. Humphrey says they sometimes played checkers, but it seems more likely that they always played political chess, with real and imaginary chessmen. The labor leaders whom Humphrey was meeting talked to him about taking specific steps toward politics, and the business and professional people who heard him speak told him he ought to think about a political career.

Among Humphrey's friends at this time were Arthur J. Naftalin and Herb McClosky. They became part of the "bunch" and are still close to Humphrey.

Naftalin was an expert in public administration and the author of many papers and textbooks in this field. He was commissioner of public administration for Governor Freeman. In his younger days, however, Naftalin was a past master of the general art of publicity, with a sort of specialty in campaigns. He knew exactly what parts of a Humphrey speech might make a headline that would do some good. He knew how to get into a newspaper office and "plant a story" by talking to newsmen or by leaving the right material in the typewriter of the right man. In his early campaigns Humphrey always enjoyed a remarkable degree of coverage even from newspapers that opposed him, thanks partly to Naftalin. Along with Kirkpatrick, Naftalin was alert very early to the problems posed for the liberal movement by the extreme left wing and the Communists. While Humphrey was awake to the realities, and knew that Communists existed—alive in Minnesota—he was always very slow to take action against people whom he had once thought of as friends, who might be unwitting fellow travelers. At one crucial point Naftalin told him, "Either you go ahead and make that statement you should make, or you can count me out. I'll resign and go home." Humphrey believes that in politics "you always have to apply Band-Aids after the fight" and he thinks one should try everything else before resorting to a blunt factional fight.

McClosky was a political scientist, a professor at the University of Minnesota, who, unlike Naftalin and Humphrey, had never gone in for public office. But off and on through the years he has been an adviser and helped on political strategy. Humphrey says, "He is a pure idealist," and McClosky, like some others, is a living conscience who tries to see that Humphrey remains true to his basic idealism.

Humphrey's "amateur advisers" urged him to try to run for mayor of Minneapolis. He had always thought his first step would be to run for Congress, but labor was interested in a new face (their perennial candidate always lost) and the "bunch" said he ought to make a try. They thought (erroneously) that he couldn't lose anything by it—they didn't realize how much money could be spent.

As with many such personal decisions, Humphrey hesitated a long time—and kept going over all the angles. Finally, according to Kubicek, "I told him, 'For heaven's sake, Hubert, you've talked about it enough, why don't you do it?'"

Hubert had waited until twenty days before the closing date to file for the primary.

The next day, with only nineteen days left to campaign, Humphrey took ten dollars down to city hall and filed.

The indecision over, his friends saw something different. It was like the spectacle of a duck that has been going up and down the shore line, looking at the waves and the sky, and then putting one foot gingerly into the drink. Finally this duck flapped his fledgling wings and waded in.

He was a duck in water.

As a campaigner Humphrey immediately and continuously startled even those who had always told him to go into politics. He did not do anything so radically different from other campaigners, *he just did a lot more of it.*

From the moment he went into the primary he seemed to think that it was natural to be out putting leaflets in apartment house mailboxes at one and two in the morning.

He made about fifteen speeches a day and expected and inspired his associates and personal friends to keep pace. Professor Kirkpatrick, Art Naftalin, and a little later Fred Kottke and Bill Kubicek, found they had become "night people." Long after Minneapolis had gone to bed they were still working.

It was during this campaign that Humphrey picked up William Simms. Humphrey and Kirkpatrick had been going through city hall, and Humphrey had been greatly taken with the likable personality of Simms, who worked in an office there. So he asked Simms to go to lunch the next day and then, surprisingly, asked him to act as campaign manager. Even more surprisingly, *Simms resigned his job the next day.* His boss let him do it but protested, "Bill, you're crazy, that young man hasn't a chance. When you are finished, you're giong to be exhausted and broke and without any future."

The boss was almost right. Simms was exhausted and broke when the campaign was over. But the future held some interesting prospects. For eleven years Simms was Humphrey's right-hand man; seven of those years were spent in the United States capital.

Humphrey's issues were focused on reform, cleaning up the rackets, and enforcing Minneapolis liquor laws. He hammered some on civil rights but that did not become a major issue with him until the end of the war.

Incumbent Mayor Marvin L. Kline had not, in retrospect, been outstanding but he had not been allied with a corrupt machine, and it was by no means easy to rake him over the coals. He was certainly not a bad mayor. Humphrey called him a "do-nothing mayor" but one adviser privately told the young campaigner that it would have been better for Humphrey if Kline had done more—then there might be something to criticize.

The tyro politician got one real break. The campaign got

extremely hot one afternoon when Humphrey thought the mayor intended to "smear" him by charging that he was associated with racketeers.

Art Naftalin brought Humphrey an advance copy of a speech the mayor was to make, in which he planned to say, "Racketeers are in this campaign upon the side of my opponent, armed with vicious and diabolical schemes to discredit what I have done."

Humphrey countercharged that Kline's campaign had plunged into "the lowest depths" and he and Naftalin and Simms decided to call up the newspaper reporters and with them descended on the mayor's office.

Humphrey was really hot under the collar and they swept by protesting receptionists to see the mayor, of whom Humphrey demanded an immediate explanation of the racketeering charge.

Kline said that *he* was being discredited, by being called a "do-nothing mayor," and that sinister interests were involved. He said there were Humphrey supporters that he might not know anything about, persons who didn't like what Kline had had to do to them. Humphrey continued to challenge him, demanding that he name one person he might have had in mind. Finally Kline named a man in the labor movement who had an unsavory reputation. Kline asked Humphrey if it weren't true that this man was to be chief of police if Humphrey got the office. At that, according to the news account in the Minneapolis *Tribune*, "Humphrey exploded." He said he had never dreamed of such a thing.

This was a stormy session, but between hostile exchanges, as they stood in front of the reporters and photographers, the two men kept giving each other embarrassed but sincere greetings of respect. The mayor would say, "I'll run my own campaign in my own way, you do the same." They both insisted they wanted "a clean campaign." Then their normal middle-class good manners came to the fore, and they both began to feel a little ridiculous.

In conclusion, after considerable dickering, they shook hands and smiled warmly toward the photographers.

Many years later an associate of Humphrey's said, "He just has to like people and have them like him and that great march we made into Kline's office ended with this warm handshake and that was the picture that got into the newspapers."

Other politicians have pointed out that if Kline had had any idea of making a big issue of Humphrey being allied with racketeers—a rather fantastic idea in light of the record, before and after this day—Kline didn't have much chance of painting Humphrey as a sinister villain after having greeted him and been photographed in a chummy pose with him. Thus Humphrey's instinct for shaking hands may after all have been the shrewdest political step he could take.

The amateur campaigners put out only one piece of literature, which in retrospect looks highly professional. Like many such pieces of literature, it breathes a general air of optimism that everything is going great. "Voters Unite Behind Humphrey," it declared. That was not an appeal—it was a sweeping claim designed to say some kind of tidal wave was already rolling. (And in Minnesota today the retort would be, "*And it was rolling*, brother, it was.")

Printed in a newspaper format, the "lead story" said:

An inspired Minneapolis resounds to the challenging appeal of the new leader!

Up and down the avenues, in the homes, in the churches and in the business places, everyone is talking about Hubert H. Humphrey—candidate for Mayor.

Spread before the people of Minneapolis is a new vision —a vision of a city united in war and preparing for peace, for a peace that will see a greater Minneapolis, clean and prosperous and more beautiful.

Columns of this rich and beautiful Chamber of Commerce vision proclaimed that young Hubert Humphrey was the man of progress and destiny for Minneapolis. One staccato paragraph said:

"Bold. Fearless. Intelligent. A man of vision. Again and again you've heard it. You've heard it from the corner grocer, from your next-door neighbor, from your friends. Everywhere persons are using these words to describe your candidate for Mayor: Hubert H. Humphrey.

The photographs showed him teaching and with his family at home—at this time Nancy was four and Skipper a charming one-year-old.

The caption read, "Campaigning is strenuous, but Humphrey still finds time for his reading and for his family"—and that may not have been 110% true at campaign time!

There was a photograph of him reading, however, to document this assertion, and the book was *One World* by Wendell Willkie; this has been cited as a typical Humphreyism. Of course even then he was very keen on a new outlook in foreign relations and he was and is a devout believer in "one world" . . . and like Willkie he can tell you specifically what he means by that. But there is also something in Humphrey that told him it wouldn't hurt him with independent Republican voters if they saw a photograph of him reading Willkie's book. Nor would it hurt him with the liberal and independent voters either.

There was also a note in this flyer to say that he had been a scoutmaster, that each Sunday morning he conducted an adult study class at the First Congregational Church, and each Sunday evening he taught at the Hennepin Avenue Methodist in a special church series called "The University of Life." It would seem that Humphrey and the "scientific politicians" around him had read their textbooks—from Plato to Madison Avenue.

Humphrey of course by this time needed no instruction in how to speak to an audience—any audience. With the fervor of an evangelist he fought for clean government and for his own election—and with the simplicity of the young he identified these two forces as identical, no doubt about that.

Yet the end result was defeat—Humphrey lost to Kline by 4900 votes.

Kirkpatrick was philosophical, but others of the campus kingmakers were disillusioned for a time. It looked so close, and yet it had almost seemed too easy. A week after election day it seemed like a crazy dream. Simms, like Humphrey, really had no job to return to. He finally went into the sheriff's office as an investigator, where he got experience that was very valuable to Humphrey's administration two years later.

Humphrey counts these frantic campaign days as one of the greatest learning periods of his life. He felt that he learned volumes about how the real bones of political organization are put together. Years later when a volunteer worker asked him how to build an organization he was stumped for a moment. "I dunno," he said. "Just get around and meet people—and get people involved." An academic associate who has struggled to define such concepts as "organization" and "leadership" thinks this is a profound intuitive statement. He also thinks Humphrey is a master at making people feel themselves committed to traveling in his direction.

In 1943, however, it did not immediately appear to the undiscerning that he was traveling anywhere. He had put up a whale of a fight. And he had lost.

The defeat was really considered a victory and more than mere semantics was involved. Humphrey had entered the primary a few days before the last date for filing. He had come close enough to force a runoff and had lost that by only 4900 votes. It was perfectly clear to discerning people —professionals and advanced amateur politicians—in Minneapolis and to many in the rest of the state that he might have won that campaign if he had started sooner. It also seemed clear that this near miss could not be accounted for by any peculiar conditions, but that Humphrey came close mainly because he was a good campaigner. If this were so, it seemed obvious the young man could campaign successfully for other offices in other places.

To Humphrey, however, the defeat was temporarily quite a crusher. In the first place, he had considered it only natural and appropriate to spend all the money he had plus all the money anyone would give him for the campaign treasury. His supporters and closest allies had gone along with him in putting in money or making commitments, when it appeared virtually certain that they would win. These young amateurs did not realize how the tremendous pressures of campaigning and the inner pressures of egotism combine to convince campaign workers that they have a good chance to win. When the contest is really close both sides become convinced they are going to win. Therefore they spend money they haven't got and borrow money that will be difficult to repay in the event of a defeat (so unlikely, in their view).

The young Humphrey family found itself with a debt of thirteen hundred dollars. There was absolutely no organization to pay the bills for radio time and leaflets and placards and the like.

During the next two years Humphrey worked at a variety of jobs. He was a professor of political science at Macalester

College in St. Paul. He was a news commentator on radio station WTCN—he appeared on 152 programs and was paid for 25 of them. Part of the time he worked Sunday afternoons and evenings in a drugstore. In addition he managed the apartment building where he lived; his duties included mending broken plaster, repairing water pipes and electrical connections, and keeping the heating plant going. Mrs. Humphrey scoured the hallways. Working at these various jobs and still keeping up the habit of making speeches, picking up a few dollars here and there, he gradually whittled down the debt that had seemed insuperable.

He assumed that he would soon be volunteering for service or that he would be drafted. Classified in 1940 as 3-A because of his small children, he was later shifted to 2-A because part of his job at Macalester College was to teach Air Force Reserve officers, and he was frozen in his job as an essential civilian. In the winter of 1943 he requested release from the job in order to get in the navy; when it was granted in the spring of 1944 he applied for a navy commission. Turned down for physical reasons, he immediately tried to enlist but ran up against the navy's no-volunteer policy of that time. He was told to wait for his draft call.

At the Democratic Farmer-Labor party convention of April 1944 there was a surging demonstration to nominate Humphrey for governor. He declined the nomination, telling the convention: "I want to go in the armed services if I am acceptable. I want to be with those other young men and women in the armed forces, and you can't deny me that privilege."

But Humphrey was never finally accepted for military service. The draft call came in the late summer and on September 6 he was at last classified 1-A. At the head of his draft of men he proceeded to Fort Snelling, only to be informed after a few days that the local draft board had reclassified him 2-A. Again he moved into the limbo reserved for those waiting for the call of Uncle Sam, and in midwinter was again called up for induction. Back to Fort Snelling he went in February 1945, only to be confronted with the news that he had a hernia, as well as calcification of the lungs from his childhood illness, and was thereby rejected. He was reclassified 1-A limited.

Humphrey has described how he argued with a colonel at

Fort Snelling, trying to get into service, and how the colonel said that "he knew where to find me if he wanted me and that he didn't want to hear any more about it."

At one point newspaper photographers had caught Humphrey in the uniform supply office and taken pictures of him with a uniform over his arm. He had been through days of physical examination and was turned down the next day, the kind of sudden turn of fate that happened to millions of others in Selective Service.

He knew at the time that he was missing one of the greatest experiences and duties of his generation, and this was dramatized vividly for him by his friend Orville Freeman, who went through plenty of tough experience in the South Pacific—and became a Marine Corps hero. And of course he realized that, in addition to serving his country, military service would be one more asset to his future political career.

His lack of a military record has never appeared as a campaign topic. When a "hate sheet" once brought it up his friends—and even political foes—answered the smear by pointing out that he had tried several times to get in the service and that none of his deferments had been sought by him.

As the years go by Humphrey feels steadily worse about missing military service and the experiences of the war. His friends think this helps to explain a number of things about him—his staunch support of veterans' legislation and his ingenious veterans' housing ideas in Minneapolis, as well as certain personal matters such as the deep feeling he has about Orville Freeman.

Throughout 1943 and 1944 Humphrey continued to be active in politics, with one restriction. It was understood that while he was a professor at Macalester College he would not run for any office. That was a condition of his employment.

Yet it was in these two years, after his defeat, that Humphrey emerged as the outstanding political leader of Minnesota.

In this period he was campaign manager of the Democratic Farmer-Labor party of Minnesota, and he helped Roosevelt and Truman to carry the state by a margin of 54,000. This was a remarkable victory, all the more unusual when one considers the stormy struggles between the Democrats and the Farmer-Labor party in Minnesota and the still more stormy times that were to follow the merger that Humphrey engineered between the two parties.

In some ways this is the most surprising part of the Humphrey story: how he came to be a successful party leader while the parties he worked for were out of office, as he was. He always got people involved.

CHAPTER VIII

Fusion and the Future

As Hubert Humphrey thought over what he had learned about practical politics in his unsuccessful mayoralty campaign, it became clear to him that he would have a political future only if he had a strong party as a base. For a score of months he devoted himself to the task of fusing the Democratic and Farmer-Labor parties into an effective unity.

Any non-Republican had a tough problem in the state of Minnesota, which during the thirties had seen the emergence of Floyd B. Olson and an extraordinary political group, the Farmer-Labor party.

By and large people who were not Republicans in Minnesota belonged to the Democratic party or the Farmer-Labor, but neither one of them was able to make much headway in the early forties.

In the first place the state was "normally Republican." For example, *a Democratic senator had never been elected by popular vote from Minnesota.*

Floyd Olson, a dramatic speaker and an unusual political figure, had appeared in the thirties as a great mobilizer of social protest and had for a time persuaded farmers and union labor to get along together. There was a day when Floyd Olson appeared on the national horizon as something of a radical Huey Long, a person who might realize the extreme left-wingers' old dream of a political force that could combine the dissident elements of both farmer and labor groups. He had made the Farmer-Labor party into a successful movement. But it did not appear to have a great future—and the Republican party had lately shown signs of a new vitality.

An influential citizen of Minneapolis, Gideon Seymour, vice-president and executive editor of the Minneapolis *Star* and *Tribune*, said some years later that he had talked to

Humphrey and made him a specific proposition at the time of his first mayoralty campaign. Seymour believed that such men as Governor Harold Stassen were making the Republican party into a truly progressive and militant group. Seymour told Humphrey in so many words that if he should get to be mayor or should run for further political office the Minneapolis *Star* and *Tribune* would give him strong support if he could eventually decide to become affiliated with the Republican party.

This was not a "deal" in which an attempt was made to pressure or swap horses with Humphrey. It was something the honorable Seymour freely talked about later. He wanted to know if Humphrey was a Republican or thinking of becoming one, because he looked like a man with a future. Seymour wanted to persuade bright young people to get into the Republican party and change it into a somewhat more liberal group. Humphrey had replied that he would have to think the proposition over a little, although he didn't really see how he could consider it. "It would break my father's heart if I turned Republican." Humphrey also had dreams of building a new party with a more forward look. He was startled that such tempting liberal talk should come from the other camp. His brain also told him to think it over carefully. The cards were rather stacked against Democrats in Minnesota, so it is not strange that he gave serious consideration to what the backing of the most powerful and influential people in Minnesota could mean. However, his heart never considered the idea and it did not really miss a beat—as Dad Humphrey could have predicted. Seymour asked him, "Are you going to go the way of Harold Stassen? Or are you going to follow in the path of Floyd Olson?" Humphrey replied that there were other alternatives besides those two. As it has turned out, he has not modeled his career on either one. But he said that, to answer the question, they could consider that he had to go in the footsteps of Floyd Olson.

In 1945 the *Star* and *Tribune* gave heavy support to Humphrey, and in 1947 they supported him for re-election, even though they knew the man they were building up was almost certain to be a senatorial candidate in 1948 or later. Fellow Republicans made it hard on Gideon Seymour but the *Star* and *Tribune* still went down the line for Humphrey. Thus to some extent he had his cake and ate it, too, as far as this particular support was concerned.

Was this luck? Or was it the natural capability of Humphrey—and the fairness of Seymour—and luck?

Many of Humphrey's best qualities were to be needed in the months immediately ahead—and, looking back, one can now see good and bad luck intermingled in a crazy pattern.

In these years Humphrey had some advantage in the fact that he had not been identified by embittered partisans as belonging to either the Republican, Democratic, or Farmer-Labor factions. Yet he also had tremendous disadvantages. He had not lived very long in Minnesota, he had not proved himself to be a winning vote-getter, he had no real party experience with either side, and he had no influential power group behind him.

In view of these things, Democratic and Farmer-Labor leaders in Minnesota are probably right when they say that one of Humphrey's greatest political coups was brought off at the start of his career when he succeeded in achieving a successful fusion.

He was working for an arrangement that looks quite simple to those in politics but certainly looks complicated to a non-political mind. We might add that it may be simple in principle and still be difficult to execute.

Humphrey wanted to convince both parties that they would be good for each other—and he had to educate them so that this would in fact be the case. The people, you might say, were not in love, they had to be brought together, educated to their responsibilities, and it was hoped that they would grow fond of each other. The marriage broker would be forever damned by all if it turned out they were not yet ready to make a go of marriage.

This is a *simple* way to describe the "fusion" of the two minority parties in Minnesota. In this "marriage" there was also a rich and powerful father of the bride.

The Democratic National Committee might be described as the distant father, rich in money and influence, who did not wish to see his Minnesota offspring tied up irrevocably and disastrously with the nationally unknown quantity of the Farmer-Labor party. The latter was then seemingly incapable of winning major elections, although it had thousands of loyal partisans. As will be seen later, there were many reasons why one might be leery of the FL party leadership; but at the time the main one seemed to be that since the death of its great leader, Floyd Olson, it had not seemed to have the vitality to grow.

To the national Democratic leadership, it seemed to be one of those sporadic developments that reflected, like Populism or Progressivism or the more recent Non-Partisan League of the north central country, a restlessness that could protest eloquently but could not quite achieve true political power.

Perhaps at this time (the middle of the war) the Democrats and the Farmer-Laborites did not have major policy differences, but they had had some in the past. There were many feuds and factions in small towns, there was a history on both sides of warm and living dislike of each other. The national Democratic leaders would have liked to see these two small groups of voters get together, but on the other hand they did not look forward to the tedious job of bringing about this fusion. They rather had the idea that Minnesota was going to be hopeless until the hatreds died out as the old partisans aged and died off.

Humphrey, as the great hope of progressive-minded Minnesotans, began to think of a set of events that might work. Both parties had to be given real hope that together they could win. They both needed to be better organized, to be "beefed up." They had to be brought to like each other a little better, to be less suspicious, to venture a little, and give a little. And at the right time they had to feel that they could get real support—without selling out—by accepting identification with the national Democrats. This courtship, as it turned out, was arranged with Humphrey as the liaison man—but it took 250 meetings or more!

Humphrey knew he would have to sell the national headquarters on the idea that something new was stirring in Minnesota. They were not eager to send in reserves if the two splintered parties could not turn out a good vote for Roosevelt and the national ticket in 1944.

In 1943, Humphrey made his second trip to Washington —staying again with Uncle Harry—where he hoped to see Postmaster General Frank C. Walker, who was the Democratic party chairman.

His account of this visit has always amused his friends and family. Once again he was traveling on a shoestring. He had written Walker a letter—in longhand—outlining his plans for the political marriage.

He could stay only three or four days, and he had no

luck at all in seeing any important official at party head-quarters, much less the Postmaster General and party chairman.

Humphrey fumed as various "decrepit-looking" people went in to see high officials, while he cooled his heels in a reception room. All this was happening despite the fact that he had sent various letters of introduction to Washington. He had also gone to the trouble of having one sent by his father's friend, John J. Exon, state chairman for South Dakota.

At one point Humphrey exploded to a minor functionary who shall be nameless—though still remembered, "Why, you folks here are taking care of all the old folks and the lame and the halt—but you ought to get wise to what's happening out in Minneapolis—we came within five thousand votes of the mayorship of the fourteenth largest city in the country!"

There is no use classing this as an Exclamation We Doubt Ever Got Exclaimed—Humphrey still has the breath to toss this off. He was and is angry that he did not get invited through the gates when he presented himself.

On his last day in Washington he tried again to break the telephone barrier and then gave up and reverted to being a tourist. After lunch, while he waited for a five o'clock bus, he went to the Willard Hotel to watch the high and mighty folks walk by. He decided he might spend fifty cents on a drink and went into a cocktail lounge, where he decided to call an old friend of the Humphrey family, Mr. Cecil Howes, formerly of South Dakota. He merely intended to say hello.

Howes was glad to hear from him and after catching up on the gossip asked him what brought him to Washington. When he heard about the great mayoralty race, the hopes for fusion, et cetera, Howes said, "Stay right there, Hubert, I'll be right down."

Howes had formerly been an assistant postmaster general and he knew how to get through the phone barrier.

He telephoned Frank Walker. "A half hour after he joined me at the Willard a big black Cadillac drew up at the front door, and it took both of us away, to a building were we met Mr. Walker."

Then Humphrey was scared. He stuttered a little as he tried to outline the hopes he had for Minnesota to become a stronghold of the Democratic party. Walker buzzed for secretaries, who located the longhand letter, and they went over Humphrey's estimate of the situation.

Humphrey was thirty-two years old and had been in practical politics less than six months. Does he now think he was rather brash to imagine that after many veterans had tried and failed to get these parties together he had a good deal of nerve to go to Washington and explain things to the Democrats' number 1 pro?

"It was a lot of nerve for a young man," Humphrey says today.

But he got the support of Walker and, as it turned out, Humphrey had the solution. Fusion worked.

Walker and others took an interest in Minnesota—and also in Humphrey. Through months of negotiations, Humphrey met the people who had or would have political interests in the state.

He went to the national convention in 1944, with a fused party behind him, and he managed the state campaign for F.D.R. and Truman. It was a successful campaign and his star was on the rise.

Thus he had become known throughout the state—and in a real way in national circles—as an articulate young man who could sometimes find solutions to difficult political problems. The fusion of these two parties was one of the great steps in his career, and took somewhat different talents than the civil rights speech—only four years in the future— that was to appear so divisive. Humphrey's first step in national politics, on the contrary, had been to take a splintered set of people and weld them together. It remains a political feat that demonstrated not only his ingenuity but his capacity for negotiation and hard work.

In 1945 Humphrey again ran for mayor and again his opponent was Marvin Kline.

What future did he have at that time? In retrospect it's easy to be philosophical. It is much easier now to say that he was certain to win this time than it was to say it then. Conceivably he could have become—not an unknown—but a lecturer and radio commentator, perhaps. He might well have decided politics was too expensive for amateurs.

The fact was that being mayor of Minneapolis was not altogether the best possible road to an important political future. Like most political hopefuls, Humphrey had thought first of the state legislature or Congress, and then perhaps

91

a run for governor. Being a non-partisan mayor might be quite an achievement, but a political figure, like a business-man, always has to think of what he will do next year to meet and overcome the competition. Being mayor of Min-neapolis did not necessarily lead to anything else. So the young man had a problem there—if he won, what would he win?

He won by the greatest majority in Minneapolis history, by a margin of 31,114 votes.

In that second campaign he made a good deal of the issue of civil rights and was warmly praised for his stand in edu-cational and religious circles and the press. The Minneapolis *Tribune* said, "He is the type of honest fighting liberal on whom the future of democratic government depends . . . evidence of his true democratic beliefs was seen again the past week in his savage attack on the conditions which breed the scandalous anti-semitism which has come into the open in Minneapolis."

Humphrey had said in his opening radio speech, "This tragic display of racial intolerance requires more than the superficial treatment of additional police . . . it requires a unified community program based upon recognition of the true ideals of democracy, wherein every person is ac-cepted as a human being with dignity and worth, regardless of race, creed or color."

Then for the first time in many years of political discus-sion his conversations were not about "what they should do" but about what could be done.

Getting things done was up to Humphrey and Company. If he could succeed he was going to cross another line be-tween the world of discussing and the world of doing.

CHAPTER IX

Mayor of the Fourteenth Largest City

As he went into his first elective job Hubert Humphrey was thirty-four years old, he had been away from Huron seven years, he had been married eight years, and he had three children. It had been two years since he entered real politics.

The Roosevelt era was ending, the Truman years beginning. Most people expected Truman's first presidential election to retire him. It was just a matter of time. The United Nations was capturing the world's imagination as the only hope against the potential atomic destruction that the average man could hardly understand. "Isolationists" still had enormous political influence, although the name itself had just about disappeared. Winston Churchill was shortly to make a speech about the Iron Curtain, and perhaps most literate people of good will would think he was too militant against the Russians. Men continued to come home from the Pacific and people idly wondered when General Mac-Arthur would come home.

The hot political topics, however, were price and rent control, housing, demobilization, and rebuilding of civilian industry.

As the young mayor settled into his job, his friends were surprised at his diplomatic and conciliatory ability. His main administrative device was the use of advisory commissions to study problems—and provide leadership.

Observers of Humphrey's terms as mayor nearly always emphasize three things: law enforcement, labor relations, and civil rights legislation.

It is rather difficult for present-day observers in Washington to realize that young Mayor Humphrey was in his own city almost as much of a racket buster as "Mr. D.A." in New York—Thomas E. Dewey.

But the Humphrey record is more involved, for even in

law enforcement the mayor of Minneapolis is not given as much authority as most mayors. Even when dealing with the chief of police, enforcing liquor-sale closing hours, or cleaning up corruption among the city police, the new mayor had to use not only powers of decision but integrity and stubbornness. He had to use persuasion not merely on the public but on the much tougher audiences of councilmen, department heads, and various committees, some of which he himself had set up. Too many of the decisions ordinarily made by a mayor are in the hands of the council in Minneapolis.

Although the police picture perhaps demanded less of his negotiating abilities, the mayor's anti-discriminatory legislation and human rights program required exceptional abilities in this line. And there were more than twenty-five major strikes in Minneapolis during Humphrey's three and a half years as mayor. As the economy was upset at the end of the war and returning servicemen came back to their old jobs, there were many strikes throughout the country. Humphrey frequently took the lead in his bailiwick in bringing the disputing parties together and working out the details of settlement. He was good at inventing face-saving devices to help both sides come down to "normal."

Humphrey's friends were accustomed to seeing him "charm the birds out of the trees," so far as mass audiences were concerned. They had also seen him center in on one person at a luncheon or party caucus and overwhelm him with personality and logic and the sheer endless flow of facts and ideas. This was still quite a different thing from the give-and-take and the judgment of personalities that one has to have when dealing with a committee of independent minds. There were formidable personalities on the city council, people who had strong preconceptions and honest uncertainties as to what really was the right course to follow. They would not have been human if some had not also been to some degree jealous of a young man who was becoming well known and was obviously being groomed for higher things than discussion with a city council. In this sort of business Humphrey began to find himself and he applied his arts of persuasion in new ways, always reserving the right ultimately to appeal to the people. He had learned a lot about negotiation in the fusion process. He was also distinctly Rooseveltian in the way he let people understand that he loved his job and meant to know everything about it and that, despite his youth, he felt a fatherly feeling toward any human being and any organization in Minneapolis. In his own family Humphrey is a dominant and rather strict father—within the limits of the time he spends at home.

Mayor Humphrey tapped an important source of strength and ideas by creating a whole galaxy of "Mayor's Citizens' Committees"—cross sections of the non-governmental citizenry of the city—to give him advice and counsel on such critical problems as housing, youth problems, and job discrimination.

The people who were close to him as mayor, some of whom have been able to observe him through the years since, were not surprised when an older Humphrey was sent as a delegate to the United Nations and favorable word came back from the marble corridors, receptions, and plenary sessions. It was not new to them, as it was to many in Washington, that in the U.N. Humphrey earned a reputation for having an understanding ear and a discreet voice, and for being an effective diplomat among people of many nations. On the surface these qualities are not so evident as Humphrey's settlement of a labor fight or the overwhelming of the city council in Minneapolis. But they were all similar tasks: to bring several different and opposing points of view into harmonious order, at least harmonious enough so that it was possible to get on with the program. It is the highest political art to do this without explicit authority, to do it by understanding people and situations.

In the realm of labor conciliation it might have been thought that Humphrey would merely take the role of champion of organized labor. Labor played a key part in launching the Humphrey career. In fact as one traces the story it would appear that union interest in Humphrey was one of the vital ingredients in his successful launching, just as surely as marrying Muriel Buck and leaving Huron were steps on the road to getting a real education. Yet for various reasons Humphrey has always maintained a certain separateness from the unions' domination. To this day he remains in close weekly or daily touch with the interests of Minnesota unions (and of course does the same with farm groups as might be expected of a man wearing the party label of Farmer-Labor). But by separateness is meant a certain distance that in the case of labor says in effect, "I am a United States senator and belong to no one particular section of the community," and in the case of Minneapolis seemed to say back in 1945, "I am the non-partisan mayor of Minneapolis, who must try to do my best for the whole city and for a fair settlement of all matters that come to my desk."

Liberals were sometimes critical and businessmen were sometimes startled at Humphrey's manners and ideas as expressed in such conciliation. But he had certain feelings and principles about government and the good of the community for which he would fight to the last ditch. Businessmen were reassured when they saw him talking bluntly in labor's own language to labor leaders. One story in particular, involving a city strike in the hospitals, was told and retold in Minneapolis. Humphrey called in the AFL officials involved and said that he just wouldn't tolerate a strike involving hospitals; he said it would be entirely different if they were striking a candy factory or a brewery. We do not know whether at that time he had ever read of Calvin Coolidge's stand in the Boston police strike, which Coolidge summed up by saying, "There is no right to strike against the public safety at any time." But apparently Humphrey came close to the same feeling as part of his personal creed; he told the unions he would fight them publicly just as hard as he could, unless a compromise were found. The strike never came off.

Minnesota had a stormy labor history and the use of the injunction had been common in the period immediately preceding the era of Governors Olson and Stassen and Mayor Hubert Humphrey. Initially, Humphrey earned the respect of Minneapolis labor leaders because he never used the police to break a strike. Today this doesn't seem remarkably enlightened or humanitarian, but the opposite policy was taken for granted in the forties.

Humphrey himself believes that in negotiation and bargaining he found his real talents and that these were his greatest areas of learning as an administrator. He preferred to get things done through negotiation and conciliation rather than through rigid decisions or frontal attacks with tomtoms of publicity and outpourings of eloquence against the opposition. At this point in Humphrey's career he began to understand the realities of American politics as distinguished from the debater's dream of "the forces of evil" being overcome by the golden voices of prophets of the people. Bryan believed in many devils and villains, and to some extent preached hate. This is the great difference between the Western "Cross of Gold" orator and the new "sunshine of human rights" orator.

There is in American politics a definite place for voices of protest, but when Humphrey became mayor he moved from the role of critic into that of the man who is responsible—and who himself would be the subject of criticism. When he became mayor he knew he was on the hot dime, as the saying goes, and if he had criticism to make—and he had—it was up to him to put his suggestions into actions. He began to sense, through all the antennae he had developed as a sensitive politician, that the American public fundamentally prefers constructive criticism. Humphrey, even while a young mayor, began to see how things could be done by compromise and conciliation, through middle-of-the-road policies, and seldom through rigid programs conceived by social theorists and executed by efficient administrators.

In any case he tried to learn about the practical matters of running a city. Here his instinct for wanting to be liked and his talent for making people like him, developed an eloquent negotiator where there had appeared to be only an eloquent voice. He understood instinctively the pleasures and principles of dissent, but now he began to understand the principles and pleasures of decision, the satisfactions of responsibility.

In his first month as mayor Humphrey wrote his uncle John:

No doubt you have wondered why anyone would want to get into political life. There have been times when I had my doubts as to the worthwhileness of the whole matter. I must confess, however, that to me, public life and political activities are the very essence of a full life. I think that I thrive on it. I know that I enjoy it. To be Mayor of Minneapolis surely is not the highest accomplishment that one could desire but I do feel that it is a first step and if successfully handled can lead to greater and better accomplishments. I have been very busy this first month I have been in office. At times I feel completely inadequate to the responsibilities and then again I know that others have been able to do a creditable job, so it is within the realm of possibility to make a name for oneself as Mayor.

This certainly shows that Humphrey was looking to the future but it can hardly be considered un-American to write to an uncle about making "a name for oneself."

In those days the young mayor never knew what would come to his desk next.

His diplomatic abilities were most severely tested in dealing with the famous Sister Elizabeth Kenny, who had attracted world-wide attention with revolutionary methods of treating polio. In 1946 Minneapolis was sorely hit by a polio epidemic—more than two thousand cases in a few months. Sister Kenny was the idol of many magazine articles and was a dedicated woman with original and sympathetic methods of treating the ill. But she was also a stubborn and difficult person, often unwilling to listen to conventional but nonetheless correct medical diagnoses. Her sympathizers had built up bitter antagonism between themselves and the National Foundation for Infantile Paralysis.

It took courage to stand up to Sister Kenny at any point, but the mayor did his best with the Kenny temperament. Once in his office she presented him with an ultimatum: if a certain situation was not immediately changed she would straightway return to her home in Australia.

Humphrey was brisk but smiling. "Very well, Sister. If you've made up your mind I'll help with the travel arrangements. . . . When do you plan to leave?"

On other occasions he said it with flowers; Sister Kenny long remembered her arrival at Minneapolis airport one day to find that Humphrey had sent her roses. Eventually she softened under the Humphrey treatment.

Many cases were coming into the city from other parts of the state and the mayor finally obtained from the White House permission to use army barracks at Fort Snelling as a hospital.

One day Sister Kenny demanded that several patients who had been moved to Fort Snelling without her permission should be returned immediately.

Humphrey gave up the slick and honeyed approach at that particular point and said, "Look, those patients are going to stay right where they are. We're running a hospital for these people, not a bus service."

Eventually Humphrey secured a Minnesota Polio Research Commission, which was to make an elaborate study of the disease at the University of Minnesota, financed by the

National Foundation, yet for years Humphrey and Sister Kenny maintained a cordial if plain-spoken relationship.

A firm stand for "law and order" became the keystone of his first wide reputation.

Minneapolis and St. Paul once had the reputation of being the best stopover for criminals and racketeers between Chicago and the West Coast. Attorney General Homer Cummings had once denounced the Twin Cities as centers of crime. In fact it was legend that in neighboring St. Paul police winked their eyes or looked the other way at the arrival of known criminals in their community so long as they merely used St. Paul as a hideaway place. If fugitives became too obstreperous they would be picked up, but otherwise it was said to be an asylum for lamsters.

Between 1934 and 1945 three scandal sheet editors, perhaps flirting with blackmail, and two labor leaders had been shot and killed on Minneapolis streets and yet there had not been a single conviction.

As a candidate Humphrey had served warning that he was going to "kick the daylights out of the rackets in this town."

To help him in this job he started a law-enforcement committee, similar to other committees he was creating, and he was successful in getting Bradshaw Mintener, a flour mill executive, as chairman. The latter agreed to serve only on condition that Humphrey appoint an FBI-trained man as police chief. The man Humphrey got became one of his greatest assets and one of the keystones of his administration —Ed Ryan. At this writing Ryan is now sheriff of Hennepin County—the Minneapolis area.

However, while Humphrey was deciding on Ryan, organized labor in Minneapolis had another man they wanted appointed. This was one of his toughest early decisions, but Humphrey felt he had to preserve some independence from his labor backing, and he was intent upon a cleanup and effective action against the joints that were giving downtown Minneapolis a raffish and raucous atmosphere as well as breeding crime.

Such appointments as that of police chief had to be cleared through the city council and the labor bloc opposed the Ryan appointment, but he finally won through. On several other occasions the mayor refused to go along with powerful labor groups. Sometimes he had to tell them, "I am my own boss, I cannot be tied to anybody's apron strings." Later he worked hard to get a new city charter which in his opinion would have cleaned up and strengthened the city government. The labor leaders bitterly opposed these reform proposals.

With Ed Ryan at his side, Humphrey made it clear that he meant to enforce the law and build a public sentiment that would go beyond mere enforcement to create positive public support of decent administration. The first order of business was to close down after-hours clubs and make clear to certain favored liquor stores that no stores could be opened except at the specified times. It is still remembered by those in the liquor business, however, that Humphrey was not vindictive or "holy"—merely firm. He gave each establishment two warnings on minor infractions of the liquor laws, sending a police officer or a letter to say that there might be some misunderstanding but that if there were a third incident final action would be taken.

Besides Ryan, Humphrey also gives credit to his Morals Squad chief, Eugene Bernath, who later was Chief of Detectives.

Humphrey says now that the most surprising opposition to such a cleanup is not that of the owners of the joints or the racketeers but the critics on the side lines and close friends and upstanding citizens who are cynical and say that laws can't be enforced.

The sophisticated laughed when the new police chief ordered certain unsavory joints to close. However, Ryan and Humphrey had the last laugh.

The young mayor also made a tremendous noise about housing and also got things done about it. He had a housing committee and he dramatized the fact that seven thousand families in Minneapolis needed better homes. And he was doing what he could about the city's "blighted areas." He sought to dramatize the approach to these problems by such actions as having a city planning commission make a city-wide tour of the "most blighted areas" and listing those that would receive first consideration.

He insisted that Minneapolis needed twenty-five thousand new dwelling units and that if the health laws were strictly enforced ten thousand persons would be forced out on the street overnight. A most conservative group called the Minneapolis Property Owners Association tried to establish the point that twenty-two hundred dwelling units were vacant because landlords were on a landlords' strike against OPA ceilings. Humphrey said he just didn't believe there was any such strike.

He thought price controls were a nuisance but that it was better to have them than inflation. You may have to take "a bushel-basket of forms to the OPA office" but that is better "than having to take a bushel-basket full of money to the grocery store if inflation gets out of control."

Generally speaking, he got excellent editorial suport for his battles on law enforcement, housing, and urban blight.

Humphrey has always shown great inventiveness. With his enthusiasm he was able to improvise and do many things that people said couldn't be done through ordinary channels and therefore couldn't be done at all.

The federal government was offering trailers for emergency housing but the flabby city government had no funds or agency to handle them. Humphrey has said, "The mayor's office took over. . . . We formed a private non-profit organization and 'panhandled' $56,000 to finance the enterprise." Soon the project housed five hundred persons and the borrowed money was paid back.

Later seven hundred additional housing units were made available by the government and $150,000 worth of bonds were issued to handle the project. Then the mayor got the city council to issue $2,000,000 worth of bonds for more housing.

He also dreamed up the "shelter a vet" campaign. He appealed to the general public and put the full force of publicity behind the idea that there should be living space in private homes for veterans getting out of the army— and turned up twenty-three hundred livable units for returned soldiers. When his good friend Orville Freeman eventually came home from the wars—he had been badly wounded and decorated for exceptional bravery—Humphrey put him in charge of veterans' affairs.

Since Humphrey had once expected to be in the service himself but had been barred from it, he felt specially obliged to see that men his age who had gone into service were treated fairly by their nation as they came home.

Law enforcement, housing, and urban blight were of course not Humphrey's only interests as mayor.

He set up the first food conservation plan in the country, which was a model for other cities. He donated space in his office for CARE and was the leader in local drives to send food to Europe. He set up a youth welfare commission and studied the problems of juvenile delinquency. He also set up health advisory, smoke abatement, and traffic advisory committees.

He was always insistent that political independents and Republicans should be brought in to help out on city programs. The chairmen of the law enforcement and human relations committees, perhaps his two most important, were both Republican. While his term as mayor promoted his political fortunes, he has not been seriously accused of running anything but a non-partisan administration. In fact many Republicans might have liked to claim him. However, it can certainly be said that his activities prepared the way for his future political career.

Another problem Mayor Humphrey attacked with energy was racial and religious discrimination.

Many people think of Minnesota as a land of wide-open spaces and openhearted people, mostly apple-cheeked blond Anglo-Saxons, democratic through and through. . . .

As a matter of fact Minnesota and Minneapolis are typically American, not because they are Anglo-Saxon or Nordic but because they are melting pots. Many nations, races, and religions are represented in Minneapolis.

With such a background, many people learn to be tolerant but others have a chance to exercise prejudice and discrimination. No less an authority than Carey McWilliams (later to be editorial director of the *Nation*) had shortly before this period surveyed the current scene and pronounced Minneapolis the anti-Semitic capital of the country. A small but articulate group in Minnesota had admired William Dudley Pelley. Now all but forgotten, Pelley led the Silver Shirts, who made futile but extremely obnoxious efforts to start a fascist uniformed group in the United States. They had appeared in Minneapolis even during the war and there had been shocking incidents of books in the university library being defaced and marked with the words "Jew" or "Communist." These incidents had made a profound impression on young Hubert Humphrey.

Back home in Spink County and in Huron there were by no means as many different races as there were in Minneapolis, but Hubert had learned in Doland to take people as they were and not according to their names, religious labels, or income levels.

102

Though he had mentioned civil rights in the 1943 campaign, it was a relatively minor issue; but by 1945 it was a major platform plank.

He had drawn up plans for a Mayor's Council on Human Relations, one of many such committees he would initiate. He was going to get something done in the community, although he did not have explicit enforcement powers that would enable him to do it by law and by direct action.

In this campaign Humphrey was so outspoken on the issues that one of his Negro friends actually warned him to go a little slower as a matter of political strategy. Cecil Newman, editor of a Negro weekly, was of course for an all-out civil rights program, but he thought the program would advance further if Humphrey were elected. He was afraid hitting the issue too hard would defeat him, so he said, "Soft-pedal F.E.P.C., Hubert, it is not a popular issue. We know your plans and you've got the Negro vote."

The next night Humphrey made a spirited radio broadcast appealing for a Fair Employment Practices Commission. He won this fight, and Minneapolis was the first American city to see discrimination because of race become illegal in factory and office.

These speeches on civil rights did not hurt Humphrey's political chances in Minneapolis. He carried through all his promises to act against discrimination and was re-elected in 1947 by a much larger plurality than he had in 1945.

Even before he took office Mayor Humphrey had in mind the man he wanted to be the first chairman of the Council on Human Relations. This was the Rev. Reuben K. Youngdahl, a Lutheran minister and a brother of Luther, who was to become a very popular Republican governor. Humphrey was successful in getting him to take this arduous job and Youngdahl gave it all he had. This Republican and the young mayor worked as a tremendous team.

One of the techniques used by the Council on Human Relations and by Mayor Humphrey was to force certain kinds of people to face up to the fact that discrimination existed. The mayor's Council on Human Relations began a community self-survey. At that time it was considered to be the most complete study of public opinions and attitudes ever officially attempted by an American city. One purpose of this investigation was to cut away the usual rationalizations and force the interviewee to give a clear-cut answer. "Do you believe in discrimination or don't you?" When put this way, the answer was seldom if ever "Yes," but it made the liars think about it.

Sociologists were not impressed with the survey as scientific research, but they were pleased that this crude but essentially accurate mirror had told Minneapolis how it really operated in these matters.

On the housing committee, the chairman included, were real estate men, and they were made to realize themselves and admit to one another that greater housing hardships fell on minority groups. The housing committee recommended that a law against restrictive covenants be publicized and that all realtors remove race and religious restrictions from deeds.

The committee also noted that large numbers of Negroes and Jews had passed industrial training courses for skilled employment during the war; in fact proportionately more Negroes and Jews than white Christians were well trained in these categories. But when the veterans came home the Negroes particularly were forced to return to predominantly unskilled jobs. No one wanted to discriminate against veterans, but it appeared that thousands of people, some of them vitally needed for their technical skills, were being forced out of the lifetime careers they might have had.

A representative committee that looked into employment found some discrimination in labor unions but placed most of the blame on employers.

The employment and labor committee called for a state F.E.P.C. and asked for more publicity on the Minneapolis city ordinance. Very soon nearly every large firm eliminated the questions on race and religion from their application forms. The Urban League's long campaign to put Negroes in department stores as clerks finally got results and every large department store in Minneapolis hired some Negro clerks. In the past Negroes had been quietly tucked away in just one corner of one of the four federal housing projects in Minneapolis. Eventually the Council on Human Relations found the man who was responsible for this policy and proved to him that there was no federal rule against integration. This man switched over and discrimination was ended in these projects.

The most interesting on-the-spot job performed by the Human Relations Council, however, was on behalf of sixty Negro actors and actresses from the Broadway musical *Carmen Jones*. When their show was scheduled for Minneapolis they were refused rooms in nearly every hotel. Just a week before the troupe arrived Mayor Humphrey authorized the executive secretary of the council to make reservations for the cast by simply asking hotels "to set aside some rooms for guests of the mayor." No names were given.

Five hotels found rooms for "the mayor's guests" and just before the actors arrived the council's secretary went to each hotel manager with pamphlets on tolerance called "Outside the Home." These leaflets were to be given to any guests or employees who objected to seeing a Negro treated as a customer in the same way others were.

Four of the hotel managers "got very hot under the collar" but none refused to receive the guests they had already accepted through reservations made for the mayor. One manager was so angry, however, that he insisted that he would never again accept a Negro guest. The others later said they found no objections from guests or employees, and discrimination in Minneapolis hotels began to decline.

Even today, many years later, no one would claim that Minneapolis has lived up to the title that supposedly belongs to Philadelphia, "The City of Brotherly Love." Discrimination still exists for temporary periods, in defiance of law and of the American spirit, in places where the law cannot quite reach. But there seems to be no question that something began to happen. Even people who were not emotionally changed by the reforms went along with them, because a strong spokesman and a widespread public movement were taking the initiative away from those who believed in discrimination. The leadership was in the hands of people who really wanted to end discrimination.

An amusing side light, which showed only a partial understanding of the human relations program, was made by a veteran policeman. This old cop was overheard saying to a new man, "And don't arrest too many Negroes, the mayor doesn't like it."

In this period Muriel began to realize that wives had to make great sacrifices for husbands in politics and that *her* husband's method of operation meant that she was going to have to make greater sacrifices than most. Today everyone who has known them for years realizes that if she hadn't shouldered the responsibility of taking care of the small children as cheerfully as she did it would have meant an enormous change in Humphrey's future. But Muriel Humphrey has extraordinary qualities of endurance and patience and much the same approach as her husband's toward getting along with all kinds of people.

She still thinks it is a lot of fun to live with Hubert Humphrey and she can still laugh at his jokes. From an old file of the mayor's personal papers comes the following, a letter that Hizzoner wrote to Mrs. Humphrey.

Dear Mrs. Humphrey:

In view of the fact that I am no longer permitted to enter your home (which, I understand, is torn up by doctors, and good looking ones, contractors, and I understand he is good looking, too, plasterers, painters, plumbers, and electricians, all of which I understand are not too good looking), I am taking the liberty of informing you that on my recent visit to your domicile, I picked up a letter addressed to you which requests your presence on Wednesday evening, November 21, at a dinner being given in honor of the wives of the Minneapolis Aquatennial Association at the Nicollet Hotel.

Party begins at 6:30 with cocktails (two is enough for you) and dinner at about 7:00. There is a P.S. in same letter which suggests that you bring Mayor Humphrey with you. Of course, since he is now a resident of the Nicollet Hotel, this can be readily arranged with appropriate ceremonies, etc., following the dinner.

Put this in your date book.

Cordially yours,
HUBERT H. HUMPHREY
MAYOR

The children had been quarantined and it had been suggested that he stay away from home for a while. Otherwise the city's mayor would have been quarantined with the kids. So when the quarantine was lifted he thought he would take her out and this was his invitation. He has written similar notes to her when he has just been extremely busy or on a long campaign trip.

These were exciting days for Humphrey. Not all his friends agree, but he himself believes his best talents are administrative and not personal or political in the campaigning or crusading sense. He likes to think he is greater as a team chairman than as a one-man band. Most of his days since he was mayor he has been both.

Today he looks back with nostalgia on the days when he was learning a great deal about city government. He was meeting all kinds of new people and sitting in an administrative place where interesting things happened and where it was possible to initiate programs and see them brought to fulfillment. In a way, the job of being a senator is almost one brush fire after another. Many programs are followed through to completion, but there are many more that have to be forgotten or are doomed to be voted down. Or they are changed and enacted under someone else's name, until the original author has little reason left for pride of authorship. But as mayor Humphrey could start and finish some major projects.

He has remained keenly interested in metropolitan areas, which he believes have become an increasing social and political problem in the United States in mid-century. He feels this is a major task before the United States: to manage the wealth and welfare of the cities.

Invited to speak at the annual conference of mayors in Los Angeles in 1959, he pointed out that even when he was running Minneapolis he and his team met some of the major problems of the day. He listed them as urban blight, the unmet needs of education, housing, and health piled up by the war, law enforcement and delinquency, human relations conflicts, and the struggle to reform local government and properly finance it.

He told the mayors, "About two thirds of our people now live in metropolitan areas. . . . In a few years the two thirds will grow to three fourths." He told them that the democratic processes had not so far recognized the "growing urbanization of America," and therefore we did not give the "great urban majority" in the United States its proper representation in our state legislatures and in Congress.

To Humphrey, "if the trouble is political, the answer, too, must be political. It lies in arousing all the people of America—not just the city folk—to the needs of urban America. Only when this is done will it be possible for cities to receive the recognition from state and federal governments to which they are entitled."

He pointed out that he was a great exponent of federal revenues sufficient to pay for federal help to cities on an accelerating, not diminishing, scale.

For ten years he has been sponsoring legislation "to correct inequities created by federal installations that pay no taxes yet require many local services. Present payment practices are a hodgepodge of arrangements for various kinds of payments in lieu of taxes or for no payments at all. In order to make a start on this problem, I have a bill to authorize certain kinds of payments at once and to establish a commission to look into other claims so that we will have a better understanding of the nature and extent of the problem. I am happy to report to you that there are good prospects for the enactment of this measure by this Congress."

He has also, of course, been quite strong for FHA, including all of its authorities, such as the provisions that enable it to insure private mortgages. He considers this essential for a proper urban renewal program. Another proposal in his program for cities is that "the federal government should stop treating the cities as stepchildren or poor relations and bring them into the inner councils of policy and administration."

He told the mayors that we must find some way "to require that federal agencies engaged in administering such programs coordinate their plans with one another and with local officials. And however this is done, there must be a single official with authority to knock heads together to make decisions binding on the federal officials concerned."

In his opinion, the President should have a "planning staff" capable of advising the White House and then Congress on "the best uses of our resources, to achieve the high priority purposes of the national security and the national welfare."

Humphrey has strongly attacked President Eisenhower for bringing pressure through conservatives in Congress to beat down the housing and urban renewal bills. He said that he was "shocked" when, after many concessions had been made to meet the President "more than halfway," the President vetoed the bill as "excessive" and "inflationary." The bill would have authorized the spending of $900,000,000 for urban renewal for the next two years, although the mayors had estimated that $600,000,000 for ten years was needed to clean up the decaying parts of American cities.

Humphrey feels deeply about the way the downtown areas of American cities have gone to pot, so that housing is bad, delinquency is a problem, the main streets that were once show places have turned into cheap Broadways with a carnival atmosphere. Some of this concern may have its roots in the way he and his father felt about the waste of buildings, time, and human resources when the dust storms and the depression went like scourges down the main streets of Doland and Huron. Humphrey always feels, when he sees an abandoned store or an old hotel or a row of cheap boarding houses in a once good neighborhood, that there is great human tragedy and waste. He knows from the inside what it means to see a thriving street go to pot and decay. So he has emotions about "urban blight."

And his conscience tells him that it is immoral to throw away homes, shops, and stores that have not really outlived their usefulness but have merely been permitted to rot away for lack of proper planning. Once a place has really become a slum, of course, he is in favor of slum clearance. He just thinks America has better uses for her resources than to build up whole sections of cities and then, in great moves to the suburbs or through improper planning of railroads, factories, and so on, let the cities become "smoky blots upon the landscape," to use his own term.

He likes to point to Pittsburgh as an example of intelligent planning. Its downtown area, which once was "covered with rust and soot," by proper planning and co-operation of voluntary associations as well as the government has been rebuilt until "it has gone from one of the ugliest downtowns to one of the most beautiful downtowns in America."

When Humphrey gets to talking in public or private about this sort of problem it is clear that there is more than one reason why he might like to hold an administrative post again. A powerful reason would be the fact that he greatly enjoyed being mayor of Minneapolis. Achievement is one of the main satisfactions of administrative responsibility.

By the time he was well into his second term as mayor, Minneapolis politicians saw Humphrey as an inevitable candidate for the governorship or the Senate—probably the Senate. A few felt he might have brighter prospects than that but hardly dared to mention it even to their mirrors. By this time Leon Henderson and Paul Porter, both liberals in the ADA wing of the Democratic party, had mentioned him as a Democratic vice-presidential possibility. Chester Bowles was one of the first to include him in a list of possible presidential nominees.

Referring to discussion of the senatorial race at this time, the mayor said, "If the papers keep talking about my political ambitions they may give me ideas."

A Minneapolis commentator had said that the mayor was not specifically running for the Senate, except that "he is running for everything all the time."

Humphrey's ambition to climb the political ladder has always had a certain transparency. Some people found it repulsive that any man should show his driving ambition so plainly. Others found it disarming and reassuring that he made so little pretense. At the same time some fundamental modesty or insecurity seemed to contradict his ambition; by his manner he appeared to be saying, "Of course a country boy like me could not be a U.S. senator." Perhaps what most appealed to the voters was the knowledge that he truly came from the rank and file and needed help if he were to rise in the world. Some candidates, strange as it seems, do not convey an urgent sense of their need for votes. They ask for votes, they want them, but they don't behave as if their need is real. Humphrey's audiences—at least a large majority of them—seemed to believe that here was a man who was working hard to please them and who humanly expected to be grateful to them and to have them grateful to him. In the Senate chamber or on television, the well-known "political observers" of Washington do not see the sympathetic radar between the senator and a live audience of people at a state fair, for example. When Humphrey speaks about the farm or the kitchen or the "rent money," they certainly know he is a democrat with a small *d*.

CHAPTER X

Commies and Civil Rights

In the fall of 1946 Hubert Humphrey got a very angry letter from a friend of his who had been offended by some anti-Communist remarks Hubert had made. The friend said:

It is very well to decry those who wait for the line to be handed down, but for God sake [sic] read originals, or has your scientific training in political science been lost on you? There was no need to make any comments . . . does Stassen make war in public on his enemies in the Republican Party? He just says "no comment." My God man wake up or you'll ruin yourself politically.

Hubert's answer began:

Your letter has had me doing a good deal of thinking. I appreciate your willingness to speak straight from the shoulder and call me to task when you believe I am in error.

Now look, don't get so alarmed about what you read in the Minneapolis *Star*. I had a good long talk with Henry Wallace. In fact I spent better than three hours with him and I am sure that he and I would both agree that there was some merit to each of our points of view . . . but one of the things which disturbed me about Wallace's statement was not so much what he said . . . but the blind worshiping of his words by some of the fellow travelers. You will note . . . that it took the Commies three days to make up their mind whether Wallace was a faker or a hero. . . . I believe him to be a highly intelligent, sincere . . . leader . . . that doesn't mean that I have to agree with every word he said. This damn hero-worshiping just does not make sense to me. If I can afford the luxury of a good scrap with my wife occasionally, I ought to be able to enjoy the same thing with some of the political leaders of the day.

One other item . . . I think you ought to catch on pretty quickly that neither Art nor Bill nor any of the other fellows around here runs my life or governs my mind. The arguments I have with some of them are much more serious than those I have with public leaders. . . . I enjoy frank discussion. . . . Thanks—for being such a good friend as to tell me some of the things that are not always so easy to take. . . . I appreciate it.

This letter really flipped his friend right over. Virtually by return mail his red-hot critic replied:

Thank you for your most kind letter, you are a "big man." What I should do more often . . . is render praise. For every seeming backward step you make there are ten forward—for which I have not commended you . . . it is my opinion this city has never had a Mayor like you. That after all is more important than the political church you may belong to and I think a great majority of people believe this, too. All hail to the chief!

We may note a couple of things about this exchange. First, Humphrey's letter very successfully kept in the family fold a man who had been sympathetic to talk describing Humphrey as "a red-baiter." Second, the letter is both genuine and at the same time terribly smooth. His admirers make the observation that Humphrey applies the same skill at communicating with people to writing letters, making speeches, or presiding at meetings. Like most leaders, he seems powerless to analyze how he does it. It is intuitive. So his admirers say, if politics is an art, he is a master artist.

Behind the incident was a much larger story.

On the surface, Humphrey was breaking in this year of 1946 with Henry Wallace and some other people, but underneath, he and all his allies were in a bitter-end struggle with those whom they considered to be Communists, fellow travelers—or their dupes.

Objective observers say there was no doubt that the liberal forces in Minnesota, notably the leadership of the DFL, had been thoroughly infiltrated by the Communists well before this time. National observers, including this writer, felt that the older advisers to Henry Wallace were being displaced and that he was being surrounded by what

Walter Reuther has called the "valet service" of the American Communists.

Humphrey in this period organized many meetings at which he urged conciliation, many steps and battles and appeals, and finally made statements in which he publicly denounced the opposing faction as led by Communists.

So far as Humphrey was concerned, his relationship to Wallace was a sad story indeed. Along with many other liberals of the period, Humphrey had thought of Wallace as ranking with the greatest of New Dealers—as a man who might well make a fine President.

As late as July 1944 he was an ardent supporter of Henry Wallace for the vice-presidential nomination. The Minnesota delegation to the convention was pledged to Wallace. Humphrey was state campaign director and wrote to Harold Young, assistant to Wallace, to make a personal request: "I would like to place the name of Vice-President Wallace in nomination, and if that is not possible, to give a seconding speech in support of his nomination."

As it turned out, there was a celebrated battle that year in the corridors of the White House over the nomination for Vice-President. Wallace was dropped by Roosevelt, and Byrnes was passed over, with resulting bitterness that lasted for years. Harry S. Truman got the nod, the nomination—and eventually the presidency. So Humphrey never had a real chance to nominate Wallace and although he was highly vocal for Wallace at Chicago no one noticed or even seemed to remember it—except, of course, Henry.

The liberals in Minnesota were somewhat surprised to learn that after Wallace's famous postwar Madison Square Garden speech Humphrey had broken off with Henry, saying that he was "totally irresponsible." From 1946 to 1948 the right and left wings of the DFL fought like cats and dogs. By 1948 Humphrey and his friends dominated the state DFL convention, in contrast to previous times when they had been outmaneuvered by Communists, fellow travelers, dupes, or various kinds of left-wingers and/or admirers of Henry Wallace. In '48 this group held a rump convention of its own, while the regular DFL convention nominated Humphrey for the Senate by acclamation. But it was a rough and bloody battle in those two years.

Humphrey is the only major American political figure who has personally tangled in political combat with Communists determined to defeat him and his friends.

Other Americans have, like Humphrey, gone to Russia and met Rusian Communists on their home grounds. And many Americans have negotiated with foreign Communists at Geneva or in the United Nations. But Humphrey was involved in a life-and-death struggle with American Communists in his home state, and the battle deserves more detailed treatment than can be given to it here.

When Humphrey emerged as the leader of the Democratic Farmer-Labor party he could reasonably have felt that his main task was to build that party into a strong enterprise and ultimately to make his stand for office somewhere as a Democratic Farmer-Laborite. But instead he got into hot water almost immediately. The main outlines of this struggle help explain important aspects of Humphrey's later career.

Several students of the time have written documented accounts establishing that Communists were important in Minnesota in those days.

The Farmer-Labor leader, Governor Floyd Olson, was never a Communist and in his later years was certainly aware that Communists existed and that they used certain ugly tactics. For a time, however, he felt that he could work with them, as did many politicians of this and other countries in that period. Humphrey and others believe that if Olson had lived he himself would have routed the Communists from his party.

In the thirties the state of Minnesota for various reasons, one of which was the emergence of a coalition of farmer and labor elements previously not seen in such a coherent form in the United States, was a prime target for the infiltration of Communist agents. Communist or extreme left-wing sentiment is not created only by the intellectual or organizational activity of purposeful agents! Minnesota had been through severe times. She was going through an uncertain period at the end of the war. Poor housing, inflationary prices, race trouble, and labor conflict produced Communist sentiments in some Minneapolis citizens just as social stress did in some citizens in London, or Berlin, or Calcutta. In 1945 and 1946 key posts in the Democratic Farmer-Labor party were captured by people whose statements and tactics seemed to some liberals to be clearly Communist. Humphrey himself had not foreseen in 1944 that the real party adherents in the DFL would be so difficult to dislodge from power or so rough to deal with while they were in power.

Humphrey was not the earliest political leader to see what Communist sympathizers were doing to the liberal wing. But he was comparatively early, and he became one of the most effective "Commie fighters" of the country. One political observer says, "I just wish I could have seen the look on the face of that South Dakota debater, already a roaring success as mayor, when he discovered just how rough and tough and dirty it could be to fight the Communists."

Many American organizations, labor groups, scientific societies, and semipolitical groups were at this time having some form or other of what the men around Humphrey call "the Commie fight." It was to result in producing many shades of opinion, as most literate readers know; some fellow travelers left the fold and became liberals, others left and became bitter reactionaries, while others pursued a dizzy course, fleeing from the reactionaries into the arms of the Party and then out to become disgusted neutrals, or perhaps later to slide completely over and become even more bitter reactionaries.

In the DFL, after some major defeats and some curious surface compromises, a strong anti-Communist element emerged with Humphrey as its leader. He has remained moderate and forgiving toward persons who did not join his group in the anti-Communist fight or who in fact had extreme left-wing convictions but then mellowed. However, it became apparent to his friends that he was shocked by their tactics, for he had long thought of Communism as not merely political opposition to the American way of thinking but an immoral approach to social change. Thus it seemed one of the few subjects on which he might be said to have rigid and lingering animosity. But that was only for the "hard core." Before the battle was over he managed to regain the friendship of many who originally thought he was a "red-baiter." Many ex-Communists or fellow travelers came to admire or go along with a man who had become a United States senator a few months after the conflict finally faded away. Humphrey has welcomed those who have now departed from knowing or unknowing fellow traveling. But he has never got over his emotional repulsion and moral disapproval of the central beliefs and tactics of the hard-shell Communists, those who never gave in, and in his opinion never played fair.

Years later, an ex-Communist was to tell him that when he first appeared at the university the Communists marked "Little Hubert" as a likely young man to be taken into the fold. It has occurred to conservatives at the other end of the political scale that Humphrey might easily have "socialistic notions." Sometimes they lump him in their minds with "left-wing professors"—he seems to be very close, in their minds, to the kind of people who are close to the Communists, in the popular stereotype. This is so far from the facts as to be ludicrous. Humphrey has never been doctrinaire for *any* doctrine and never been close even to the socialist line.

Humphrey and those close to him for many years say that he never toyed with the idea of becoming a fellow traveler or a Communist. In his most formative years at the university Floyd Olson was first a living figure, then a vivid memory. At the time Humphrey turned twenty-one Franklin D. Roosevelt was elected to his first term as President of the United States. Roosevelt and Woodrow Wilson were almost too great to serve as models, but Olson was definitely of human size. Olson and Roosevelt were his governor and his President—and while both of them had profound commitments to social change, at the same time they had basic beliefs in the American credo of fair play, majority vote, education for all, and free speech. Both Olson and Roosevelt, be it noted, had in great part won their followings and made the social changes they were able to make through their great gifts for persuasion and political improvisation. These were Humphrey's models rather than the European socialist or Communist who greatly resented the ruling class and believed that manipulating people with propaganda would lead to the seizure of power.

One of Humphrey's teachers had a favorite saying, which for years was a favorite of Humphrey's: "Power goes to him who seeks it." While this might sound like Machiavelli or Khrushchev, it is not too far from the ordinary Kiwanis philosophy, that if you work hard you are very likely to be named chairman of the committee. In any case Humphrey might logically have been used by left-wingers, although he never was. But he never would have joined them. When Humphrey was forming his opinions and general coloration in politics he was guided by people who had a general skepticism toward all political slogans and most specifically those of the far left.

116

In the end Humphrey and his friends decisively defeated their foes within the DFL party—and went on to defeat Republicans for the statehouse, Congress, and the Senate. Among these friends were three people who became part of the circle of Humphrey advisers. This was *never* a closed circle, never a "club," and as it widened and fanned out Max M. Kampelman, Eugenie Anderson, and Eugene McCarthy were included in it.

Mr. Kampelman was a lawyer who also had a background in political science. He was around the edges of the basic circle in war years but did not get particularly close until after the war. During the "Commie fight," Max and Naftalin and Eugenie Anderson made many forays through the countryside seeking allies, helping to build up the DFL into their vision of a truly liberal party. At the time Humphrey was elected senator, Kampelman was a professor at Bennington, Vermont, but was called down to the Humphrey office to help organize it and recruit staff and so on. "He came for three weeks," says Humphrey, "but I kept him for years." His leave of absence gradually became permanent, and he stayed on with Humphrey as assistant and legislative counsel until 1955, when he resigned to go into private law practice. He still keeps in close touch with Senator Humphrey and advises on policy and political strategy. The Communist Control Act was his idea, and his mark is on much other legislation, where his legal and strategic abilities were invaluable.

Mrs. Eugenie Anderson, of Red Wing, was an early DFL campaigner and of course active in the Humphrey senatorial campaigns. She later became nationally known as a Democratic committeewoman and was appointed Ambassador to Denmark. She was active in the "Commie fight."

In 1958 she was bitterly disappointed when three of the "old bunch" were all thinking of running for the senatorial nomination. She and Karl Rolvaag and Eugene McCarthy were all contenders, and she did not, as she might have expected, receive the support of old DFL leaders such as Humphrey. The latter pursued a policy of making no choice among his old friends, so of course none of the three contenders was completely satisfied.

Eugene McCarthy was a bright young economics teacher from St. Paul who after the war came into the inner circle and soon was one of the most influential. He ran successfully for Congress and in 1958 won his place in the Senate. Thus

117

Minnesota has sent two teachers to the Senate, and the DFL is just about on top of the world, holding all the top spots in the state.

But the scars of the fight are still on the DFL party, and there are members who are cool to each other to this day. As is the case with similar battles in other organizations, some feel that others showed themselves to be dupes or that they "got off the train too late"—or "too early," in which case they might be termed "premature anti-Communists"! And there are some who feel that their colleagues were zealous against the extreme left-wingers but were not very squeamish about their tactics and used deplorable means toward the desirable end of establishing a DFL more representative of its members.

Humphrey today feels that he learned at first hand what Communists are like and that his youthful idealism met up with some very rough and tough tactics as well as some awesome hostility. He recalls one party council where he and such friends as Kampelman and Naftalin were physically segregated on one side of a room—on the other side were people who actually booed and hissed them. Humphrey had never expected American politics to be like that, nor has he found much like that since.

He says the Communists certainly showed their foes how to work—they got up early and late. They knew how to get the people out, something Humphrey, like any other politician, respects. But he was shocked one night in his own precinct to find so many people at his own neighborhood meeting. His foes had packed the hall, in the sense that they had called up everyone they knew in the precinct. Humphrey was mayor at the time but could not be elected by that precinct as a delegate to party councils because "the word was out" to the leftists to vote against him. He and Naftalin and Kubicek and Simms and the others had to get up early and work late to explain what was happening and round up all their allies, so *their* adherents would pack the necessary meetings. So he learned that the "bad guys" could defeat the "good guys," even when they were in the majority, unless that majority went to work to use democratic methods for all they were worth.

Humphrey also found that many persons in politics not only enjoy rewarding their friends, but once they start doing hatchet work on their foes, they enjoy that too.

Humphrey does not enjoy bitter rows. Today he still feels that looking after friends is more important than "cutting up" your foes. An associate says, "Critics think Humphrey just loves everybody, and he ought to hate more people, but he isn't good enough at hating."

Humphrey's feeling is that you have to be careful to avoid factionalism, remember that people change, and that you must not shut the door so that they can never come back.

His attitudes then and now are interesting in view of the fact that in our foreign relations we deal with many countries that have strong Communist parties.

He is honestly puzzled as to how humanitarians, even though they may not believe in any religion, can view Communism with favor. He considers that a godless materialistic philosophy is not only mistaken but immoral.

So he does not think about Communists merely in terms of politics or national power, and certainly he does not consider Communism to be the hope of ultimate democracy or brotherhood for the human race. He has suffered personally from Communists, he believes he knows various twists and turns of their immoral philosophy very well from firsthand struggle with them, and so, although he remains an ardent New Dealer, enthusiastic about the use of government to promote human welfare, he remains stubbornly against any philosophy with a tinge of totalitarianism.

His basic attitude then—and it is not much changed today—was that Communists and their friends had to be fought, night and day, and one had to learn that their rough tactics had no place in a liberal party. He does not and never did believe that one can create what used to be called a "united front" composed of social reform parties, including the Communists. But he abhors treating fellow travelers or even Communists as if they were an entirely different kind of people who are totally beyond the reach of persuasion, and he is firmly set against vengeance and vindictiveness. He considers that "the hard-core Communist" has no place in the American political scene, or in any country that desires a democratic government, but he thinks —and the Russians seem to agree—that very few human beings are capable of being dedicated Communists.

It was in this period that Americans for Democratic Action was started, with perhaps two main missions—to express a truly liberal Rooseveltian view in political discussions, and to fight American Communists. In the course of the Minnesota fight a live-wire ADA was formed there, and Humphrey came to the attention of many Democratic liberals nationally through the ADA. In 1949 he served as national chairman of ADA, and he has remained with it through thick and thin. Professional politicians consider this a great liability, and he has said that perhaps it is but the ADA has given him a great deal and he cannot bring himself to pull away from it.

His friends feel he showed leadership and courage in going with the ADA trend of thought, first against opposition from the left, and years later in sticking with it against opposition from the right. Thus they feel that Humphrey is a man of character, and "you know where to find him, he won't duck when the heat is on."

This quality was becoming apparent to national observers as 1948 brought other events.

Mayor Humphrey's future was changed for the better in a single night at the Philadelphia Democratic convention of 1948.

The background was a troubled outlook for the Democratic party. Truman was considered certain to lose to Dewey, a man who had tried and tried again for the presidency.

Truman up to then had often been considered a weak President, even by many Democrats. A sizable wing of the Americans for Democratic Action thought that Dwight D. Eisenhower would make a stronger and more liberal President. In his first years in the White House, as the faces associated with Roosevelt departed, it had seemed as if they were being replaced by a "Missouri gang." Still in the future were some of Truman's major decisions, such as the move to go into Korea, General MacArthur's discharge, and other steps that were to show that President Truman had a real philosophy of the presidency. And of course there lay ahead a great surprise victory over Governor Dewey, but the delegates in Philadelphia did not know that.

Truman had always, somewhat surprisingly for a Missourian, spoken clearly for federal action in the field of civil rights, but leading party politicians were at odds over the issue. They regarded it as dynamite, in a year when Henry A. Wallace was going to nibble away at Democratic strength from one side, to take a stand that would permit conservatives to nibble away at the party from the other side.

Humphrey and other members of the Minnesota delegation, however, were pledged to the strongest possible stand.

Humphrey already had a national reputation in civil rights circles because of his Council on Human Relations and the fact that Minneapolis was the first city in the country to pass a Fair Employment Practices Act.

As the platform committee wrangled late into one night it sometimes appeared possible that an "acceptable" compromise would be reached, one that would somehow reconcile the views of liberals with those of the die-hard Southern delegates who were already threatening to walk out on the party if a strong civil rights plank were adopted. Humphrey, contrary to the public view he often presented in those years, was privately counseling moderation. In his discussions with other delegates he was using his best conciliatory tactics to seek some compromise that would not throw minority rights to the wolves but would not prove hopelessly divisive.

His closest advisers included his father, a delegate from South Dakota, proud and excited, and doggedly telling Humphrey that when the chips were down the son simply could not accept a plank containing such broad and bland language that it would really mean nothing at all. Brother Ralph was on hand too. He has contributed time and effort and money to his brother's political campaign, but he is not personally absorbed in politics.

Humphrey told the people working on the platform that he and other liberals would hold their fire until the fight for a reasonable compromise appeared hopeless. In the small hours of the morning, as those who were to become Dixiecrats appeared more and more intransigent, another close adviser, Orville Freeman, kept insisting that compromise was impossible, and from time to time Humphrey made notes for a speech he would try to make to the convention in the morning.

Humphrey naturally thought over the political angles of the civil rights issue, but he did not really think it was politically smart to stir up a floor fight over it. Even a White House assistant told a Humphrey aide not to urge Humphrey into futile battle. "He won't get fifty votes, you are making a fool of America's future great liberal." But Humphrey thought this was a moral position that he—and the party—had to take. That still left many tactical angles to consider. If their proposal didn't carry, the results might be worse than a compromise.

Humphrey's conscience is large enough and strong enough that he worried about what he was doing to the party and to people whom he admired but could not join in their political beliefs. But his conscience would have made it too hot for him if he had gone the other way.

Toward dawn he made up his mind, in the direction his father had expected all along. Writing the speech for no compromise began in earnest, but he still had no very good idea how it would be received.

Eugenie Anderson had the idea of reminding everyone that Mr. Truman had taken a strong stand in favor of civil rights. So an effort had been made to associate the proposition with the Truman goals.

It might be noted that big city "bosses" of the Democratic party, the men from Northern industrial centers, regarded a strong civil rights program not as a wild-eyed idea but as a very practical one for strengthening their ticket in home precincts.

Even when he was ready to go, Humphrey was still apprehensive about his course. On the way to the bunting-draped platform, in the crowded and excited convention scene, he ran into a veteran politician, Ed Flynn. The latter had been boss of the Bronx for many years, and a close personal friend of Roosevelt's, though personally he was about as liberal as James A. Farley; but when he realized what Humphrey was planning to do he nodded approval and gave him the benediction of a hard-bitten politician: "It's going to be all right." Humphrey still remembers this, for he was inwardly shaking in his shoes as he met this great moment in his career—one that would be remembered to his credit or discredit for many years.

Once he started speaking his confidence mounted and his eloquence was electrifying.

His timing proved correct. The majority was ready to face the fact that on some issues the party could not accommodate such widely differing views. It was a short speech, one of the shortest Humphrey has ever made. But the course of the Democratic party—and in particular the path of the die-hard Southern delegates—was clear by the time he had finished.

Mayor Humphrey said in part: ". . . There will be no hedging, and there will be no watering down, if you please, of the instruments and the principles of the civil rights program.

"My friends, to those who say that we are rushing this issue of civil rights, I say to them, we are 172 years late.

"To those who say that this civil rights program is an infringement on States' Rights, I say this, that the time has arrived in America for the Democratic party to get out of the shadows of States' Rights and walk forthrightly into the bright sunshine of human rights. . . .

"Let us not forget the evil patience and the blindness of the past. In these times of world economic, political and spiritual —above all spiritual—crisis, we cannot, and we must not, turn from the paths so plainly before us."

The convention went for the civil rights plank—and many Southern delegates went for the door. Spiritually and physically, they walked out into a summer rain as fate would have it. Soon they formed the Dixiecrats and ran their own candidate for President.

Politicians still differ as to whether this move of Humphrey and the convention was *politically* smart. It developed that after Humphrey had won his moral victory Truman went on to win re-election in an electoral vote victory. Some feel that Truman won but that Humphrey lost forever any chance of being a close contender for the nomination.

Tradition has it that the Democrats do not nominate Southerners for President, although they frequently nominate them for Vice-President (six times out of the last seven tries). But tradition has it that the Democrats do not nominate people who are personally or ideologically anathema down South—in spite of Truman's victory.

One way to figure the outcome of '48 is that Truman did indeed lose 38 electoral votes in the South but was enabled to overpower Dewey (and Wallace) and hold the line in California, Illinois, and Ohio, where he picked up 78 votes. Thus, in one view the Dixiecrat movement ended in an autumn rain—of votes.

One of the happiest hours of Humphrey's entire life came as a surprise when he returned to Minneapolis the Saturday after the Philadelphia convention closed.

With a few phone calls and considerable hurried painting of signs to be carried by paraders, his cohorts had organized a demonstration—not that it was hard to get people to turn out to welcome their scrappy mayor home from his civil rights victory.

The *Tribune* said the crowd of more than two thousand rooters made the biggest wartime railroad station crowd look puny. There were brass bands playing and a great crowd of university students carrying signs, most of them reading, "Humphrey: Champion of Human Rights."

At that night's reception at the Nicollet Hotel, Humphrey told a crowd of five hundred people he didn't want to bring anything political into the meeting. "We all know this is just good-fellowship," he said. However, he did give a half-hour talk outlining his fight for the civil rights plank.

George Murk, the politically active head of the musicians' union, led the crowd in group singing and said, "One song I hope we will all sing is 'Somebody Else Is Taking My Place' and we will dedicate it to Joe Ball." When Humphrey finished his talk there was a three-minute ovation.

Cynics said that Humphrey's fight at Philadelphia would not have succeeded if delegates had been more optimistic about the Democratic party's chances that year. If they had thought they could *win* with Truman they would have gone to greater lengths to keep the Southerners in the family. Some men now say that Northern Republican leaders, worried about losing their own states and their own congressional districts, figured they could take a chance and let the presidential election go where it was going to go anyway, down the drain. But they could fight better locally for the ticket if they had a civil rights plank in the national platform.

Others said this was a step that had to be taken by the Democratic party sometime and it might as well be in 1948 as well as later. Others thought it was good Minnesota politics for Mayor Humphrey, who had often been mentioned as a candidate for senator. From this point of view it was an effective step toward picking up some of the votes of Wallace supporters. It mitigated the chances of there being another liberal candidate, under the Wallace ticket, in the field against Humphrey.

When Humphrey was a student of political science and decided to run for mayor, it might have seemed like a crazy idea, but in fact he was known to masses of people and well liked by some quite influential people. And he had friends in labor, business, university, and church circles. Who *should* run for mayor?

By the time he had become a famous mayor and was thinking of running for the Senate, it probably would have been more surprising if he had not run than his deciding to try for it. He was a mushroom who had come up overnight, but there was no denying he was there.

When he was ready to run for the Senate he was well known through the length and breadth of Minnesota. He had already been to Congress several times to testify on such topics as rent control, housing, fair employment practices, and high prices.

He had made excellent appearances nationally on such radio programs as "America's Town Meeting of the Air" and "People's Platform," and increasingly he received invitations to speak from all over the country.

While he was mainly known in Minneapolis as a nonpartisan mayor it was hardly a secret that he was a New Dealer; but he certainly was not a theorist working for a planned society as the Republicans loved to characterize the New Dealer of the cartoonists.

He was a firm supporter of the United Nations and the Marshall Plan—and that was a major issue on which Joe Ball had voted the other way.

He was also known to farm audiences as someone interested in the soil conservation plan and rural electrification, which the Republican Congress had cut down.

It is startling to think how little time had elapsed from his first election in 1945 to his running for the Senate in 1948, but he was a most obvious choice for the nomination. He was a campaign manager, he had put the party together, he had gotten national attention at the convention, and he was the very opposite of a dark horse so far as the DFL nomination was concerned.

In addition to everything else he was known for the way in which he could work twelve, sixteen hours a day and thrive on it.

As he went into a campaign he could work eighteen and twenty hours a day being mayor and running for the Senate. He said then, "On a typical day I make three to five speeches in addition to my regular round of official business. I get back to the office from my last meeting around 11 P.M., then

I work until 1 or 2 A.M. and I'm back to work at nine-thirty in the morning." This was to be his steady schedule for many years.

He had become, perhaps to a greater extent than he realized, the liberal leader of Minnesota. He was not only a good candidate, he was a person whose advice was sought and taken. In party councils he was recognized as an adept negotiator and conciliator. He was not a boss and he did not have a machine or organization, and all the details of party machinery bored him to some extent. But when people finally got him interested in a "situation," what he did about it worked out well.

Humphrey's strength in Minnesota, like the way he does his thinking and the way he manages his Senate office, is a real one-man affair. He does not have a whole number of cogs in the machine throughout the state—or the country— who will do his bidding. He has a lot of friends and a lot of people who for practical purposes are friends or behave as friends because they like what he is able to get done in Washington. You don't find Humphrey agents or puppets or mouthpieces. You find that Humphrey's friends and cousins, once a crowd of five hundred (Doland, pop. 500), has somehow enlarged to thousands.

In the Senate campaign he took off to make new friends, and he campaigned in eighty-four of Minnesota's eighty-seven counties.

Once again Humphrey was running against a rather colorless—or at least quiet—man, as Mayor Kline had been. No one seemed to consider Joe Ball terribly good or terribly bad. He had been a fairly conservative senator but not extremely reactionary. He had two main issues in which he believed; he had voted *for* the Taft-Hartley law and *against* the Marshall Plan. Humphrey met him foursquare on both of them.

Repeatedly he challenged Ball to joint debate. This is a proposal that the holder of an office never likes as well as a man who is running to grab the office. There is always the chance of inadvertently saying the wrong thing or in the heat of rebuttal delivering a fiery phrase that will come home and haunt you. Of course either man may make such a mistake in a verbal free-for-all, but the officeholder is the one who has the job in hand and has more to lose. Ball had all the Minnesota daily newspapers and all but 18 of the 460 weekly newspapers in Minnesota with him, so he had his views set forth.

Humphrey by statistical count could speak three times as many words a minute as slow-speaking Ball. Ball never put his head into the noose of debate. But at more than one meeting, while he was speaking in his careful and methodical manner, Humphrey would be going through the audience shaking hands, smiling at the ladies, cheerfully chucking children under their chins, and remembering the names of everyone he had ever met. Thus Ball made the speech on some occasions and Humphrey met the voters.

Humphrey sometimes gave more than a dozen speeches a day, and he traveled thirty thousand miles, or a little more than it takes to go around the earth at its widest point.

He attended more than fifty county fairs. No one knows how many hamburgers and hot dogs he ate, nor how many gallons of pop he put away, after throwing how many numbers of balls at how many wooden milk bottles in side-show games. The crowds loved it and of course Humphrey loved it. The Russians have been known to practice "physiological warfare" on our diplomats by throwing elaborate dinners at which our people are hopelessly outclassed when it comes to consuming all the borscht, caviar, pastry, and vodka to which the Russians are accustomed. In this respect there are very few cast-iron stomachs that would compare with Hubert Humphrey's. If this were the main point of the cold war, there is no question who should be our champion. He can drink gallons of "orange drink," mixing it with quantities of fried chicken, hot German potato salad, hot dogs, hard rolls, and a shot of bourbon with the local politicos in the hotel suite afterward by way of settling the stomach. It is not true that Humphrey never has a twinge of stomach trouble. He does. He has been known to take a soda mint as he leaves one dinner, where he has had a plate of soup and made a speech, and heads for another dinner, where he may get a little ham and some salad and make another speech. After that he goes to the final speech of the evening and a cup of black and acid coffee.

However, even if his stomach occasionally gives him a twinge by way of reminding him that he is human, Humphrey's schedule is more than equal to the heartburn front of the cold war.

In this campaign against Joe Ball, Humphrey made Labor

Day speeches in three widely separated towns. He made two in Rochester and Faribault in the southern part of the state and then flew to make another in Duluth, several hundred miles to the northeast.

And what did he say? A lot of things with which the voter —and at least the reader of this book—are familiar. That all people are human, all Americans have basic rights. That farmers are part of our economy and entitled to their full share in it—and their product, like the rest of our productivity, should be used as strength for waging peace. And more—for an hour or two. And the crowds loved that too.

His first senatorial campaign was the first occasion Humphrey had to take a real responsibility for broad-scale opinions of foreign affairs.

In one letter to the Minneapolis *Tribune* he sounded certain themes that were dominant in his mind.

He explained why basically he was for the Marshall Plan and for expanding it (whereas Senator Ball had voted against it).

Further, he did not think the objective of the Marshall Plan and our foreign policy should be merely to "contain" Russia. He felt that the Marshall Plan was "a broad, dynamic plan which was meant to lift up the people of Europe, to nourish democracy everywhere, to obtain a just, prosperous, and enduring peace."

He was criticized for the statement in which he said that rather than "contain" Russia we should "lead" her. As far back as this campaign, Humphrey felt that we should compete with Russia in peaceful production and imaginative ideas. Not "containment" but "competition" was his key word.

A short while before, President Truman had briefly considered the idea of sending Chief Justice Fred Vinson to Moscow to talk personally with Premier Stalin. The President had let it be known that he was considering this and then from his own party and advisers (and from Republicans) he had received a storm of criticism. To Hubert Humphrey this was a reasonable idea, to try to establish personal contact with the Russian Premier. One of Humphrey's favorite phrases in the first campaign was that we should "get off the diplomatic defensive and create a diplomatic offensive."

A real program of help for the farmer was also a main part of his campaign.

He predicted that he would win by 77,000 votes. But before election he cut the figure to 50,000. This perhaps indicates that, as one friend says, he suffers from underconfidence. It turned out that he won by a margin of 243,000!

So the first Democratic senator from Minnesota in a century took off with a plurality of nearly a quarter of a million.

Ball's campaign workers tried to toss off this crushing defeat by saying that Senator Humphrey was simply a tremendous brash salesman "who would have made the greatest vacuum cleaner salesman that ever lived." This is true as far as it goes. That, of course, is one of the things they think about Humphrey back in Spink County, South Dakota, where he and his father did go from door to door and were considered the greatest salesmen for miles around. But today even the supporters of Joe Ball would agree that there is a great deal more to this salesman than they thought. This bouncing consumer of hot dogs and producer of oratory knows how to please a crowd, but the crowd may see a good deal else in the man they sent to Washington to cope with the complexities of government in the atomic age.

Perhaps these crowds thought that Humphrey had a special spark.

PART III

The Nation

"You people always write that I talk on every subject. I do—I *like* every subject. I can't help it—it's just glands."

HUBERT H. HUMPHREY

CHAPTER XI

Gabbiest Freshman in the Senate

From the moment Humphrey entered the Senate it was clear to himself, his family, and everyone in range that he was going to enjoy the job just as much as he had hoped. In that first year he fairly wallowed in being a senator, and his colleagues and the members of the press found this a disturbing element; they could tolerate only a certain amount of the brisk and brash young man who seemed so determined to let the world know he was on his way.

One long-time assistant of Humphrey's says that for many years Humphrey really never got over his surprise at finding himself—"Little Hubert"—sitting "in the seats of the mighty." There can be no doubt, says his old assistant, that he is fundamentally humble and modest. Further, because he felt somewhat insecure about his abilities, he developed for a time a superbrashness and bravado that often created an entirely false impression. "His basic fault was never overconfidence," said this assistant; "if anything his basic fault has always been underconfidence. He cannot really believe that he is as well qualified as anyone else who is likely to get the job to be a senator, and he still rattles inside when there is serious discussion and consideration of him as a candidate for President."

One of Humphrey's most engaging traits, an assistant of the present day believes, is that he does not appear to take himself too seriously, an impression in remarkable contrast to many other public figures. In his early years in the Senate the Humphrey bravado may have covered his modesty and "underconfidence." Today he is less brash, this assistant says, because he has now moved successfully in the very highest echelons of government.

A liberal newsweekly said that his election was "a one-man miracle wrought in defiance of all the political laws and probabilities." In retrospect this seems to be putting it a little strongly, because even Republicans in Minnesota had admitted to themselves that Ball was not a strong candidate in 1948—and Humphrey was. Nonetheless Humphrey had won a stunning victory, and though it seemed to be part of a national upset, Humphrey's colorful personality made him the subject of special attention—for example, an extended profile and his picture on the cover of *Time* magazine.

He was a guest on "Meet the Press," then a well-known radio program. With his astounding and colorful answers to Larry Spivak and the other panelists, he was a resounding success. J. R. Wiggins of the Washington *Post* asked him if he were not chairman of the Americans for Democratic Action. Humphrey said, "That's right," and Wiggins said, "And do you recall an ADA pamphlet which stated that Truman had not won the minds and hearts of the people and declaring that this grave moment needs a new face and victory can be won by drafting Eisenhower and/or Douglas?"

"Yes, I do, sir," said Humphrey, respectful to the well-known newspaperman.

Wiggins: "Do you still think that you and the rest of the ADA were right in wishing to ditch Harry Truman?"

Humphrey: "I think we were dead wrong and I think confession is good for the soul."

Wiggins, a little stunned by this, said, "I think that's magnificent."

Those who remember Humphrey as always cocky when he first came to the Senate simply forget that at other times he was modest to excess and rather self-deprecatory.

On that famous "Meet the Press" program Spivak asked him, "What do you personally plan to do as far as the national FEPC goes? Are you going to try to put legislation through Congress on those issues?" Humphrey replied, "May I just say that I recognize that I am a newcomer to the Senate of the United States? I'm the junior senator from Minnesota and I have an awful lot to learn and I know it, and I'm looking forward to the opportunity of becoming much more informed on many national issues and I'm going to be a co-operative member of the United States Senate. I'm going to support President Truman and his program. If he asks for a program—which I think he will, he didn't mince any words about it—on civil rights, I'm going to support that. I'm surely not foolish enough, may I say, to think that some young fellow from out here in Minnesota is going to come down and upset the Congress of the United States, nor do I have any intention of trying to do so."

Spivak persisted. "In short, if he lets the civil rights program drop, you're going to let it drop along with him?"

Humphrey: "Oh no, I wouldn't say that, I don't think the President is going to let the civil rights program drop and we're not going to let it drop."

Then he was asked: "Well, I gather then, Senator, that you don't expect to introduce this civil rights legislation in Congress yourself?"

Humphrey: "Well, I frankly haven't had much time to think about introducing any legislation into the Senate of the United States. I intend to be down there and I will surely co-operate with those that want to go along with such a program in their six-year term, may I say, and maybe in six years a man will get his feet pretty well on the ground."

In recent years Humphrey sought particularly to avoid being self-righteous toward Southern Democrats. He did not pronounce moral judgments on them and avoided castigating them personally. He was aware that many well-educated and well-traveled Southern leaders were themselves unprejudiced and enlightened men who were doing the best they could to advance their civil rights problem in the gradual way they sincerely believed to be the best. Humphrey could not be called a "gradualist," but even when he disagreed most strongly he did not step up on a pedestal and take the attitude that one big vote in which "people stand up and be counted" can materially advance human rights.

A freshman senator in 1949 was supposed to keep comparatively quiet during his first months or years of office. In fact there was an unwritten rule that it would be better if he did not make any speeches for the first six months. (This rule has largely gone by the boards, as the inflow of new senators from the West in 1958 swept away most of the barriers.) The average citizen has no idea how closely the United States Senate tries to observe traditions, how seriously it takes itself as a kind of club in which the members must observe a certain code. It is easy to picture the Supreme Court as a place where rituals are followed, all regulations carefully observed, and tradition is enormously respected. The citizen looking at the Senate, however, remembers something he saw in a television hearing, or visiting the gallery as a tourist and seeing people aimlessly milling to and fro, or a particular senator out campaigning at a corn-husking contest and in an undignified way belting the daylights out of his opponent in a Fourth of July speech. Nonetheless, the Senate in its own home in the Capitol is a very sedate and solemn place. And most certainly every senator is considered to have a duty to the Senate as well as to his constituents and to the nation.

Young Senator Humphrey, before he was well settled at his desk, was asked whether he was going to be able to keep quiet in his first few months and whether that silence wouldn't kill him. He said that he was going to speak out when he felt like it and that you couldn't govern speech and political issues merely by the calendar. So much for the old six months rule!

The old king buffalo of the Senate, it must be believed, were not one bit worried about the impact of this latest example of "the sons of the wild jackass." It would not be true to say they were not irritated, but they were not truly upset. They thought—correctly as it turned out—that this young man would very shortly get his comeuppance. The Senate through many decades has developed ways of dealing with people who are a little too rough about rocking the boat.

Perhaps even more distressing, so far as his political future was concerned, was the fact that Senator Humphrey was less than perfect at making himself understood by the Senate press corps. In Minneapolis, Art Naftalin had shown him how to manage his press relations smoothly. He had had good publicity even in his first amateurish campaign in 1943. Yet in a poll in which Washington newspapermen voted for the most able senator, the most popular senator, and so on, the junior senator from Minnesota was shown to be personally unpopular with several influential Washington reporters. Perhaps this was fortunate because it made clear to Humphrey that he was doing something wrong.

He called in veteran newspapermen and asked them what he should do to improve his press relations. (In much the same way, on his extraordinary tour of the Middle East in 1957, he made it a practice to call in reporters to get their candid appraisals of the local situation, as perhaps opposed to those of the State Department.) Those who have been on the transmitting end of such an exchange say that he can be as exceptional a listener as he is a talker. He does not argue, he races ahead to ask the next question, but he hears very clearly the points that are made.

Many interviewers through the years have found that Humphrey can use his glib articulation—perhaps unconsciously—as a smoke screen. But he can also relapse into candor so complete that even hardened journalists feel he should be protected. They find themselves softening his remarks so that an interview that seems to have developed into a private conversation won't be printed.

In his early appearances on the Senate floor Humphrey was hitting a new stride as an orator and to some extent he still has this extra fire, although he may not see his villains and his heroes in the same black-and-white way. As he moved onto the national stage he was more nervous but also more confident. It was inevitable that sometimes he would be over-confident.

Owing to the prolonged interruption in his education, Humphrey was slightly older than people usually are when they first go into politics. He didn't get into the political arena until relatively late, and some of his spirit—some of his assets and also some of his early mistakes—can be attributed to the fact that he was still a novice. When he reached the Senate, for example, he had been in politics only about six years. How could he be expected to know the rules and the manners? He was not a seasoned and experienced politician, and some of the things he did sprang not so much from his basic attitudes as from the enthusiasm and radical do-it-now enthusiasm of a newcomer.

This was a period when he would say while attacking the Taft-Hartley law: "I submit that the processes of democracy are as relentless and ever flowing as the tide itself . . . the American people, the working people of this country, the people who have been oppressed by this law, are determined that they are going to remove this kind of punitive legislation from the statute books, and are determined that they are going to have something to say about the processes of government, because this country is their country, as well as it is yours and mine."

He also would go after "the bankers" in his original primitive way: "Mr. President, I am one who believes this nation is as strong . . . not as the Chase National Bank, not as the stock market, not even as the great powerful corporations, but the nation is only as strong as the productivity, the intelligence, the health, and the education of its people—and, I repeat, of its people. I believe that if we put more emphasis upon the human element we will take care of the financial element."

On June 14, 1949, he said, "Mr. President, too many times

in this country we have been fooled by the golden glow of the painted domes of high privilege. Too many times we have been fooled into believing that because so many people were wealthy the people of the country were strong." He would ask, "Mr. President, who are these high and mighty people who think there is anything in this country besides those who really produce, the men who work in the shops, in the factory, on the farms? They are the producers. Business cannot continue unless people have purchasing power."

He would say, "This nation is only as strong as its working people . . . whose boys and girls need homes, need pork chops, need clothes." And he would say that when we consider such major questions as labor-management relationships we should realize that "the eyes of the world are fixed upon us, the people of other countries want to know whether people of this great America are concerned about people or about the golden calf."

Surprisingly to some, Humphrey in such speeches as this always made the same plea for little business that he made for the farmer or the workingman. In debate on amending Taft-Hartley he said, "Business deserves a fair profit . . . but when I speak of business I speak of the kind of people I have known—those who made this country, the drugstores, the grocery stores and the clothing stores. They are the ones who made America . . . the big boys have tried to pit little business against labor, they have tried to tell the little businessmen, like the little contractor in California, that his enemy is the union. Someday he will find out who his enemy is . . . the little businessman will wake up and find out that the only important customers he ever had were those who worked in overalls . . . there are not enough corporation directors to keep every store in America busy."

Humphrey also made a plea in his discussions for the real history of the country to be taught in the schools—school children should learn about unions and "about the Haymarket riots, as well as about the Mexican war." He said that the average American was being given the wrong impression of that "period in American history from 1920 to 1929, the period of normalcy, the period of prosperity. What was happening? This country was being ditched, damned and drained; a little money was being made in the stock market by a few, the unions were destroyed, farmers were liquidated, small businessmen were destroyed by the thousands, banks failed all over the country. It was a great period. It is strange about these great periods. They seem to be great to a handful of people who are not so great."

In those first months as senator he surprised everyone by spending a great deal of time with his constituents, even on apparently trivial matters. Every senator is pleased to meet and be photographed with a touring high school senior class, the visiting choirs, and the 4-H Club winners who descend on the capital, particularly in the spring tourist season. But Humphrey remains one of the few senators who will take time out of his frantic schedule to discuss national and world affairs with high school and college students. They pose for the photographers, to be sure, but then Humphrey starts the discussion. He soon puts them at their ease, although sometimes they don't get too much of a chance to ask questions. They ask one good question and the senator is off. In a few moments he has led them through the United Nations, the underprivileged countries, the importance of grass-roots democracy, the separation of powers in the American government, and perhaps, as his opponents claim, a couple of references to the Magna Carta and the Gettysburg Address. At the same time, in a curious way, he seems to pick up information from these visiting delegations even while he is talking. "That pickup must be by radar and telepathy," said one observer, who cannot be called an admirer.

Sometimes the senator likes to put a cynical or "smart" interpretation on what he does. He will apologize to a visitor, who is perhaps arranging a national television show: "Of course you've got a big show you are putting together here, but those high school kids were from Minnesota where the votes count." This is said with a disarming and deprecatory smile, as if to apologize for the fact that a senator has to remember where his support comes from. Lots of times, of course, the visiting students really do not have any votes (indeed, many of these groups are from Eastern colleges), while the television show may reach tens of thousands of persons in Minnesota. The senator is just pretending to be concentrating on support. He doesn't always like to admit that he just loves an audience, particularly if it is sincerely interested in fundamental questions about national policy and war and peace.

Humphrey often humorously describes himself as a "refugee from the classroom," and comments to college groups that his "present job" is so precarious in tenure that he wants

138

to make sure his "credentials are still in order." The truth is that he has almost a compulsion to teach, is a "born teacher," and apparently most enjoys himself when discussing issues with young people.

In 1949 and 1950, while the old-line senators were taken aback by the new junior senator, they had to admit even against their will that in the give-and-take of debate on the Senate floor he was among the very best of this generation. In due time they would see him engaged in absorbing verbal duels with such masters at the late Robert A. Taft. Taft had a debating skill that few cared to challenge, but Humphrey met that test. There were memorable exchanges between the two men over the question of amendments to the Taft-Hartley Act which veteran senators like to recall "as verbal duels which were like you think the Senate ought to be and which it very seldom is." This statement does not mean that either had an overwhelming edge in knowledge or debate or articulation; they were both first-class performers, and the Senate appreciated that among their other qualities.

Humphrey's first months in the Senate would make a fascinating study for any political scientist, psychologist, or citizen seeking to understand our form of government.

His own explanation of how he has changed since those first months is that he has learned more, that obviously his attitudes are different now that he has been in the Senate for a while than when he first entered it, and that his early methods and speeches were probably all right for that stage in his career. To some on the left it has sometimes appeared that he compromised his basic views or at least "became more like the others." And to critics of the center and right of the political spectrum, it has appeared that he changed into a mature and responsible power in the Senate.

It is interesting and more than a little frustrating to see how the fact that a man has changed confuses some of his audience and some of the voters. There are those who feel that Humphrey is and always was a "wild man," and there are others in the liberal blocs of the party who feel that he has become an important working part of a governmental scheme of things that is not pushing needed reforms. He has lost friends at both ends of the Democratic party but he seems to have kept most of his early support and won new support from moderate elements.

Humphrey believes that people in politics get stereotyped too quickly. He says he used to be considered a flaming radical and that he almost had to live up to that; he "had to act that way" and make "tough" speeches or he would not have been perceived at all. As he moderated his method and tone he received hundreds of letters from voters over the country asking, "What happened to you?" or "Have you sold out?" Humphrey's view is that to some extent a politician becomes a prisoner of people's expectations. Those who have supported him as a certain kind of person have some right to expect that he will remain that way, but Humphrey reserves the right to learn—and to change! His integrity and ability to learn from experience required him to change some of his basic attitudes and to make several major changes in his methods. Naturally he and his friends believe these were changes for the better, changes to meet realities.

When he was new in the Senate the main thing that liberals knew about him was that he was a dynamo of energy with basically right attitudes on civil rights, housing, Taft-Hartley reform, and other liberal objectives of the day.

There are many people in Washington who will seize upon a new face, "a new leader," and do their best to feed him material, introduce him to people, find people who will write his speeches, and so forth. For a time Humphrey was besieged by liberal lawyers, labor people, government experts, organizations, and lobbyists for causes. They would give him research material, facts, and briefings on all their causes. And they still do so today; various groups—the Quakers, the fallout experts, the proponents of federal aid to education —consider him the senator who listens most knowledgeably.

His staff agrees that he always feels a final decision is up to him: it is not going to be decided by a group and he is not going to be budged too far by any clever argument, nor is he ever going to be dominated by a person on his staff. Therefore, in a logical but paradoxical way, he is perhaps freer than other bosses to listen and to let an adviser make his point with as much freedom as he wishes. His general attitude might be summarized thus: "I want to know precisely what you think, it won't bother me any if it is opposed to my ideas; when I sit down to decide what I think I know I will do it all by myself anyway, so tell me freely what's on your mind." The foregoing words are *not* quoted from the senator but are descriptive of his attitude as described by his assistants.

Humphrey did not have then and never has had any one particular adviser or even two or three who are genuine quarterbacks for his team. Franklin Roosevelt had Louis Howe and Harry Hopkins and in another way Sam Rosenman. At different times many persons had the ability to sway the President quite considerably, even though Roosevelt, too, was an independent operator who knew what he wanted to do and how to do it. Though his advisers had an enormous influence, they did not approach the unparalleled influence Sherman Adams had on the domestic policies of President Eisenhower.

There are a number of persons for whom Humphrey has the greatest respect and to whom he listens with interest, but none of them has ever approached the position of really master-minding what the senator will do next. In the first place Humphrey does not often calculate his future course. He is more of a lone operator, it would seem, than any recent presidential contender.

However, he does not suffer from lack of candid advice. He has been told that many of his speeches are "too corny" or "too long." Humphrey, perhaps deliberately, often warms up the average audience with broad jokes and "inspiring references" that can only be compared to commencement addresses or Fourth of July speeches. In the latter part of these addresses he *may* become much more serious and move to a higher plane. He claims that these are good tactics and logical, and that one has to win an audience and "get them on your side" before they can be led on to a particular proposal or a vote for a particular man. He also disagrees with what he considers "overly sophisticated people" who do not realize just how popular commencement speeches and Fourth of July talks are with the great American public. Many people consider them boring, but the commencement speeches are here to stay. Humphrey should know because each year he gives not one but a *dozen* commencement speeches.

His assistants have also lectured him for years about being on time. They say that of course it is pleasant for his audience if he lingers after a speech to shake hands and meet everybody. And if he is getting into a taxi and a police officer asks him something about Russia, nothing could be more democratic—and vote-winning—*at that spot* than for the senator to explain some of the finer points of negotiation with the Russians. But as his assistants have pointed out, this little discussion with a few people on the curb is making him late at another meeting hall where four hundred people are waiting for him. Fundamentally, this is a rudeness to the four

141

hundred people, who have been promised a Humphrey appearance and are becoming restive.

Humphrey listens attentively to these lectures. But time after time he leaves one place late for another, arrives late and dashes in full of energy, his coattails flying. If given half a chance he speedily makes friends all over again with the people who have become impatient.

"I will say this," said one assistant. "He has never been late for a network television broadcast and he has never been late for an appointment with the President. But as regards the White House, a couple of times he has just about given me heart failure." It would be considered quite a serious affront if a senator showed up late for an appointment with a President. When it comes to leaving airports, his staff has been known to telephone and ask that a scheduled flight be held up a few moments; the senator is on his way but will be a few minutes late. When he gets there he may very likely make the entire planeload feel amused and then grateful for the wait.

Various people have tried to set him straight on punctuality and the related matter of speaking too long. Sometimes he appears to agree with them on the latter point, but emotionally he disagrees; there is something about a longer speech that is quite different from a "talk." He believes that people in the Middle West have a tradition of long political speeches. "It helps them to judge a man, to see what intellectual and physical endurance he has," says the senator. "Perhaps they want to see how his mind works when he has been on his feet awhile and *has run out of notes*. They know about ghosts—notes could be prepared by a staff member—but when a man has been on his feet beyond an hour —then he'd better be able to think for himself." It would seem that Humphrey believes a man who is a good speaker on his feet has some of the prime qualities needed in politics. These points come to his mind when he thinks of Nikita Khrushchev, as we shall see later.

Humphrey likes to learn new things and there was a period when he tried voraciously to assimilate facts and programs on all phases of government and proposed reforms. He made many speeches and seemed to convey a chip-on-the-shoulder attitude. Other senators might not have minded his speeches being fiery and cocky, but they certainly did take exception to his self-righteously implying that sometimes his opponents were in the grip of "special interests."

142

Not only did he constantly advise the Senate on what it might do, and through the press corps try to counsel other parts of Washington on what ought to be done, but during the 1949 recess he toured the country, speaking and raising money for Americans for Democratic Action. This organization has a special place in his heart. At the present time it has scarcely no political power, but Humphrey will not say so in so many words and he never, even when it was most unpopular, thought he should resign from it. He believed in what it stood for, he was proud of some of its accomplishments. He was impressed originally because of its success, in many instances, in establishing liberalism in organizations and communities after bitter battles in which the non-Communists and non-fellow travelers had met and routed Communist sympathizers. Later he was elected chairman of Americans for Democratic Action, and to some extent he brought a more practical political line into that group of intellectuals and "eggheads."

In 1949, ADA was anathema to the old-line political pros. Skating around the country on behalf of ADA did not increase Humphrey's standing in the Senate.

But "Little Hubert" was involved in much more than that in his early Senate days.

He had been outspoken for the reform of political parties. In fact he espoused ideas that would have allowed Congress' seniority system to be scrapped. He urged that Senate rules be changed to allow debate to be cut off and filibustering abolished, so the legislation to create FEPC could be passed. He was in favor of tighter regulation of lobbies and political campaign funds. He himself introduced legislation for these things and for presidential preferential primaries.

Some of these proposals would greatly have upset established political forms and conventions if they had been acted upon and they struck rather directly at his fellow senators' familiar channels of support.

So he was considered a disturbing influence in so far as he had any influence. And most galling of all was the uncompromising way in which he often behaved when senators approached him. He now admits he could be quite unbending in those days. But the Senate works by means of hundreds of deals in which one group says, "If you vote for this we'll vote for that," or "We'll hold back on this if you'll go for this later." Most of these do *not* involve giving up a chance to win on a point of principle.

Humphrey really became quite unpopular and it was said that sometimes the Republicans would lie low waiting for Humphrey to speak for some subject. They knew that this would pick up Southern Democratic votes for them faster than any speeches they might make.

Some people bitterly disliked him and it was not only those who were "in the grip of special interests."

Looking back on this period, Humphrey feels that he certainly made some mistakes. But most of the things for which he fought he still believes in and he felt that it was important to make a public fight for them. More than that, so far as his own position and his present power to get things done are concerned, he rather tends to feel that through this speaking and infighting and initiating of proposals he established a public reputation to some extent on a national scale. By the time he began to get along better with fellow senators he also had some reputation behind him. No one can argue with the proposition that on the Hill today are many capable senators, serving their first or second terms, who have been rather quiet, who have observed all the rules, but who are not well known and never will be. Humphrey's name is not a household word from coast to coast but his name is reckoned with in all professional political circles. He feels this is due partly to the fact that when he arrived on the national scene he arrived working and talking and fighting and appeared to be in a hurry to get things done.

Some observers say that a senator can emphasize his constituency back home or he can see the Senate itself—or the nation or a particular part of it—as a constituency. Humphrey planned to be a leader of the liberal voters of the nation, and the liberals were his constituents. Once he was firmly established in that position, he could give more emphasis to his Senate constituency, and for years now he has paid attention to all of his "districts."

The dislike and distrust that some powerful senators had for him did not turn out to be fatal—and in fact was not permanent: today he is one of the most popular men in the Senate. However, his critics still say that he came close to talking himself not into fame but into oblivion. It is also said that a certain amount of mistrust of him exists in top political circles. At least his friends and foes and he himself agree on the low point of his Senate career.

The United States Senate sometimes appears careless of its integrity and dignity. It has tolerated many different kinds

144

of people, including outrageously dishonest demagogues. Yet the traditions of the Senate, human and fallible in execution, seek to preserve a certain code. These few score men must work with each other for years at a time, often under stress. There is a ritual and respect for fellow senators that tradition deems essential to the management of their complicated and often burdensome responsibilities.

Of course there is room for argument as to whether the Senate is not sometimes concerned with dignity when it thinks it is concerned with integrity. And at other times it seems to strive for a façade of false dignity at the very time it is most disorganized. In the case of Senator Joseph McCarthy, it was widely noticed that McCarthy had done untold damage to the executive side of the government, to this country, and to its people, but it was only when the Senate felt that he had brought shame upon the Senate that at last a vote of censure was taken. This may show a parochial sense of dignity, but does it show a sense of proportion?

In any case, senators do have a sense of dedication to the Senate. Long-term senators sometimes become devoted to that temple of government as their spiritual home and consider its rules and traditions as important as those of the constituents who sent them there in the first place. In this sense Senators might be compared to those ambassadors who have served a long time in one country and become so sympathetic to its ways and language that they have to be recalled. So one might ask, Isn't the Senate part of the United States? Yes, but it sometimes behaves as if it were a small but very powerful country of its own.

The Senate has many ways and degrees of putting a member in his place. So, after a year, many old members of the Senate felt that Humphrey's self-righteousness and manner of proposing measures that would shake up their basic sources of strength called for some form of discipline. Their rationale was to show him that after all he had to live with them.

Then in 1950 Humphrey took on a fight with Senator Harry Byrd of Virginia. While Byrd and Humphrey are both Democrats they are at opposite ends of the political scale. For years Senator Byrd had been chairman of a joint committee on non-essential expenditures in the executive branch. Unofficially, Byrd was practically a competitor of the Budget Director of the United States, in so far as his reputation and achievements for economy and thrift were

145

concerned. He had conducted many investigations on "non-essential expenditures" of the government. Quite often those he considered frivolous or unnecessary were welfare programs close to the liberal heart. Byrd is also quite different in personality and temperament from Humphrey and, far from being interested in a hundred different things, had become virtually a monomaniac on the subject of thrift in government and elimination of waste.

There is another committee, the Senate Government Operations Committee, of which Humphrey was and is a member. This also looks over the general administration of government and Humphrey got the idea that Senator Byrd's committee was a duplication—it was superfluous and redundant and could be abolished. Very likely he was right—in the abstract. But in the Senate he was way off the beam.

Many New Deal senators had cordially disagreed with Senator Byrd through the years, but he had been a Senator a long time and had even been chairman of his pet joint committee during Republican-controlled Congresses. Humphrey was striking at Byrd although he meant mainly to strike at the committee. He wanted to make a positive contribution to a more liberal assessment of government expenditures for liberal causes, but the point the Senate saw was that he was striking at a revered figure, implying that his work was superfluous.

Humphrey had observed the courtesy of notifying Byrd, who was at home in Virginia, that he was to speak on the subject, but he did not wait for Byrd to arrive in the Senate before he introduced the resolution and made his remarks urging that the committee be disbanded. Thereafter from time to time Humphrey placed additional arguments in the appendix of the *Congressional Record*.

Finally, on March 2, 1950, Senator Byrd arose and for an hour and a half defended his committee and castigated Humphrey. Other senators would interrupt Byrd in a benevolent way with the kind of flowery questions designed only to show their support or to bring out an additional point to bolster Byrd's arguments. Reporters began to fill the gallery as word got around that something unusual was happening. Obviously the old buffalo of the Senate had decided to join shoulder to shoulder to present an almost solid front against the young buffalo from Minnesota. Senator after senator chimed in with Senator Byrd, with purple passages beginning with façade questions, such as, "I would like to ask the senator from Virginia if it is not also true that the beneficial result of . . ." All these are ways of saying, "Me too," so the senator who has the floor will be reinforced. "I thank the junior senator, he is quite right, et cetera, et cetera."

While this flood of viscid prose became ever wider, but not necessarily deeper, Humphrey was vainly trying to get the floor but was not being recognized. When all possible compliments had been exchanged, Byrd yielded the floor to Humphrey.

The best debater Spink County ever saw rose and began his counterattack, but he was dismayed to see that Byrd and almost all the other senators were walking pointedly out of the chamber. They had planned to give him his comeuppance.

Humphrey made his speech to a dwindling number of reporters in the press gallery and a few liberal colleagues such as Senator Douglas. Other senators and Humphrey himself agree that this was the low point of his Senate career. The old buffalo had made a deliberate and successful effort to humiliate the newcomer and teach him a lesson.

The old buffalo watched with interest to see how he would take it and whether he understood that they thought they had had to do this for his own good and that of the Senate.

The young buffalo limped away from this encounter and did a good deal of thinking. He was badly bruised but not crushed flat. There were worse things they could have done. There were more minor things they might have done if he had been more minor. From that point on he began to gain in popularity with his fellow senators. He cut down on his speechmaking and tried to cover a few subjects more thoroughly instead of many subjects rather quickly and superficially.

Humphrey has always liked to win. As an assistant has said, "He likes to be right, but he likes to win; he really does not enjoy being right and losing." By 1954, according to the clerk of the Senate, Humphrey had his name on more amendments, many of them crucial, some of them initiated by him, than any other senator. He had learned a great deal about the realities of getting particular measures through the Senate. By the time he returned, solidly re-elected, in 1954 many other senators were turning to him for advice. He had become something of a diplomat, the man whom conservative senators asked to speak to the liberal group, the man to whom the liberals entrusted their case, to secure whatever concessions could be secured from the conservative group. There is little question among other senators or the press gallery that Humphrey today enjoys the esteem of the Senate. His fellow senators can readily tell the difference between oratory or merely clever debate and that rarer thing, the speech and discussion of a man who is saturated in a certain subject. The Senate greatly admires a man who tackles a complex subject and who knows how to present its intricacies clearly and forcefully toward a given end. Humphrey, like the late Senator Taft, or Vandenberg, Millikin of Colorado, or the late Senator McMahon on atomic energy, is listened to on a number of subjects, as a man who knows what he is talking about.

This is quite an achievement, and it is the more remarkable since Humphrey still remains a personal operator, a soloist.

The art of being a senator requires independence, a strong personality, and individuality—and that a man be able to get along with other individualists. But even in this gallery of special men, nearly all of whom are capable of operating as independent persons, Humphrey is distinguished as a lone operator.

Only he knows what he may do next. Nearly always it will be something that he wants to do and believes he should do. Very seldom will he do something of which a team or an adviser has convinced him against his will. The Senate now respects this quality in him, and he pays other senators the courtesies of the Senate and since that comeuppance day he credits them with some degree of integrity too.

Through a series of rare circumstances Humphrey changed committee assignments twice in the 83rd Congress. This is exceptional for a man in his first Senate term.

At the beginning of the 83rd Congress he was given a post on the Senate Foreign Relations Committee, an assignment most senators would covet, and in which Humphrey of course had a special interest.

In January there had been a meeting at the White House between three members of the outgoing Administration—President Truman, Secretary of State Acheson, and Mutual Security Administrator Averell Harriman—with the then Minority Leader, Senator Lyndon Johnson of Texas. They discussed the fact that Senators Robert Taft, William Knowland, Homer Ferguson, and William Langer, all considered isolationists, were to be given places by the Republicans on the Senate Foreign Relations Committee. It seemed obvious that Taft would dominate the committee unless he were challenged.

Truman and Acheson felt that there should be an energetic, articulate, liberal Democrat on the Foreign Relations Committee and Humphrey was the man they wanted. Johnson checked with Humphrey and arranged to have him assigned to the committee if possible. However, Humphrey would have to give up his position on the Labor and Welfare Committee, which would be serious for him in view of the importance of labor legislation and labor support. He would, however, be able to keep a seat on the Government Operations Committee where liberal Democrats were also needed. At this period McCarthy had begun to ride high and the Government Operations Committee needed men like Symington, Henry Jackson, and Humphrey to do whatever they could to stem the McCarthy tide.

With the Republicans coming into power after the elections of 1952 in which Eisenhower won by such a sweep, the Democratic senators would be reduced from three committee posts to two and it had been decided that if a senator were put on one of the most sought-after committees—Appropriations or Foreign Relations—then his other post would be on a so-called minor committee. Thus Humphrey knew that when the new Congress convened he would have to lose his prized membership on the Agriculture Committee. When the Truman-Acheson move started him toward the Foreign Relations Committee he realized that he was also going to lose his membership on the Labor Committee. It was quite a serious behind-the-scenes thing for Humphrey and he had to make up his mind rather swiftly.

One factor that predisposed Humphrey in favor of the change was the thought that Congressman Walter Judd, a foreign affairs expert, might be Humphrey's opponent in 1954 and in running against him it would be important for Humphrey to have foreign relations experience.

As William S. White put it in *The Taft Story*, it was clear that Taft was now going to take "a very great interest in foreign affairs."

Taft had sacrificed a place on his beloved Finance Committee to move over to Foreign Relations and, according to White, "he went . . . in the spirit of a man who is leaving what he likes for something he has always disliked; in the spirit of responding to the grim call of duty. He regarded the Chairman of Foreign Relations, Republican Alexander

149

Wiley of Wisconsin as far from 'safe.' He once told me as much . . . thought the Chairman was by any standard too pliably internationalist. . . ."

Lyndon Johnson was able to get both Humphrey and also another new senator commonly considered a liberal, Mike Mansfield, spots on the committee. Johnson later said that he was criticized by Texas newspapers for giving such a choice assignment to a man like Humphrey. Characteristically, Johnson arranged a new policy of giving each new senator a major post.

Before the final meeting of the steering committee that was to make the arrangements, Humphrey did his best to reach the most interested national labor leader by phone, without success. Humphrey's legislative assistant, Max Kampelman, who had many personal contacts in the labor movement, called other labor people in Washington to explain the shift and was told by one that it could be fixed up with the number 1 man—because "what's good for Humphrey is good for us."

There were a few labor leaders in Minnesota who felt that Humphrey had made a mistake and left them behind when he moved over to Foreign Relations. But Humphrey has continued to interest himself in labor legislation and his labor record is still considered outstanding.

Humphrey got from Johnson a promise that he could get back on the Agriculture Committee if a vacancy occurred. This came up in May 1954, with the death of Senator Clyde Hoey of North Carolina. Then Humphrey really had choice assignments in which he could learn and work. He had to leave the Government Operations Committee, but he had Foreign Relations in which, to use his words, he could "be a statesman," and he could and did make farm policy his chief legislative and political emphasis for some time.

By this time he was also on the select Small Business Committee, which has been a long-time interest of his.

There was a time early in his Senate career when Humphrey was not overly informed on farm problems and the intricacies of the flexible farm price support proposals. But he had fought for a liberal farm policy for many years, he had lived in a farming community and in fact spent summers on the farm, so that he never regarded farmers as *them* but always as part of *us*.

When he was appointed to the Agriculture Committee shortly before it was coming to key work and key votes on the price support program, he knew that his would be the deciding vote. This was the time to get a better understanding about farm policy, which he had been studying and working on for two years. Moreover, he is particularly emphatic about the family farm—he agrees with Jefferson that the small landholder is a backbone of democracy. Humphrey believes, paradoxically, that there should be many kinds of government help, to keep this independent farmer prosperous.

It was late in 1952 that he decided agriculture would be the chief campaign issue for 1954. He spent a lot of time talking about his farm program in speeches in his home state; in fact most of his effort was concentrated on the farm vote. His decision has been corroborated in many ways and no doubt it contributed to the large majority by which he was re-elected.

Many people study Humphrey, and several of these students have maintained that "Hubert is many things, but there is one thing he never is—he is never *calculating*."

According to this theory, Humphrey looks ahead and plans but he does not really scheme. He does not *calculate*, he does not work hard to manipulate people in a premeditated way.

This writer asked him, "Do you agree—that you aren't a calculating person?"

He hesitated a little, and allowed that yes, that was probably true.

But an hour later he said, "I'll tell you, there are two or three things I really believe I have calculated, I believe you could call them calculating."

And here is one of them—"the Youngdahl appointment."

One of the strangest political and social acquaintanceships of Minnesota's history existed between the mayor of Minneapolis and "the Youngdahl family." But no one foresaw what it would eventually lead to: a striking play involving the legislative, judicial, and executive branches of government—and including the President of the United States.

Humphrey had long been acquainted with the Rev. Reuben Youngdahl, who served as chairman of the Council on Human Relations while Humphrey was mayor of Minneapolis. At this time he also knew, rather slightly, the minister's brother, Luther Youngdahl.

Luther was becoming one of the top Republican leaders, the greatest vote-getter Minnesota Republicans had had in recent times. When Luther seemed to be headed for the governorship, Reuben suggested to Humphrey that it was inappropriate for him to continue to serve. Of course, the council, working on civil rights, had no partisan political tinge. The Youngdahls were all Republicans, and Humphrey knew that when Reuben was appointed. But one doesn't think of a minister's politics, and the whole idea of the council was alien to politics. Even after Youngdahl defeated Humphrey's friend Charles Halsted and became governor, Humphrey would not hear of Reuben resigning, although the minister sincerely thought his staying might hurt Humphrey or his brother.

"I really need you, it makes you more valuable than ever," Humphrey said. "I want this council to be clear above all politics. Of course it would be embarrassing if I got into public controversy with Luther . . . but I won't! About the only issue would be some municipal matter—something the city wanted from the state—and city-versus-state arguments are more or less normal. I'll tell you what. At any time I think I might have a head-on collision with Luther I'll let you *both* know in plenty of time for you all to decide what to do about it. But I don't think it will ever happen."

This approach only drew Humphrey closer to the Youngdahls.

As time went by, however, it appeared more and more likely that Humphrey and Governor Youngdahl would eventually square off—and in the most head-on collision one could expect in politics.

More and more Republicans saw Youngdahl as their best man to run for senator in 1954, and they thought he had an excellent chance to defeat Humphrey. As Humphrey tells it, Youngdahl had liberal views, many of them the same as Humphrey's, and they both knew it would be a tough campaign, a fight neither of them wanted. Neither would feel right telling the voters that the other man would be a disaster if elected. Ray Ewald, a Minneapolis businessman, acted as an intermediary between the governor and the senator, in giving each a subtle sense of the other's interests.

So when Humphrey read one day that a federal judge, T. Alan Goldsborough, had retired he knew exactly what spectacular play he hoped to bring off.

Months before this, Humphrey had heard that Youngdahl's health was not absolutely tiptop, that his doctor had urged him to take things somewhat easier. Humphrey had also had the word that if Youngdahl could ever be considered for a federal judgeship he might be extremely interested. At one point, long before the actual judicial vacancy came up, Max Kampelman, as a strategist for Humphrey, went with the senator to a White House appointment. Near the end of the conference Humphrey asked, "Do you know our governor, Mr. President?" Mr. Truman was already impressed by Youngdahl. Nothing was spelled out at this time, but Humphrey was encouraged to go ahead planning his stratagem— and keeping his eyes open for an appointment that might be filled by Governor Youngdahl.

Democratic senators do not ordinarily work hard to advocate the appointment of Republican governors to the federal judiciary. And was there anything in the picture to suggest that Harry S. Truman, one of the most partisan Presidents in history, would care to appoint a Republican to the bench?

The astute political observer would say *yes*—because every President would like to have another senator for sure. And it happened that Youngdahl, like Truman, was a national leader in the Shrine. There was more to it than that. Truman had visited Minnesota, he had met Youngdahl, and he liked him personally. And there was something even more emphatic in his favor so far as Truman was concerned.

When Truman dismissed General Douglas MacArthur many Republican leaders had assailed him as an irresponsible civilian presumptuously taking out of Korea one of the greatest military men of all time. Some Republican governors had even signed a statement condemning the dismissal. Governor Youngdahl had not only refused to sign that condemnation but had gone out of his way to write Mr. Truman a letter approving his action as perfectly logical in the American tradition of the ascendancy of the civilian power over the military. The President is the Commander-in-Chief of the armed services, and Youngdahl had been able to see this perfectly clearly in spite of the smoke screen of partisan battle.

Seeing things clearly is the finest trait one could wish for in a federal judge, Truman may well have mused to himself. The President had a fine memory for anyone who had ever befriended him (or, for that matter, opposed him).

When Humphrey telephoned him, his neat idea appealed instantly to Truman, who urged that Youngdahl be brought into town immediately. "Of course I must meet him and talk to him right away, and of course there must be nothing said about the matter to anyone."

Both men knew that if news of the proposal leaked a storm might blow up from both the Republican and the Democratic camps.

Very few people besides Bill Simms, Muriel, and the President knew of Humphrey's idea when he telephoned Youngdahl.

The governor was on vacation, at a hunting lodge far in the northern Minnesota country. When Humphrey reached him he was speaking over a country party line. The connection was poor, and Humphrey knew that the whole countryside might be listening. He still laughs out loud when he thinks of that phone call and his efforts to speak in code.

"Luther, if you read the newspaper you'll see that there is a big chair waiting for somebody. . . . Luther, can you come to Washington right away? I want to take you to see a very important friend of mine, Luther, I mean a *very important* friend. . . ."

Eventually Humphrey impressed upon the governor that he must call back immediately on a private phone, and then the senator was able to make arrangements for their early morning call at the White House. Under the code name of Smith, Humphrey got the governor a room at the Mayflower Hotel. They were to enter the White House by a side door, so that if nothing ever came of this Mr. Smith could go home without anyone knowing that his name had almost changed from *Governor* Smith to *Judge* Smith.

Humphrey did, however, alert the Washington correspondents of Minnesota newspapers, and it still rankles him to think that they did not immediately get excited about this "blind date." "You would think they would have been keen to go up there," he said, "if I told them their senator was going to see the President and *might* have something to say afterwards." The reporters were hot that morning for a postal rate hearing that involved some Minnesotans.

The conversation with the President didn't take long, and quickly covered MacArthur, the Shrine, fishing in Minnesota, and legal background. Truman of course had had Youngdahl's education and experience checked through the usual channels. The matter was soon settled, the offer made and accepted.

Then an ebullient Humphrey and Youngdahl, both of

them facing a more secure future, went out to give the news to the startled press. The Minnesota papers gave it a somewhat larger play than the postal rate hearing.

Humphrey's voice becomes high-pitched as he remembers, "And the Republicans just went crazy!"

The Democrats were also surprised, but the story went by the grapevine to the last county chairman in a matter of hours, so that they fully appreciated what this meant in terms of the party hold on the job of senator. It has proved to mean a great deal through the years.

Those who always want to ask one more question may be somewhat puzzled as to *why* Youngdahl did it. Many reasons could be advanced. There are very few lawyers who would not leave almost any other future in order to become a federal judge, with a good salary, position of status in the community, and wonderful retirement pay. And health may well have been a factor. He certainly has seemed robust since he came to Washington, but the hurly-burly of elective office might have been bad for him.

One should not overlook the possibility that Humphrey felt that Luther would make an excellent judge, and Luther felt that Humphrey was doing a perfectly good job as senator from Minnesota.

Thousands agree with both judgments.

The reader should put *that* into his calculations. And the Minnesota DFL party is forever indebted to General of the Army Douglas MacArthur, for without him Youngdahl might never have written Truman that fan letter.

CHAPTER XII

Champion of Bills

As some observers see it, compromising or striking a balance isn't just *sometimes* done in the Senate, it is the very key to understanding how the Senate ever gets anything done. This, they insist, is the essence of learning to be an effective senator.

This view is stated explicitly by William S. White in his book on the Senate, *The Citadel*, where he discusses Hubert Humphrey's change and maturity as he saw it.

White expresses it thus:

. . . Humphrey had found, and now he illustrated, one of the ultimate truths of the Senate. This is that one *cannot* forever refuse there to make any compromise at all and remain a good, or effective, member. The art of high negotiation is an absolutely necessary part of Senatorial equipment. For the Institution, as it was at its beginning, is something more than a parliamentary body engaged upon parliamentary work. It is likewise an assemblage of diplomatists, in which each State in a sense sends Ambassadors to the Federal Republic, and the function of Ambassadors is not to reach proud, violent disagreement; it is, of course, to find acceptable agreement.

To accomplish this and yet not to let down one's principles, one's ideals, one's State—this is the unique achievement of a good Senate man. Because this is the highest requisite, it follows that this is no place for the man who has *only* principle; for every genuine political fanatic is simply awash with principle as he understands the term.

Though White seems to believe that the civil rights problem is eternal, he says: "It cannot readily be denied, however, that the more moderate Humphrey of the late fifties had, in consequence of all that had happened to him, put himself in infinitely better position to bring the Senate to adopt *some* bill in that area."

Not every student of the Senate agrees with these observations. Speaking of compromise and "the art of high negotiation" as part of senatorial equipment, they say, "Yes, he is talking about something that goes on, but what he means is 'the art of low negotiation.'" To borrow an example from safely across the Atlantic, Winston Churchill reached one of his finest hours soon after Munich, when he did *not* soften or moderate his views or compromise with those honorable colleagues whom he considered honorable dunderheads. Churchill was an ambassador *from the future*; and at that low point of British appeasement he considered that his function was to make clear his "proud, violent disagreement."

So, to many observers, the gentle art of compromise, basic art of politics, and the very fine art of the gentlemen of the Senate is still not felt to be the essence of advancing new ideas into government. One could not compromise with Hitler or with an atomic war. And as the Negro said about eating in a fine Southern restaurant, "I don't know how to compromise—with the table half in and half out of the door?"

These observers see Humphrey as an idealist who should keep fighting for new ideas—and sometimes lose after "violent disagreement." Humphrey sometimes agrees with them. There are finer things in this world than "Senate types," and evil as well as good in ritual and tradition.

Senator Humphrey's slogan, sometimes used in campaigns, has been, "He gets things done." Humphrey will often "compromise" in the sense that he would rather see only a part of some program implemented than none of it. But his purpose is to get something done. In the remainder of this book we shall see in some detail just how much work a project may entail. And no brief account can mention all the hundreds of people—from the Farmers' Union to the attachés of the Indian Embassy—who may be connected with it. Far, far more is involved here than dealing with other senators, compromising or not compromising with their quirky and craggy personalities.

One suspects, watching senators do their hardest work—*not* on the floor or in the cloakroom—that there are not many of them who want to be "senator types" or "ambassadors" to the federal republic. Each is the head of a small, incredibly busy agency, each is also a cog in a very large government.

Therefore, when Humphrey fights for one of his major projects it is not strictly a solo performance—like Manolete against the bull. It is more like a campaign of education and persuasion and psychological warfare—directed not just at the other senators who have the crucial votes but at all sorts of people who can influence those senators or contribute in any of a half dozen other ways.

Calls are sent out for experts. The library of Congress is ajangle with Humphrey's myrmidons hunting monographs.

Associations don't always have to call Humphrey, he calls *them*. "Here's what you ought to be doing."

Speeches? Yes, speeches—in Minnesota, of course—but in many other places where some influence may mobilize.

The executive department gets a buzz: "What's behind this statement on X? That isn't what the man from Y told me this morning. . . ."

Articles are written as well as read. Television comes into play; the senator usually puts on a cracking good show and leaves some facts in a few million living rooms.

Hearings are held—and Humphrey needs no prompters to feed him sharp questions. His assistants may show up but he is capable of asking good questions of people in fifty different fields.

Thus Humphrey does his work as a liberal who knows he has to fight for his projects most of the time.

Personal relationships with other senators are important, of course, but this operation is not much like chess, with people as pawns and kings. It is more like a company that is launching a new product. There may be not so much a real need for the product as a great desire on the part of a large group of customers—voters.

But in any case it is first decided to launch the product. Then there is research—and invention, and Humphrey is one of the most inventive legislators of our time.

Then there is experiment. What can be done with this idea? How can we try out a piece of it, how can we ask a sampling of customers what they think of it?

Then there is more research, more practical engineering.

Then there is education, and sales, sales, sales.

Of course there is competition—and perhaps conflict with other inventors, other customers!

And perhaps the inventive head of the company has some dramatic encounters with his competitors—or his partners.

But it is more like work than like "Playhouse 90." The build-up goes on for weeks—or months. The maneuvering for votes takes less time, the speeches and the roll call are over in days and minutes.

As Humphrey has become more respected and influential with his fellow senators, the principal change in his attitude, he thinks, has been the simple understanding that they, too, have important ideas on legislation and other projects. He feels that his own aims and convictions haven't changed so much as his willingness to give some priority to the views of others. Now he is apt to see several sides to most questions and he thinks that liberal periodicals do not give all sides, merely all of one side.

It has been suggested that in the Senate itself a man's personal qualities, such as character and basic integrity, are more important to the esteem of the rest of the Senate than the matter of party loyalty. There is some support for this idea in the box score kept by the *Congressional Quarterly* for the years in which Humphrey was becoming a Senate leader. The *Quarterly* devised a "party unity" score that is determined on the basis of whether or not the man voted with the majority of his party in cases where the two parties were really opposed to each other.

Humphrey "followed the party line" most devotedly in his first year in the Senate, 1949, when he voted with the majority 94 per cent of the time. Since then his score has never been above 92 per cent and in 1950 was 88 per cent. In 1953 it was 89 and in 1954 it was 88 per cent again. As the *Quarterly* computes such things, he was well ahead of the party in all these years. The average Democratic senator was with the party about 75 to 80 per cent of the time. Yet the early years were the ones when Humphrey was considered to be "out of line." Another point this record makes is that the Democratic party has some conservative members who cross the line and often vote with the Republicans.

Humphrey believes that other senators look to him for several kinds of specialized knowledge: on all phases of agriculture, civil rights, disarmament, and negotiation; on his little specialty, food and drug legislation; in various areas of foreign affairs; and on specific proposals like the food-for-peace plan.

Today he thinks the best way to win acceptance from other senators is to show them that you are being "constructive," which doesn't mean that you "compromise" or conciliate. Another factor is old-fashioned work; the Senate respects a man who takes an assignment and studies it, goes to the hearings, holds conferences, explains it "on the floor," and otherwise follows through. Obviously the Senate can judge whether a man is working as a subcommittee chairman or "dragging his feet." To get any project through requires an endless series of phone calls, meetings, buttonholings, and explanations to one side and then another.

Humphrey feels that from the time he was a mayor he has been more of a bargainer and adjuster and diplomat than the press or public give him credit for. His associates are somewhat discouraged because the public doesn't see this, but by its nature diplomacy goes on quietly whereas the civil rights fight, the last-minute scrap for the vice-presidential nomination, and the flaming speeches of the first year and a half in the Senate were all quite public.

Humphrey is still interested in all sorts of things, and some friends and critics agree he is interested in far too many things. This doubles his work load.

Humphrey says, on the contrary, that a politician should be curious about everything. He was impressed that Nikita Khrushchev was interested in all sorts of things and had a smattering of information about virtually every subject they discussed in their famous eight-hour session.

Civil defense, fallout, Israel, housing, child health care, problems of the Middle East—he believes that all these are matters that a United States senator should be interested in.

Sometimes when irritated on this subject he has snapped, "I didn't become a United States senator to become the nation's leading expert on the boll weevil."

He has a hardy contempt for those senators who take one subject, sometimes a surprisingly minor one, but related to their constituents, and make it a lifelong specialty.

He continues to attack most subjects with almost unabated energy. However, he is human and his friends think there is some slight evidence that he does not maintain the same round-the-clock pace that he once did. One would not expect his program to be as strenuous at fifty as it was at thirty.

Here is a sample day as observed by Rowland Evans, Jr., a quite objective reporter for the New York *Herald Tribune*:

Recently, the man from Minnesota, who is now 47, got up at 6:45 in the morning, his usual hour, helped one of his four children with homework, and hurried into town in his 1955 Cadillac from his suburban house at Rock Creek Knoll to breakfast with Mrs. Franklin D. Roosevelt, Edward R. Murrow and a host of other panelists attending an Exchange of Persons conference.

Actually, the Senator got tied up on so many early morning phone calls at home that he arrived at the conference after the breakfast dishes had been cleared away, and ate nothing at all. The conference lasted until 11:45.

At 12 noon, the Senator moved onto the floor of the Senate and introduced four bills during the period called "the morning hour." The bills would set up a Youth Conservation Corps, liberalize the passport laws, enact a "food for peace" resolution and outlaw certain kinds of water pollution. He also made brief speeches for civil rights and against President Eisenhower's farm proposals.

Sen. Humphrey then gobbled a sandwich and a glass of milk.

During the afternoon, he conferred hurriedly, always running late, with his staff experts on the Disarmament subcommittee, of which he is chairman, a Government Operations subcommittee, which he also heads, and the Senate Agriculture Committee, of which he is a member. He kept appointments with Kirby Ramsdell, chief editorial writer of "The Los Angeles Times," who wanted to interview him, and attorney Pat O'Connor, a prominent citizen of Minneapolis.

At 5:30, he was scheduled to go to a television network studio to do a special program for the Institute of International Education, but he arrived there half an hour late. From 6:45 to 7:45 he shook hands with the auxiliaries of the American Legion and the Veterans of Foreign Wars at a downtown reception.

He then dashed back home in his car, pulled on his dinner jacket, collected wife Muriel and rushed back to a private club in town for a dinner given by Doris Fleeson and her husband, Dan Kimball, for Sen. Clair Engle, the new Democratic Senator from the politically potent state of California, and Mrs. Engle. He arrived very late, was called away from the table by an urgent telephone call, and again missed some of his meal.

161

As Sen. Humphrey once said, "I can't keep a tight schedule. Each day is unto itself and we live each day." He got home late on the night in question, but early enough to assure his normal five to six hours of sleep.

The four telephone lines into the Senator's office carry up to 350 calls each day, by recorded count. His mail on a big day runs around 412 letters.

His performance on this "hectic" day was really first-class. He received many enthusiastic letters and remarkable tributes from persons who heard his impromptu remarks at the Exchange of Persons conference. Humphrey has done a great deal to promote more interchange between persons of all countries in the cause of peace.

Rowland Evans happened to select a "typical day" in which Humphrey introduced three bills that were to become of real significance in the work of the 86th Congress. Their history is instructive of the way Humphrey operates in the Senate and illustrates three continuing legislative preoccupations of his: conservation, opportunity for youth, and constructive use of agricultural surpluses.

The Water Pollution Control Act illustrates Humphrey's method of giving Senate leadership to legislation originating in the House—in this case legislation drafted by Humphrey's close friend, Congressman John A. Blatnik, from the Iron Range country of Minnesota. Blatnik is in an influential spot on the House Public Works Committee. The bill roughly doubles the size of the existing Blatnik program for matching-grant federal assistance to communities in the construction of sewage treatment works. In this case Blatnik, with his close ties to the House Democratic leadership, could be counted on to move the legislation through the House, but leadership in the Senate was needed to make sure that it did not smother to death in the press of "more urgent" senatorial interests. Had the legislation been assigned to one of the Humphrey committees he could have moved directly in its behalf but, failing this, another close friend and political colleague, the newly elected Senator Eugene J. McCarthy, happens to be on the Senate Public Works Committee. Because of his previous years of experience in the House, McCarthy has a certain amount of seniority on the committee, sufficient to move legislation through committee with far greater dispatch than one would expect from a freshman senator. With a Blatnik-Humphrey-McCarthy sponsorship, the bill had the advantage of a key sponsor on the appropriate committee of both houses, plus an articulate and aggressive spokesman who could be counted on to sway the Senate leadership into a favorable position on the bill. This is precisely what happened, and as the first session of the 86th Congress wound up at 6:23 A.M. the day before Chairman Khrushchev arrived in his TU-114, the bill had been passed by the House, had been reported favorably by the Senate Committee on Public Works, and was on the Senate calendar with the enthusiastic blessing of the Senate Democratic leadership awaiting a Senate vote in the second session.

The Youth Conservation Corps proposal, introduced by Humphrey on the same day described by Evans, was also a companion to a House proposal by Congressman Blatnik in the House. This is a bill that few observers gave any chance in the 86th Congress. It was the third version of a proposal that Humphrey had been introducing for several years. Now he wanted to make a real drive to push it through committee. Version number 3, while it contained important changes derived from a good many months of intensive correspondence and discussion, represented an old basic idea that Humphrey was not going to give up. He intended to get it passed. The previous years' bills had been part of what Humphrey likes to call the "educational process." He believes that it is necessary, without the power of the White House behind a proposal, to build up rather overwhelming public opinion behind an idea. This takes time. And the senator, though he sometimes appears to be an impatient man, can be both patient and persistent. He has learned to try—and then to wait. A search of his legislative record indicates a pattern of legislation introduced and reintroduced, frequently modified, but bearing the basic Humphrey stamp. The question is sometimes asked: Why does he introduce some bills—many bills—when he knows they have no chance, or, like the Youth Conservation Corps, practically no chance? The history of the YCC bill helps to answer that.

It started out as a trial balloon—a modest "pilot plant" proposal for 50,000 boys to be enrolled and put to work in the national parks and forests doing conservation work— part of a package of bills introduced by Humphrey, designed to provide more opportunity for young people. Incidentally, this package and the subsequent package in the 85th Congress also contained bills that in modified form were incorporated into the National Defense Education Act of 1958. (Much of the language of that Education Act is taken from old Humphrey bills.)

Encouraged by the interest expressed by various groups, Humphrey then drafted a full-scale Youth Conservation Corps proposal for 150,000 youths, enlisted the support of virtually all the voluntary organizations in the field of resource conservation, and secured the personal support of the grand old man of conservation in the Senate, Senator James E. Murray of Montana. He also wrote a rousing article about the idea for *Harper's* magazine (which by arrangement appeared the day Humphrey introduced the bill). When he introduced the bill he also offered a major Senate resolution setting forth specific resource-conservation goals for the federal government.

Something about the proposal "hit" the American public. Humphrey's sense of timing is remarkable, and apparently it was operating on all cylinders this time. Not only did the conservationists rally behind the bill, but an entirely new galaxy of organizational support appeared: juvenile court judges, school superintendents, welfare authorities, reformatory wardens, who saw in the Humphrey proposal a way to do something constructive about preventing juvenile delinquency. Humphrey's mail reflected virtually unanimous support for the idea, by actual count more than 99% in favor. The overwhelming response indicated that the time was ripe to proceed, and he circulated his idea throughout the Senate. He also saw that each member of Congress received a copy of the *Harper's* article and other material.

On the day described in Evans' column, Humphrey had a phalanx of Senate Democrats and Bill Langer, the maverick Republican from North Dakota, "on" the bill as cosponsors. Version number 3 of the bill went into the legislative hopper as S. 812 of the 86th Congress—with a lot of horsepower.

Unfortunately, there it met a cold chill from the right side of the aisle, presaging a Republican boycott and campaign of opposition. In fact Senator Jacob Javits of New York, who had indicated he wished to cosponsor the bill at one point, withdrew his name from the list of cosponsors within a few days after introduction.

At this point an interesting and complicated interplay of personalities began, involving many personal negotiations and telephone contacts on Humphrey's part.

The bill was assigned to the Committee on Labor and

Public Welfare, over which presided the distinguished gentleman from Alabama, Lister Hill, perhaps the senator most admired by Humphrey, and a long-time friend. But the committee was locked in an internal struggle concerning the school construction bill and the question of integration in this field. Furthermore, the labor management reform bill was pending before the committee. The resultant legislative log-jam was a formidable enough barrier, without the handicap of Humphrey's no longer being a member of the committee.

He had, however, taken pains to encourage several of the committee members to be cosponsors of S. 812. One happened to be a new senator, Jennings Randolph of West Virginia, who had in the course of long service in the House been one of the principal movers in the original Civilian Conservation Corps of the first Roosevelt administration. Randolph, approached by Humphrey, indicated genuine enthusiasm for the task of shepherding the bill through the committee, but both men agreed that without the chairman's support the idea was strictly academic. Humphrey thereupon undertook a quiet campaign of brief letters both to Hill and to other members of the leadership, tentatively suggesting that it would be a good idea at least to have hearings on the measure. Finally one day he walked over to Hill on the Senate floor, sat down beside him, and suggested to him that Senator Randolph might be prevailed upon to take over the time-consuming task of conducting hearings. Humphrey also offered the assistance of his personal staff and forwarded a similar proposal from Senator Murray. Hill agreed then and there, called Senator Randolph over from his chair, and hearings were scheduled.

Then the accumulated weight of public opinion—or organizational strength—so carefully measured and encouraged in the past three years, had a vehicle through which to express itself, and it did. Letters and statements poured in through four days of hearings. In the meantime Humphrey was busily bombarding Lyndon Johnson with reasons why the bill ought to become part of the Democratic record in the 86th Congress. Finally, buttonholed on the Senate floor, Johnson allowed as how it was a good bill and if HHH could help round up the necessary votes he would do what he could to get it past the Senate. In due course the Randolph subcommittee recommended passage of the bill, the full committee favorably reported the bill (on a strict party-line vote), and S. 812 went to the Senate calendar in the closing weeks of the session.

At this point a head-counting operation began that was to last more than five weeks, with constant checking and rechecking between Humphrey, Randolph, Murray, and Johnson. They finally agreed that if they could "see" forty-nine votes they would bring the bill up for a vote; if not, they would carry it over to the next session. In a series of complicated cloakroom maneuvers during which arrangements were made to "pair" the opposing votes of several senators, the tally mounted. With Senator Langer, the lone Republican supporter of the bill, out of the Senate program owing to his wife's recent death, and with a large share of the Southern Democrats refusing to come along, the sponsors began to despair of securing the necessary majority. Finally, Humphrey corralled Senator Milton Young of North Dakota, a Republican who often votes with Humphrey on regional matters, and talked him into supporting the bill.

With what appeared to be the necessary majority, Johnson quietly motioned the bill up from the calendar. Then some fast footwork on the Senate floor averted what was clearly meant to be a crippling amendment to be introduced by the Republicans. Then the bill was up for a straight up-and-down vote.

In the swift moments of the roll call it became apparent that two of the votes that had been "counted" were not there at all. But while waiting for his late-on-the-roster name to be called, Republican Senator Alexander Wiley of Wisconsin—who had no love for an Administration that had not lifted a hand to save him in his last primary battle with the right wing in Wisconsin—strolled by.

"Hubert," he asked, "is this your bill?"

Humphrey said, "I need you on this, Alex." And Wiley went to his seat and cast a "yea" vote. Freshman Senator Ed Muskie (D., Maine), not entirely convinced of the necessity of the bill at that time, had voted "nay," but now came to Humphrey and talked to him about it. When they had finished, the tall New Englander rose to his feet, asked, "How am I recorded, Mr. President?" and changed his vote to "Ay." These two surprises saved the day.

The third major bill introduced on the day described by Rowland Evans had the theme of "Food for Peace," and will be dealt with in a later chapter.

As a freshman in the 81st Congress in 1949, Humphrey was able, as chairman of the Subcommittee on School Construction of the Senate Labor and Public Welfare Committee, to secure passage of the first Federal Aid for School Construction Act. His proposal, S. 2317 (P.L. 815), provided federal grants for school districts overcrowded by children of defense workers and federal employees. Such districts are defined as "federally impacted" areas. Companion legislation (P.L. 874) provided federal aid for *maintenance* and *operation* of schools in these "federally impacted" areas. Both of these laws, pushed through by Humphrey, were major breakthroughs toward greater national responsibility for meeting local school needs. By going "through a side door" the senator had taken a real step nearer federal aid to education.

When Humphrey gave up his membership on the Labor and Public Welfare Committee he also gave up most of his opportunity to push through educational legislation with the Humphrey label. But he continued to work closely with Senators Hill and Murray, who have been leaders in the field of education legislation. In the 85th and 86th Congresses Senator Humphrey introduced Youth Opportunity Programs, including new versions of proposals he had supported since first coming to the Senate.

The Youth Opportunity package of the 85th Congress, S. 868-872, included proposals enacted into law by the National Defense Education Act, which Senator Humphrey also joined in sponsoring. These proposals included graduate fellowships, loans to college students, and loan "forgiveness" for borrowers entering schoolteaching. In the 86th Congress Youth Opportunity proposals S. 1087-1091, Senator Humphrey repeated his previous proposals for federal scholarships, school construction aid, tax benefits for those financing higher education, and assistance to colleges and universities for expanding facilities to handle bigger enrollments. These proposals were not included in the National Defense Education Act as finally signed into law, although the Senate approved a scholarship program that was deleted by the House. Provisions of the National Defense Education Act previously sponsored by Senator Humphrey included:

Loans to college students and loan forgiveness to borrowers entering elementary or secondary school teaching, graduate fellowships for students preparing to teach at the university level, vocational aid grants to states, and grants for improving state statistics on education.

An effort to add school construction aid to the Senate bill was made on the Senate floor and supported by Senator Humphrey, but this amendment was defeated.

Senator Humphrey works closely with Senator Hill, chairman of the Labor and Public Welfare Committee, which deals with education legislation. However, it is fair to say that Humphrey's record shows that he strikes out on his own, ahead of the legislative leaders in education, to make proposals that are eventually embodied in committee legislation.

Senator Humphrey's interest in education and his concern for aiding underdeveloped nations resulted in his 1959 "Education for Peace" proposals, S. Con. Res. 68, to co-ordinate an expanded effort to help develop educational systems.

He has a long legislative record of support for medical research and education and construction of medical facilities.

Since he came to the Senate in 1949, Humphrey has sponsored legislation to help voluntary non-profit associations offering prepaid health service programs to secure necessary facilities and equipment through long-term low-interest loans.

These proposals reflect an awareness of the growing role of prepayment of health expenses and health insurance in financing the medical-care needs of the American people.

Senator Humphrey has also joined in sponsoring legislation to expand local public health activities, medical education facilities, and medical education aid for public health and nursing training. His successful sponsorship of pollution control legislation is part of this general concern for public health.

During the second session of the 85th Congress the Senate approved Senator Humphrey's proposal for a study of international health and medical research by his Subcommittee on Reorganization in the Senate Government Operations Committee. It was this study that took the senator to Moscow in 1958, and it has pulled together a lot of information on international health problems, which previously had never been put into a pattern.

Senator Humphrey's proposal S.-1151 to provide hospital and nursing home care under Social Security reflected an awareness of the acute health care needs of the "over sixty-five" population, which are so difficult to meet with the low incomes of this group. Since prolonged hospitalization is the major health cost burden for these older citizens, the proposal would help to solve one of the most difficult problems of health financing. This problem is one that Humphrey appreciates in human terms, and on which his many friends in health, medicine, and social welfare work keep him informed.

Another favorite project of Humphrey's, and in many ways a typical "minor project," is a humanitarian and perhaps grandiose idea for a "great white fleet embarked on peaceful missions." The original idea came from someone else, which is not typical, though quite often Humphrey enthusiastically picks up an original idea from someone. He is willing to give full credit and he is seldom bothered because it was someone else's idea.

This concept came from a U. S. Navy commander, Frank A. Manson, who had the idea while on overseas duty, and when stationed in Washington decided to try to do something about it.

As Humphrey summarizes it, "Once before in American history a fleet of American ships in peacetime dramatically signaled a turning point in American history, when President Theodore Roosevelt sent the first White Fleet on a three-year round-the-world voyage. A new White Fleet, sent forth over the seas of the world to the coasts of Asia and Africa and South America, could dramatize America of the mid-twentieth century as it brought American help to the disaster-stricken and American knowledge and teaching to the merging peoples of these continents, a symbol not of American power but of American good will, friendship and maturity."

This dramatic idea was not really fully formed when Manson brought it up on the Hill in 1958 and went to see Humphrey. After a short interview Humphrey immediately saw that this could be quite a project, and he asked Manson to prepare a memorandum and work out the logistics of the plan.

By July 1959 Humphrey—joined by thirty-five other senators, and with concurrent resolution introduced in the House—was ready to introduce a resolution calling on the President "to establish a fleet of de-mothballed ships and aircraft put to the service of humanity—a great White Fleet embarked on peaceful missions, equipped to render prompt and vigorous assistance in natural disasters, and to serve as a permanent vehicle for public health training and other technical assistance programs undertaken by the United States Government and the private voluntary agencies."

The announcement of this came from Senator Humphrey's office, as well it might, and it credited Frank A. Manson.

Meanwhile the attention of the Luce publications, *Time* and *Life*, had been attracted. They seized upon the proposal as so photogenic an idealistic and dramatic idea that they all but gave one issue of *Life* magazine over to the idea, including a smash cover painting depicting "The Great White Fleet" of the future in action.

But in the course of getting the article ready they had suggested to Senator Humphrey that it really ought to be a non-partisan project and not one brought out solely on the Democratic side of the aisle. Humphrey was agreeable to the notion and he brought in Senator George D. Aiken, Republican of Vermont, as cosponsor in the Senate. It was a source of bitter amazement to Humphrey's associates that as *Life* magazine plugged the great white fleet idea week after week credit was properly given to Manson but never to Humphrey. This kind of occurrence is often cited when Humphrey's friends say that he is really not "calculating." He truly wants to see a great white fleet established, for humanitarian reasons. He is far from being averse to having his name attached to the proposal, but he is simply far too busy to arrange this and half a hundred other projects in a cold-blooded manner so that they reflect credit on the Humphrey name.

Time after time he has had an idea and perhaps even introduced a bill, and in the end someone (probably a subcommittee or committee chairman) has introduced a similar bill that has gone through, and yet the heart of the proposal came from the Humphrey brain or the Humphrey camp.

Civil Rights

What has Humphrey been able to accomplish in the Senate by way of civil rights legislation? The answer, was: *probably as much as anyone could.*

Humphrey was readily accepted as a key leader of the civil rights bloc in the Senate from his very first days. He and Senators Herbert Lehman of New York and Paul Douglas of Illinois worked together closely on the civil rights front until Senator Lehman's health prevented his running for re-election in 1956.

The first floor fight for civil rights during Humphrey's senatorial tenure occurred in 1950. Senator Humphrey, who as mayor of Minneapolis had put over the first municipal FEPC bill, was strongly in favor of doing the same thing on a national level and the year 1950 found him working diligently for the enactment of an effective FEPC law. But the obstacle then, as it has been ever since, was the filibuster by Southern opponents of civil rights. Twice Senator Humphrey joined with those who wanted to close debate and get action on the FEPC, but both times the civil rights forces found themselves stymied. A substantial majority of more than fifty senators twice voted to close debate, but neither time could the civil rights forces command the two-thirds vote necessary to do so.

Senator Humphrey did not take this defeat lightly. It seemed illogical as well as unjust that a majority favoring a bill like FEPC (even voting to close debate on the bill) could be defeated by the minority who opposed the bill. Humphrey was determined to find the answer.

In the following two years he kept questioning friends, associates, experts of all kinds about what could be done to stop the filibuster. The answer was always discouraging. The Senate's Rule 22 not only prevented closing debate except by a two-thirds vote but prevented any closure whatever upon a change in the rules. The situation looked hopeless. But one day Joseph L. Rauh, leading force in ADA, made the suggestion to the senator that at the opening of the Senate of a new Congress the majority could write the rules just as they saw fit. This was not an absolutely new idea but it had not been tried for a generation. Its freshness appealed to Humphrey; he was not going to be blocked by slogans about the Senate being a "continuous body." In practice this meant no more than that the dead hand of the past could prevent a majority of duly elected senators from getting on with their job.

On the opening day of Congress in January 1953, Humphrey joined with his colleagues Lehman and Douglas to lead the fight for a motion offered by Senator Anderson to take up rules for the Senate of the new Congress. Only a handful of votes were obtained for the proposition but Humphrey and that handful were determined to carry on the fight again and again until they were successful. Biding their time in 1955 when civil rights seemed at a low ebb, Senators Anderson, Douglas, and Humphrey renewed their attack on the rules at the opening of Congress in January 1957. This time forty-one senators registered their belief that the Senate of the new Congress could adopt any rules the majority wanted.

The alarm signals were up for the Southerners. They knew that they would have to give up something or their prime last-ditch defense, the filibuster, might be abolished.

So when the House-passed civil rights bill came over to the Senate in 1957 the Southerners restrained their impulse to filibuster the motion to bring the bill before that body. Instead they threatened to filibuster final passage unless Majority Leader Lyndon Johnson succeeded in deleting Part III of the bill—which would have given the Attorney General power to institute suits to enforce the Supreme Court's desegregation decisions—and unless an amendment providing for jury trials for contempt of injunctions to enforce voting rights was tacked onto the bill. Senator Humphrey joined with Paul Douglas in urging his colleagues not to listen to the threat of filibuster, arguing that Part III was essential to any bill and the jury trial amendment damaging to voting rights. But most of Humphrey's and Douglas' Democratic colleagues yielded to the threat of a party-splitting filibuster and voted the two amendments that the Southerners demanded as their price for silence. A few urged Senator Humphrey to vote against the bill on final passage, but perhaps most liberals went along when he calmly cast his vote for the diluted bill. His typical reasoning was that one can't be against progress simply because it is not all the progress one had hoped to see accomplished.

Though Part III was deleted from the civil rights bill of 1957, Senator Humphrey believed that the fight for this provision must go on. In 1958 he joined with Senator Douglas and others in introducing a bill to bring about desegregation in the public schools through assistance and persuasion and through enforcement under the old Part III where assistance and persuasion failed.

The Douglas-Humphrey bill has had the full support of all the civil rights organizations and they repeatedly urged action upon it in the 1958 and 1959 sessions of Congress. Senator Humphrey literally pleaded with the Senate for action to show the colored two-thirds of the world that the

United States means its preachments about all men being created equal.

He even suggested before the United Automobile Workers' Convention in late 1959 that a special session of Congress would be appropriate to take up both the Douglas-Humphrey bill on school desegregation and a proposal for federal registration of voters where the 1957 law had failed to do the job. Senators Humphrey and Douglas are both leading the fight for constant strengthening of the legal protection of basic human rights.

CHAPTER XIII

Humphrey and the Witches

This book has made frequent mention of conservatives or Republicans who have differed with the senator, and naturally he has many critics because of his dramatic and explicit statements on civil rights.

Their criticism has been no sharper, however, than the disagreement and disappointment with Senator Humphrey expressed by *liberals* over his sponsorship of the law that "outlaws the Communist party."

The senator has never followed up this law with similar proposals, and liberals otherwise find his record on civil rights to be 100 per cent clear, so the law and the episode are superficially of minor importance, but the story may give us useful information about the subject, and the principles and strategy involved are of major importance, and were so considered at the time.

Senator Humphrey, like many other liberal senators, was angry and opposed to everything the late Senator Joseph R. McCarthy of Wisconsin did to promote hysteria in the name of fighting Communism. He had even more reason than most Democrats to disapprove and dislike his goals and his methods.

It was particularly disgusting to anti-Communist liberals, who had fought and bled in battles with the Communists in their own organizations, to find themselves branded as "reds" just as they had once, a few years before, been branded as "red-baiters." Some few persons suffered simultaneous attack from both sides. Another turn of the screw was the indisputable fact that McCarthy, in his rise to power against the incumbent Senator Bob LaFollette, had accepted the support of Communists in Wisconsin. But, as could be said of other liberal senators, Humphrey's private anger was not accompanied by a desire to get into a public wrestling match with the Wisconsin senator.

Humphrey did make statements—some at ADA meetings, some on the Senate floor—deploring McCarthyism and other witch-hunts.

In June 1953 the sixth annual ADA convention adopted a strong statement on McCarthyism, and Humphrey played a leading part in seeing that this, like other ADA policies, was discussed where it might do some good. The statement condemned McCarthy's "assaults upon our democratic birthright" and it commended Senators Humphrey and Herbert Lehman of New York for their "determination to fight this new despotism."

In April 1954 Humphrey made the keynote speech at an ADA convention in which he really attacked McCarthy and his followers as a new kind of "know-nothing party." He first pointed out ADA's anti-Communist record, then went on to attack those who "pretend to be the leaders of anti-Communism and the saviors of our liberty. . . .

"What they have actually succeeded in doing to an appalling degree is to divert our national attention from the clear and present danger of Soviet aggression, to undermine the respect we once held in the world community of free men, and to stifle the processes of national debate through which a great democracy should be confronting the desperate issues of our time. At a moment when all our national wisdom should be employed in the quest for solutions to the awesome terrors of the Hydrogen Age, we find ourselves plunged into venomous and often irrelevant fratricidal conflicts that dishonor and debase our traditions. We are compelled to spend so much time challenging the big lie that we seem to have little chance to search for the basic truths that might help lead mankind out of the present world impasse. Worst of all, at an hour when we should be exalting the institutions of freedom, we are allowing them to be tarnished by this madness of know-nothingness."

In his conclusion he referred to hooliganism and said, "But to your and our friends abroad, let me say this: I believe the tide has begun to turn. America is not to be found in the headlines, nor is its spirit and faith to be discovered by Gallup Polls. Even the fearful must admit that the condition of freedom in our country today, despite the continuing assault, is more promising than it was a year ago. When we last met many felt that this was a pretty lonely battle. Now men in all areas of our national life have begun to speak out." The liberal road in these years, Humphrey told this

ADA convention, is often "a two-front war against tyranny abroad and reaction at home."

By August of that year McCarthyism was at its height; it was a time designated by some Washington intellectuals as "the year of the terror."

The late Republican senator from Wisconsin was of course not the only Republican engaged in witch-hunting, headline-gathering, and political haymaking. (There were also Democratic witch-hunters.) It seemed to many Senate liberals—not to mention even more angry conservative Democrats—that the Republicans had made brazen but astonishingly successful efforts to brand the Democrats as "soft on Communism," in the present, as well as guilty of having harbored "traitors" and "Communists" in the past. It was apparent to any reasonable man that very few Communists were being found in government, and it was perfectly obvious to Republican leadership that the Democratic leaders they had known for many years were not "soft on Communism." But it was not a time when reasonable voices gained their proper audience, and many demagogues were using this issue to the great detriment of the country's prestige.

With November elections approaching, it was also particularly obvious that this issue would be used to the detriment of Democratic candidates for office, most particularly in the Senate.

Max Kampelman, a lawyer and an anti-Communist with experience of battles against them in labor and in the DFL in Minnesota, conceived the basic idea that the Communists were really not a political party. As a political strategist for Humphrey, he further reasoned that a law that outlawed them as such could go through the Congress—and it would be good for the country as well as the Democratic party.

Humphrey went for the idea and introduced the bill—which went over with a tremendous bang. It may or may not have been a poor law, or a poor piece of politics, but it cannot be said that Humphrey was alone in his reasoning. As soon as it was introduced other senators immediately understood the double mission of the bill. It was aimed at destruction of the Communist party, and it was aimed at protecting, presumably forever after, the name of every senator who voted for it. He would always be able to cite his record—that he was so anti-Communist he had voted to make them outlaws. Later critics have said that Humphrey and the others were overexcited and misjudged the temper of the

176

country, exaggerated the threat of the Republican attack, and therefore overreacted. If so, Humphrey was not alone.

The rationale of the senator as set forth in a memorandum at the time said this was "a proposal to declare the Communist Party an illegal conspiracy working, in cooperation with a foreign power, to overthrow the government of the United States by force and violence."

Further, the senator explained, "such a conspiracy should not under our laws receive immunity or otherwise be free of the consequences of its position simply by attaching to itself the label of 'political party.' Under our laws, political parties receive certain rights and privileges in a democracy. These rights and privileges belong to a political party but not to an illegal subversive conspiracy. The Communist Party . . . did not meet the standards of a political party in a democracy in that it did not compete for votes, did not attempt to achieve success by depending on majority support, was not subject to membership control, and was part of an international hostile force aimed at subverting the democratic processes of our system."

Liberals and even many quite conservative but liberty-minded lawyers thought the law ran counter to basic American freedoms. If a Communist is a spy, there are laws against espionage. If he is planning to blow up an atomic production plant, there are laws against sabotage. There are laws against conspiracy to overthrow the government. There are laws to require agents of a foreign power to register with the federal government. But in America it has never been against the law to belong to *any* party or to hold meetings for *any* kind of political discussion. Liberals of course were surprised to hear this proposal come from Humphrey, and thought he would surely realize that the law would be unconstitutional. But he saw it just the other way.

The memorandum of August 1954 said this on constitutionality:

It is Senator Humphrey's judgment based upon consultation with leading Washington attorneys that his measure to outlaw the Communist Party is not only desirable, but also constitutional. When he drafted his resolutions, the first member of the Senate to whom he took the resolution for consultation and discussion was his colleague, Senator Morse of Oregon, noted constitutional lawyer and noted Dean of the University of Oregon Law

School. Senator Morse not only enthusiastically approved of the bill, but asked for the privilege of co-sponsoring it. He was soon joined with 18 members of the Senate who asked for the opportunity to co-sponsor it. It is the opinion of the leading Washington attorneys that a democratic system has the legal and constitutional right to defend itself against internal subversion. The evidence that the Communist Party is an international conspiracy to overthrow the government of the United States by force and violence is overwhelming. Judicial decisions support this view. It is likewise clear that this action is in no way a precedent by which the Congress could or would illegalize other political parties or movements for the Humphrey proposal specifically points out that the Communist Party is not a political party in the legal or democratic sense of the word. The Congress, therefore, is not outlawing a political party—it is outlawing an international subversive conspiracy.

The New York *Times* had once suggested such an approach, in these words: "Many people believe that it might be approaching the Communist problem more frankly and openly to outlaw the party itself as the conspiracy it is, in accordance with the sanctions now applied so universally to party members. It does not seem impossible to find a constitutional way of doing this."

Some friends of Humphrey consider this the single blot on his liberal record but are inclined to forget it as part of the hysteria of the times. One companion of twenty years' standing said, "I gave him hell about this—before, during, and after the whole business. I was never so angry with him. I told him we could all excuse his departure from principle over something like voting for bills which hamper the development of oleomargarine—he knows perfectly well that margarine ought to be on a better basis of competition with butter—but he votes against it. I can understand that because it is a matter of his survival as senator from a dairy state. But the right to join other people in a political party is a basic American freedom."

To supporters of the bill, however, it seemed at the time to be even more important to be anti-Communist in the United States than it was to be anti-margarine in Minnesota. And it must be remembered that Humphrey had a political history that (a) convinced him the Communists were not really a party and (b) at the same time made him a particular target for conservatives.

This writer asked Humphrey in the autumn of 1959, "Do you now feel you were oversold on the danger? Do you think the law has done any good?"

Perhaps he was merely speaking for the record, but Humphrey said he felt that passing the bill had saved several liberal senators who might have been defeated, "certainly at least two." He thought the purpose of the bill—to take Communist-hunting out of headlines and committee circuses, and put it in the courts—was sound.

The elements are mixed in this man, as in all men, and it does seem that to the end of his time some practical politicians will fear that "practical politics" will never contain him completely, and idealists from time to time will have reason to cringe over some of his words or deeds.

CHAPTER XIV

"How about You, Hubert?"

In 1956 the solid senator from Minnesota was involved in one of the worst fiascos of his career.

Humphrey's advisers sometimes wonder how he would operate in a real defeat or major setback. Occasionally they mention the frantic and bitter struggle of the closing hours of the 1956 Democratic convention.

It is traditional in American politics that the man who is chosen as candidate for President has the right to choose his vice-presidential nominee. He almost always exercises that right. As people interested in politics well remember, Franklin Roosevelt always chose his man, and in the cases of Henry A. Wallace and Harry S. Truman he greatly disappointed many professional politicians at the convention, who would have preferred him to choose someone else. When Adlai Stevenson was nominated in 1952 he chose John Sparkman. You may not remember that in 1956 he departed from that custom. But professional politicians remember it well.

Stevenson had been engaged in rough-and-tumble primary battles with Estes Kefauver. The Kefauver supporters had gone to the convention determined to win the nomination for their man, and Stevenson was their leading enemy. When Stevenson declined to name a candidate, leaving it to "the floor," the convention was thrown into a hectic twenty-four hours, in which Kefauver and John F. Kennedy (with Hubert H. Humphrey in the rear) fought like cats and dogs for the vice-presidential nomination. That Humphrey was so far in the rear was Stevenson's fault, according to many Humphrey partisans.

To this day many Humphrey supporters, some of whom were present at conferences in which Stevenson and Humphrey met and discussed the vice-presidency, feel that Stevenson had clearly—well, maybe unclearly—indicated that Humphrey was his preference. On the other hand, supporters of Stevenson say that, yes, Mr. Stevenson had indicated that he would be glad to run with Humphrey, but that he had never given a clear word. In fact, they say, he had long had the idea, particularly as 1956 produced such bitter infighting among the Democrats, that it would be best to leave the choice to the convention at Chicago.

Six weeks before the convention, leading Democrats in Washington had gathered for a party to honor Senator Walter F. George. After the festivities Humphrey and Stevenson got together for a huddle about the vice-presidency and Humphrey was on top of the world when he left the room. He had the firm impression that Stevenson would designate him as first choice. After discussing various names, Stevenson had turned to Humphrey and said, "And how about you, Hubert?" And he had indicated that few things would please him more. It was about 4 A.M. when Humphrey got home—and woke up Muriel to tell her all about it.

When the convention opened Humphrey was still optimistic and he had worked hard for Stevenson. Minnesota was interested in running Humphrey as a "favorite son" candidate, but Humphrey had passed that up and instead made speeches for Stevenson. Then Kefauver had swept through Minnesota, putting on a campaign in Humphrey—or Harry Truman—fashion. He walked down the main streets of Minnesota towns shaking hands with practically everybody. So Kefauver won the primary in Minnesota and Humphrey's prestige in his home state was hurt because of his stubborn insistence that Stevenson was his man. He had fought a good fight, he and his team had suffered for their leader.

When Stevenson and Humphrey met in Chicago there were other contacts between them that are still subjects of acrimonious reminiscence. One Humphrey supporter has said that he himself never heard that Stevenson explicitly told Humphrey that he was his choice, that he would stay with that choice to the end. There was enormous pressure on Stevenson on all sides, and it is well known that Mr. Stevenson likes to wait sometimes until the last minute before he makes up his mind. Therefore, said this Humphrey supporter, at Chicago it was expected that Stevenson might think it over, but he said Stevenson and his advisers quite definitely assured Humphrey that if there were *any other action* by Stevenson he would absolutely let Humphrey know in advance. This would have been quite important to the Humphrey camp, because Humphrey would have been able to decide whether he should under the circumstances make a last-ditch fight for which he was not prepared. If he were forewarned he would retire gracefully and let Kefauver have the vice-presidential nomination. Although Kennedy had a surprising number of votes, the professionals thought it would absolutely go to Kefauver if there was a floor fight.

It is thought that if Humphrey or Kennedy had gotten the number two spot in '56 it would have helped immeasurably to make them known to the public from coast to coast in 1960. The same is not true of Kefauver because it is felt that he "had shot his bolt." Kefauver had been campaigning before the public for some years and he had staked everything on trying for number one in 1956. But the vice-presidential nomination was very important for the Kennedy or Humphrey people—at least it certainly seemed so at the time—with 1960 (or later) in their minds.

Stevenson at the last minute decided to leave it to the convention and televiewers may remember a very stirring set of votes, roll calls in which young Jack Kennedy apparently came within an eyelash of winning the number two spot. The voters did not realize, however, that Humphrey felt *he* had come within an eyelash of winning it by the more usual means: being selected by the presidential candidate.

A few hours before Stevenson made up his mind he had asked a number of prominent Democrats at one meeting whether he should make his choice or leave it to the convention. Unanimously they had told him, "Pick him yourself." When Humphrey heard this he assumed that everything was going along according to plan.

He never got a call saying that Stevenson had changed his mind—if that is what Stevenson did. It would probably be more accurate to say that Stevenson had finally *made up his mind* and that in all honesty he had never intended to fix on Humphrey, much less give a group of people that impression.

This was probably the most severe shock Humphrey has ever had in the give-and-take of politics. It was unexpected and left him in a poor position to take any next step. He couldn't even quit very easily, although he had no organization.

He decided that he would make a fight, although some of his advisers warned him that it was hopeless—as it proved to be. He had come to the convention without even the favorite son candidacy of his delegation, and certainly with no organization throughout the convention delegates. In the crisis he thought that his friendship with Lyndon Johnson might

182

sway that party leader to help him out with Southern delegates. He "knew" that he had agriculture pretty solidly behind him, and he had every reason to get the endorsement of labor. But as a matter of fact Walter Reuther and other powerful labor politicos went for Estes Kefauver. Johnson's followers (or perhaps in this case they were the leaders) went into the Kennedy camp and so did Johnson.

Farm delegations generally split their votes between Humphrey's rivals.

Altogether the 1956 convention was not Humphrey's finest hour. He had hoped to deliver his Minnesota delegation to Stevenson but Kefauver had run away with it. He had indicated out loud that he would like to be the convention keynoter, but a Southerner had been chosen instead. He had arrived in Chicago an open candidate for the vice-presidency, and yet he did not even have a convention pass. It all lends credence to the statement of some professionals that "there is something incorrigibly amateur about Humphrey—and his advisers." Of course, the voters often obstinately overlook real amateurishness—as witness Wendell Willkie or Dwight Eisenhower.

The Stevenson aides who were present at the Stevenson-Humphrey meetings in 1956 agree that Stevenson indicated that he would give Humphrey advance warning of what he was going to do. That would have helped Humphrey to get off the hook, if he wanted to, and not fall on his face—as it turned out that he did. In the hurly-burly of the convention, with Stevenson in one of his most indecisive moments, that arrangement fell through.

Douglass Cater, Washington editor for the *Reporter* magazine, wrote, "Humphrey, lacking a floor organization, not knowing the handicaps he had to overcome, uncertain even whether a secret pledge had been made to Kefauver, was completely demoralized. At the same time, Kefauver, suspecting Stevenson of a deal with Humphrey or Kennedy, had actually started packing to leave Chicago.

"The overnight efforts of the tiny Humphrey band were pathetic. Finding the liberal-labor groups committed to Kefauver, they made a desperate effort to rally support among the Southern and border-state delegations. It was a hopeless task. Governor Orval Faubus, whose Arkansas delegation had actually been polled for Humphrey, failed to deliver. On the first ballot Humphrey got 134 votes to Kennedy's 294½ and Kefauver's 466½. One hope after another

183

faded. By the start of the second ballot, half the Minnesota delegation, which had remained uneasily loyal to Humphrey on the first, defected to Kefauver."

One of the main conclusions Cater drew from the episode was that the South's attitude toward Humphrey "had changed little in eight years, since Philadelphia."

Cater said that Lyndon Johnson had tried to stir up support for the new and moderate Humphrey but that his Texas delegation would not hear of it. Texas and the rest of the South went for Kennedy and not for Kefauver, who had also been a strong civil rights man. Humphrey today says that neither party will ever in the future nominate anyone who is not a strong civil rights man.

Humphrey made a personal resolution that never again would he lose a convention fight. It would be better to appraise the situation correctly and bow out long before there was danger of being involved in a bruising defeat, under the eyes of his political colleagues, the press corps, and millions of television viewers.

After the convention Humphrey went to bat for Stevenson with all the enthusiasm of which he is capable. Some of his would-be admirers have criticized him for this. Some Humphrey friends, who were Stevenson admirers up to then, were so burned up at what they thought was cavalier treatment of Humphrey that they "sat out" the 1956 campaign. That splinter didn't affect the 1956 election. Friends in Minnesota urged him to "punish" the Kefauver faction, but characteristically Humphrey wanted to "bind up the wounds, not put salt in them."

Humphrey's attitude—after he had recovered from this humiliating experience—seemed to be that after all it was politics, and he understood the pressures and the motives of the people who, like Johnson, had left him in the final hours.

Then he seemed to take a positive joy out of punishing himself with hard work in the campaign. It seemed as if it was almost a moral duty with him to see that he didn't crack or become bitter. Instead, he would be too exhausted, being a team player, to dwell on the fights of yesterday.

This was something of the spirit in which he worked to pay off that thirteen-hundred-dollar debt in his first try for mayor. His friends insist this will probably be his response to any other major setback: he will say little about it—certainly say nothing public that would damage his party or his country. His response to setbacks generally is to try to work twice as hard, to be the best "good loser."

Another thing Humphrey's supporters say about his response to setbacks is that he is aggressively determined to learn from them. He will tell interviewers candidly, "Oh, I make mistakes, boy, do I make mistakes!"

He now feels he made several mistakes in his convention behavior in 1956 and says, "I know exactly where the pressure points in a convention are now."

He told his supporters that he would never again be interested in the vice-presidential nomination. He has said publicly that being in the Senate is too wonderful a job to leave for another "in which you would stand around waiting for somebody else to catch cold."

With all respect to such remarkable Vice-Presidents as Theodore Roosevelt and Richard M. Nixon, it is doubtful that American history gives much idea of what it would be like to have a Vice-President with the energy and drive of Hubert Humphrey. And it is said that other leading contenders for the nomination merely look alarmed when asked if they might consider Humphrey as a running mate or as a man who would be presiding over the Senate while they presided over the White House.

So on the surface it would appear that Humphrey will never take the number two spot and that it is not likely ever to be offered to him.

"But only a high school boy or a naïve supporter of Humphrey would take all that at face value," said one of the most knowledgeable Democrats in the capital. "If once again it is the closing hours of a convention, the convention has chosen another man who is being generous and also in a great mood of exhilaration and it looks like a Democratic year, and they call up Hubert and he says, 'Hubert, I want you to know that I've just got to go out there and tell them that you've accepted and will be my running mate,' I would never bet one dollar against a hundred dollars that in that early morning hour he might not change his mind. And that doesn't mean that he is insincere for one minute. But when the chips are down and the convention is roaring, waiting to send you to some kind of spot in history, there are not many people whom you could count on to return a flat and final 'No.' "

If he did get the number two or for that matter the number one nomination, and lost, then, his friends say, you would see a man trying to become the world's title holder as "a good loser." Thus they unwittingly play into the hands of those who say Humphrey would be a great fighter to carry the banner—any year that you feel is not going to be a Democratic year. To this his friends reply that he is a long shot to be nominated, "but if nominated, this whirlwind campaigner will win."

PART IV

The World

"Today the world does not need massive retaliation, but massive doses of health, and food, and education."
HUBERT H. HUMPHREY

CHAPTER XV

Doland's Debater Meets
Russia's Champion

At two-thirty on the afternoon of December 1, 1958, Hubert Humphrey was told that he could see the "First Minister"—Nikita S. Khrushchev—at 3 P.M. *that same day*.

Senator Humphrey was in Russia as part of a European trip to study medical, health, and research problems. He had been asked by the Russians what he would like to do in Russia, and he had made some unusual requests—he would like to speak on a television program, he would like to see an automobile factory, and of course he would like to see Premier Khrushchev.

As they whisked him off to the Kremlin with escorts and a photographer, the Russians might have been amazed if they could have peered inside Humphrey's head. He was boiling over with a mixture of idealism and political thinking and plain ordinary excitement. Others may grow blasé at meeting the earth's rulers. He never will. And of course anyone might have been flustered at being rushed into such a whirlwind interview.

To quote from the senator's own account, "In a matter of minutes, I was at the Kremlin with two official escorts and an Intourist photographer. We walked at least a hundred and fifty feet down a tremendous, carpeted corridor on the second floor, then another hundred feet or so along a similar corridor to our right, and entered the outer office of the premier's suite.

"At three minutes to three o'clock I was ushered into Khrushchev's office. It appeared to be some fifty feet long by thirty-five feet wide, big but not particularly ornate or impressive. Khrushchev was seated at a very plain desk of dark wood, measuring perhaps six by four feet, just about the size of my desk in Washington. As he got up and walked around the desk to meet me with his hand outstretched, I could see that he was well groomed in a dark suit, a light tie, a white shirt with simple cuff links, and two small decorations in the form of red stars on his jacket lapel. After we had greeted each other he asked if I would mind having a few photographs taken. The Soviet photographers ordered Khrushchev and me around just as they would have done in Washington, and I said something to the effect that photographers were the same everywhere—always 'one more.' Khrushchev laughed and asked me to pose for 'one more' with him."

They did not know at the time the photographs were taken that beneath one of them would be the statement "Start of eight and a half hour session as crack Soviet interpreter Oleg Troyanovsky takes notes."

Humphrey was surprised in the first place to have gotten to the Kremlin and later was more surprised that he had stayed so long.

He had hoped to be able to take Muriel and Julius Cahn with him. Cahn was a young project director of the Senate Committee on Government Operations, who was accompanying the Humphreys on their European tour. But the Russians told him that this was a rush call, that there was only a limited time available and he would not be able to pick up Mr. Cahn.

At that time—it seems a long time ago—very few American politicians had met Mr. Khrushchev. It was always a question how one was to meet with any Russian diplomats or officials. After the censure and death of Senator McCarthy it became easier but it is still a hot political question. If Mr. Gromyko can be invited to the United Nations, surely he can be invited to dinner, and if one is going to dinner with him, surely one can shake hands with him. And yet there are politicians in the United States who have been capable of mounting a hysterical attack on an American politician for being "chummy with the Russians," and one handshake can be and has been cited as evidence.

Furthermore, any senator and particularly any member of the Foreign Relations Committee, knows that there is a limit to what anyone on the congressional side of things should do in the way of diplomacy. Conducting our country's foreign affairs is the business of the President of the United States. He has an entire department, headed by the Secretary of State, that brings him information from all corners of the globe, which the congressional side of government cannot hope to match. Foreign affairs, moreover, in

189

many ways is a more delicate and precarious business than anything done on the domestic side. Saying the wrong thing may lead to the most serious consequences.

In any case, as Humphrey was hurried to the Kremlin and into the course of an interview with the fast-talking Khrushchev, he knew that he was dealing with material that would be very hot to handle at the time, and very likely it would be hotter when he got home. As a responsible member of the Foreign Relations Committee, he knew also that he could carry messages back and forth but was not an official representative of the United States policy, although he knew that the Premier in many ways would look on him as if he were, no matter what he said to the contrary. Meanwhile, in the Kremlin, on the hot spot, as soon as he was engaged in spirited conversation with Mr. Khrushchev he knew that dealing with the Russian leader was a whole chapter in itself so far as delicacy and complexity were concerned.

For the first hour and a half Humphrey did most of the talking and Khrushchev did not display much emotion or any enthusiastic interest. As Humphrey has said, "It has long been my belief that despite the political differences between the U.S. and the Soviet Union there are many areas of non-political co-operation that are open to our governments and people. I urged him to take a personal interest in these subjects. My chief emphasis was upon the great need and opportunity for international co-operation in medical research —for example, jointly combating cancer and heart disease— the approach that I call 'health for peace.' Khrushchev agreed (or professed to agree) with practically everything that I had to say on this vital subject. Among other things he said the Soviet Union will give enthusiastic support to my proposal that the U.N. sponsor a world-wide International Public Health and Medical Research Year, probably in 1961, somewhat similar to the successful International Geophysical Year. He also promised to do his powerful best at the Moscow end to remove bureaucratic and political obstructions in the way of the cultural exchange program that the Soviet and American governments agreed upon a full year ago. With frequent ejaculations of 'Da, da, da!' Khrushchev indicated that he believes as strongly as I do that both our countries stand to benefit from the maximum exchange of visitors and knowledge."

It is interesting to note that when Mr. Khrushchev came to the United States he brought with him medical research people and that one of the main places he wanted to visit was the Institutes of Health in Bethesda. At the last moment Khrushchev's own visit to the Institutes had to be canceled but members of his delegation held enthusiastic meetings with United States scientists there and this may be taken as a result, in part, of the Humphrey visit to the Kremlin.

However, to Humphrey it appeared that the Soviet Premier was genuinely enthusiastic but that obviously he usually leaves matters of research and public health to other people; he was much more concerned with diplomatic questions.

When they had finished this part of the conversation Humphrey indicated a willingness to go but said of course there were many other topics that could be discussed.

It was Khrushchev who said, "What would you like to talk about?"

Their conversation swiftly got into subjects in which the Premier showed a much keener interest—for example, the matter of Berlin, the matter of nuclear disarmament, and the question of bases supposedly encircling the U.S.S.R.

While discussing atomic progress Mr. Khrushchev told Humphrey that Russian scientists had recently developed a "five megaton bomb" using one tenth less fissionable material than was previously required.

The Premier also discussed another secret, his 8700-mile missile. He said, "I will tell you something that you do not know and your government doesn't know, we have a new one that we haven't been able to test adequately. We have to test it in stages."

And he boasted, "Maybe we ought to have competition on rockets. You know we are having trouble testing our intercontinental ballistic missiles. They shoot too far."

Khrushchev said several things that were in the nature of messages for Mr. Humphrey to take home to Washington and to the White House. The Premier repeated often, "I have the deepest respect for President Eisenhower . . . we want no evil to the United States or to free Berlin. You must assure the President of this."

Though he spoke quite admiringly of Eisenhower, he also said, "I did not like Truman. I did not like Truman's policies, but Truman *did* make decisions."

Sometimes this got to be quite a strange conversation as conversations with the genial ex-miner who is now head of the Soviet system have a way of becoming. One moment he would smile and the next he would make some grim threat.

Soon after his Kremlin trip Humphrey reported that Khrushchev had even praised Vice-President Nixon. But Khrushchev was quite bitter about the late John Foster Dulles, who of course was Secretary of State at this time. He said, "I am sorry that the policies of the United States are made by Dulles. He is a man of a very special kind of character. This is your own internal matter, but that is not only my view. Throughout the whole world he is regarded in the same way. It is not just I who do not like Mr. Dulles. If you don't think so, read the British press and the French press and the press of other countries. However, I will tell you that the Soviet Union will survive. We have survived many Secretaries of State."

When Khrushchev characterized Dulles as "imperialist" and "warlike," Humphrey sharply disagreed. He said, "If that were so, President Eisenhower would not have him as his Secretary of State and the people wouldn't have him, either." Humphrey said, "Let us hear no more of this," and they "heard no more of it."

Later in the conversation, said Humphrey, "Khrushchev once ticked me off in somewhat the same fashion." They had been talking about "colonialism" and Humphrey had said that, after all, the Americans were "the original anti-colonials." To this Khrushchev said peremptorily, "We will not speak of this. We might disagree."

So the conversation rocked along, hour after hour. Humphrey got the firm idea, which of course was confirmed many months later by thousands of other Americans, that one had to be careful above all of "talking down" to the Premier, but that if one spoke bluntly and candidly to him he seemed not only to appreciate it but actually to like it. At one point Mr. Khrushchev said, "Let us go off the record as you Americans say." Humphrey had been taking notes for several hours but he put away his paper and pen. Then the two men had a conversation that was not recorded but covered many topics—Berlin was not one of them. Apparently they talked a good deal about the practice of politics, but Humphrey has held fast to his pledge not to report what was said in that part of the conversation. One may surmise that they discussed differences and likenesses between political methods in the U.S.S.R. and the U.S.A.

Humphrey has often said that the Russian Premier is a politician as well as a dictator and that "this is a new combination for the Russians" as well as for us to deal with. He also said that he feels Khrushchev could be either a political boss, the head of a political machine in the U.S., or he could be a candidate, "a front man" who could go out and please the population with his campaigning and debating in, say, a legislature or Congress. There seems no doubt that, so far as his political abilities are concerned, Khrushchev is admired by Hubert Humphrey and vice versa. Humphrey of course said this sort of thing long before the President said, after Khrushchev returned to Russia from his visit to the United States, "He certainly is an extraordinary character."

In Humphrey's words, "Khrushchev used some of his harshest language—but in a tone of gleeful good humor—when he discussed President Eisenhower's rejection last July of a request for credits to finance Soviet purchases of consumer goods in the U.S. Khrushchev said that in our propaganda we had been telling the Soviet people how badly off they were and how sorry Americans were for them, and that he 'just got tired of it.' So he wrote a personal letter to President Eisenhower, requesting the credits. Khrushchev continued that he was delighted when the President rejected the request. 'You helped me,' he said. 'You showed my people that you did not really care about them. You walked right into it. You were stupid, you were fools.'"

At other times Khrushchev made it clear that he did not follow the classic Marxist-Lenin-Stalin doctrines letter by letter. And in particular he said that in China it had been found difficult or impossible to manage agriculture and to direct big communal farms according to the classic Marxist doctrine of collectivism.

Humphrey was surprised, startled, and for the moment somewhat disarmed by the disposition of the Russian Premier to speak so frankly. Later it appeared that the Premier regretted some of his frankness. But at least for several hours that evening the pharmacist and the miner had a remarkable and on the whole very pleasant interchange of views.

At the time of Humphrey's Kremlin visit, however, the press was more concerned with its own impressions of Humphrey. The reaction to the Humphrey-Khrushchev conversation was sensational.

At first blush many Washingtonians and the average Moscow correspondent for an American newspaper smiled broadly. There was something about the idea of Humphrey talking for hours to Khrushchev that amused everyone. Later it was suggested by another senator, when Mao was rumored to be resigning his office, that Mao was afraid he was next on Humphrey's list, that Humphrey was headed in his direction and he might be talked to death.

More seriously, the reaction of Washington observers was that Humphrey had done extraordinarily well in presenting American attitudes. He had obviously struck some chords of understanding with Mr. Khrushchev, which up to that time no one else had been able to manage. Overnight a number of people began to say that Humphrey had become a much more likely contender for the 1960 presidential race.

The chief of the New York *Times* Washington bureau, James Reston, said that Washington had been skeptical of Humphrey for years. "He has been suffering for years from the original impression he created here as a gabby, to-hell-with-the-consequences-liberal. . . . Hubert Humphrey is still a pretty glib and cocky fellow . . . but the Senate has amended its opinion of him upward in the last six years."

Doris Fleeson, one of the leading liberal columnists, wrote, "It's a very Merry Christmas for Hubert Humphrey."

The conservative *U. S. News and World Report* reported in a startled manner that the senator "managed to start a Presidential boom from the steps of the Kremlin itself . . . he carried it halfway around the world to the steps of the White House. For a week he received big and favorable headlines. The boom remained sturdily alive."

A few months later Fletcher Knebel, a wisecracking Washington columnist, looked back and said, "It looks as if Hubert Humphrey succeeded in prying open the door of the Kremlin so that Richard Nixon could walk through on his way to the White House."

In Moscow that December night Humphrey was very careful to report the extent of his conversation to the American Embassy immediately. As a matter of fact he took his notes, which were unusually legible and voluminous, back to the embassy and there he sat down with a recording machine and for hours dictated quotations, impressions, and conclusions on his discussion. The substance of this was immediately cabled to the Secretary of State in a lengthy and detailed report. When Humphrey met reporters later on they found him, as *U. S. News* put it, "unusually reluctant to talk."

On the way home from Moscow, when his plane landed in Oslo, London, and Washington, he was besieged by reporters and he did give them additional threads of information. In Washington two hundred reporters turned out for a press conference. Some reporters felt that at this time "Mr. Humphrey added a few more suspense-making teasers." The next day the senator spent eighty minutes with President Eisenhower and another half hour telling White House reporters about his meeting with the President.

It was at this time that Eleanor Roosevelt said that Humphrey had the "spark of greatness" that the next President would need. Other people chimed in. For example, Senator Mike Monroney, an Oklahoma Democrat, at this time spoke his approval of such a nomination.

Many wondered what was in Khrushchev's mind when he picked Humphrey as a man with whom to talk or carry messages. The Baltimore *Sun* said that Khrushchev had "confided the secrets to the most notorious chatterbox in the United States Senate." Even *U. S. News*, however, felt that if Khrushchev had tried to "use" the senator for propaganda purposes "Senator Humphrey, undeceived, had promptly put the situation to his own political advantage." *U. S. News* at that time said that one of the main messages Humphrey had brought was "that Khrushchev would like to journey to Washington for a meeting with the President, if he could only wangle an invitation." *U. S. News and World Report* did not think much of that suggestion, but as history turned out it was acted upon, with implications for the entire human race.

Magazines like *Newsweek* and *Time* made the meeting their number one story of the week, and later Humphrey himself wrote a lengthy article for *Life* magazine about the experience in the Kremlin. In it he made clear that the first thing to do with Khrushchev was to take him quite seriously. It may be hard for Americans now to remember, but when Khrushchev first came to power he was regarded as a funny round little man who drank too much at official receptions and made off-the-cuff bloopers and braggadocio remarks.

Humphrey emphasized that Khrushchev was an "extremely intelligent and a shrewd man with a terrific sense of humor; he is a country boy who has made good." The move was appraised internationally as a new pattern on the part of Khrushchev to seek some understanding with the West. Earlier in 1958 Khrushchev had invited Adlai Stevenson to a two-hour talk and at that time the boss of the Kremlin was well aware that the voters were turning to the Democrats, something they did in the November elections. Khrushchev had seemed to believe that the big Democratic victory in the off-year elections was a "repudiation" by the American people of Secretary Dulles' cautious way of dealing with the Russians. (The Democrats did not see it that way.) According to *Newsweek*, Khrushchev was "launched on a full-scale diplomatic offensive to woo the Democrats, split asunder the bi-partisan foreign policy of the U.S. and lull the West while Communism rolls on." If this was Khrushchev's theory he did not stick to it very long. For along with the reaction to Humphrey's speeches and articles his trip came an angry outburst from the mercurial Mr. Khrushchev.

On February 5, 1959, Khrushchev went to address the Communist Party Congress.

He said that he considered Humphrey a peddler of fairy tales and a "fabricator."

He said further, "You will remember that this senator recently visited the Soviet Union and I had a talk with him. In the expectation of a noisy sensation, Humphrey, in his speeches and articles, told fairy tales—three bags full of them —such as the story that he had brought a special message from the Soviet government to President Eisenhower—of course no such message existed at all—and that I had confided two important secrets to him.

"Indeed, I could find a better partner to share secrets with than Mr. Humphrey.

"Senator Humphrey's wild imagination ran riot when he began to make up his inventions about the relations between the Soviet Union and the Chinese People's Republic. In this he even exceeded the well-known compiler of fabrications, Baron Munchausen.

"And now the Yugoslav revisionists have taken this fabricator unto themselves as a witness. The very idea that I could have been in any way confidential with a man who himself boasts of his twenty-year struggle against Communism can only serve to raise a laugh.

"Anybody who has the slightest knowledge of politics, not to speak of a knowledge of Marxism-Leninism, will understand how unthinkable a confidential talk with Humphrey would be on questions of the policy of Communist parties, on our relations with our best friends, the leading people in the Communist party of China.

"Evidently, matters are going so badly with the Yugoslav revisionists that they are picking up all sorts of ridiculous inventions. This reminds me of the way newspaper peddlers sold their gutter papers in tsarist Russia. The newspaper seller would come running along shouting: 'Extraordinary occurrence! Woman gives birth to a girl with whiskers!'

"And the inexperienced reader, of course, would grab the newspaper and look for the report of that event and not find anything of the sort. But the newspaper peddler had sold his paper and he had done his job.

"It seems to me Senator Humphrey and the Yugoslavs have something in common with the salesmen of the yellow press."

So Humphrey concluded that he had apparently "touched a very sensitive political nerve" when he passed on to the world the statement that the Premier made to him about not following the Communists' classic doctrine down to the last eyelash. The Kremlin leader is supposed to be the world prophet of the Communist faith and therefore he must never deviate—and in any case his relations with China are his number one problem. So Khrushchev, who had not bothered to jump on Humphrey at the time his reactions were publicized, apparently did so after he began to hear repercussions from China and Yugoslavia.

Humphrey, feeling that he should not engage in a shouting match with the Soviet Premier, issued a restrained press statement saying, "It is rather significant that Mr. Khrushchev's now adverse reaction was not made known when my remarks were first publicized; rather, his denials are only now coming forth, in the midst of the Communist party's policy meeting, after the Soviet First Minister has been criticized by some of his satellites.

"Mr. Khrushchev appears particularly sensitive, and understandably so, to having some of his remarks about Red China's communes publicized. Yet it might be well to remind him that his first deputy, Mr. Anastas Mikoyan, made similar comments while he was in this country, reaffirming what Mr. Khrushchev had told me.

"My only suggestion is that Mr. Khrushchev recall one point in our conversation on which we agreed—that the cause of peace would be better served if we quit 'name calling' and concentrated instead on ways we might better work together toward a joint and lasting peace." It is interesting to note that Humphrey passed up an opportunity for quick profits in the anti-Communist business by holding his rebuttal to a moderate tone. He wished to keep open the communication channels to the Soviet leadership—channels that a future White House resident would find useful to the nation.

After the racket over the talk had died down it became clear to seasoned political observers that the Khrushchev incident had caused people to take another look at Humphrey. When they appraised the Humphrey of the present day, instead of their memories of Humphrey as he had been some years before, it was generally realized that he had become one of the most influential men in the national capital.

So far as bringing home vital information or changing the foreign policy of the United States goes, this visit was but one more of the several unusual contacts Americans have had with the Soviet Premier. Of course it did show that apparently the Premier would respond to a certain kind of blunt candor, a point that was underlined when Vice-President Richard Nixon made his trip to the Soviet Union.

But what happened so far as Humphrey's reputation was concerned was not based directly on what he had accomplished there, except that he had made spectacular news. When everybody in Washington had talked about the event for a few days they found themselves revising upward their opinion of the senior senator from Minnesota.

The *New Republic* had said before this, "Humphrey . . . busily proving himself on issue after issue . . . in foreign affairs especially, he has become a pace setter for his party . . . identifying himself with controversies which more often than not are shunned by his colleagues as too risky. . . ."

After the visit to Khrushchev, James Reston wrote in the New York *Times* that the senator was "beginning to get the political breaks and he is now just old and experienced enough to know just how to exploit them . . . about all this does for the moment is to bring Mr. Humphrey forward far enough so that he will be studied more carefully than he has been in the last few years. But this is important."

Doris Fleeson said, "Senator Humphrey's report on his travels . . . was no ordinary turnout . . . the press galleries have long known Senator Humphrey as a talented and resourceful politician . . . in Monday's conference they appreciated the fact that he had utilized those talents effectively within the walls of the Kremlin itself. . . ." Chalmers Roberts wrote in the Washington *Post* that "Humphrey represented the kind of executive vigor so lacking in Washington. Khrushchev apparently sensed this as something he had not encountered before in the leading Americans."

It is interesting that Mr. Khrushchev was criticized in Communist circles and among satellites of the Soviet Union "for talking too much." In passing judgment on the whole exchange between the two men, it would appear that on this occasion the voluble senator from Minnesota was not the one who talked beyond his depth or said too much in a delicate situation. Mr. Khrushchev may well disagree, and when he came to the United States he and the senator never got together or attended the same function. Mrs. Humphrey was invited and went to the Soviet Embassy on Sixteenth Street for their most gala party and reception—the one attended by the most glittering crowd of diplomats and celebrities, including Van Cliburn, the pianist. But on the day that Khrushchev had a long session with the Senate Foreign Relations Committee Mr. Humphrey was in Worthington, Minnesota, addressing the annual turkey day festivities where fifty thousand rural Minnesotans—most of them voters—turned out to hear him. That night Humphrey flew back to Washington to attend an important reception of the Democratic National Committee, but he never saw Mr. Khrushchev or got in touch with him personally in any way.

However, some of the things that were discussed in the Humphrey-Khrushchev talk in the Kremlin—such as further exchange of persons and co-operative medical research, and a resumption of trade relations—appear to be well under way as this is written in the winter of 1959-60.

When Humphrey was in Khrushchev's office he made a point of telling the Premier that he had fought Communism for twenty years, beginning with the great battle inside the DFL on the streets of Minneapolis, and through the prairie and countryside of Minnesota. This was the point to which the Premier alluded when he spoke to the Party Congress, but Humphrey did not find it a drawback to their negotiations that Khrushchev should understand that Humphrey was familiar with his philosophy and was against it.

On the other hand Humphrey believes in equal directness and some candor concerning things he admires and likes. When he wrote about this angle of the cold war he put it this way:

Nikita S. Khrushchev is a complicated human being with many moods. He is also a consummate politician, with many motives. . . . A few years ago an American official spoke of the Russians and the "Oriental mind." This implies that some human beings are just naturally different.

This sort of nonsense does us a great disservice. The Russians are human beings, like the rest of the human race. We may find the Russians hard to understand, because their value systems are different from ours, but they are human beings, they have human minds precisely like ours, and we must find humane ways to communicate and to compete.

Mr. Khrushchev in particular has a receptive mind and very human traits.

During his visit, he will undoubtedly make many seemingly offhand comments, which appear unpremeditated. Americans should remember that he is not only speaking to his hosts and to the American people but he has in mind other countries, the neutrals, the satellites, and always the men at home in the Kremlin. Some things in America he may be delighted with, but he will know that he simply could not express great enthusiasm for them without causing repercussions at home or in the ranks of some ally, such as China. We may forget this, but he will not forget it.

The nature of the cold war creates such pressures on all sides. Americans coming home from Russia will not be as enthusiastic or as candid about some things there as they might be, because such enthusiasm may be criticized at home. This is part of the tragedy of the cold war. This circle has to be broken or civilization will explode.

Both of us must speak some plain truths in public and private.

Premier Khrushchev is the leader of a world-wide political movement, the prophet of a fanatic faith. The Chinese, for one example, suspiciously peer over his shoulder to see that he remains "pure in the faith," that he does not become dominated too much by Russian national motives.

Khrushchev is also chief of a reluctant empire, the symbol of tyranny to millions of enslaved people in the satellite countries.

Meanwhile, Khrushchev is production chief of all the factories and farms of a nation which is competing with us, night and day. The title of Khrushchev's latest book, a Russian best seller, of course, is *Towards Victory in the Peaceful Competition with Capitalism.*

Finally, Khrushchev comes to us as a politically sensitive leader of millions of human beings. I do not believe Mr. Khrushchev can totally ignore the average Russian, who passionately hopes, as does the average American, that the hydrogen bomb will never be used by any nation upon any other.

We should listen politely and speak candidly to all of these Khrushchevs—the prophet, the human being, the production chief and the dictator-politician.

We should listen with caution born of experience, but greet him with courtesy born of confidence. The eyes and the hopes of mankind are upon us.

A key to all of Humphrey's dealings is the fact that to him people are first of all human beings. This may sound to a cynic like an old and worn-out cliché, but it means something to the typists who work hours overtime in the Humphrey office, and apparently it meant something to Nikita S. Khrushchev.

As Humphrey thought over his extraordinary evening with Khrushchev he knew that he might take the easy way out. He could go home and give out the general line, "I've seen this ruthless man and I know again just how evil Communism is." If he behaved in this way he might find it was the safest course, politically. In America today one cannot be sure that the people will not turn at some future date and seek to punish those who have sought to negotiate with the Russians. However, to take this course would probably have endangered the future exchange of informal conversations between the Russian Premier and other leaders of the West. Humphrey reasoned (correctly, as it turned out) that Khrushchev was quite sincere in saying he sought further informal conversations of a rather candid nature. Of course Mr. Khrushchev is known to be a master of propaganda and the Kremlin under his regime has often done one thing and said another, but on many occasions Mr. Khrushchev has been surprisingly frank in stating his purposes and his fears. Humphrey saw this and decided that he had to take the chance of reporting candidly and rather fully, in spite of the political risk this would bring at home.

Between the time Humphrey got home and the time the Kremlin turned on him and attacked him, the extreme conservatives did start to haul Humphrey over the coals. The magazine *Human Events*, a journal of opinion, said, " 'The liberal' Democrats, triumphant in the recent election, have their Kremlin-blessed candidate." Unfortunately the writer does not have at hand what *Human Events* had to say after

Mr. Nixon was given such a warm reception in Siberia and Poland.

Others made fun of Humphrey's emphasis upon the strength, intelligence, and resilience of Mr. Khrushchev. Douglass Cater quotes an elder statesman who said, "You have been in the lion's den and described the lion for us, but Hubert, we already knew there was a lion in there."

And while some of the Washington wiseacres among the newspapermen had criticized him for talking too much about the visit, he also had the same criticism from Mr. Khrushchev. Of course Humphrey knew that it is impossible to deal with Mr. Khrushchev in any way that will please the entire American public. It is also impossible for an American to deal with Mr. Khrushchev in a way that will never lead him to become angry, or at least to pretend to be angry. These would seem to be self-evident propositions and can be applied not only to Humphrey but to any other American who goes into the lion's den and tries to bring out something useful for freedom-loving peoples.

It may be of interest to our story, however, to examine Humphrey's judgment of Khrushchev and the Russians. Before Khrushchev came over here, before he made many speeches to explain himself, Humphrey, on the basis of one interview and subsequent study of his policies, made some exceedingly interesting observations.

Humphrey's friends and supporters say there are dozens of such examples in his record, and they think it a prime requisite of a *leader* that he learn things before the crowd does. They believe Humphrey perceives the situation far more quickly than the average man, and therefore is equipped to make decisions on momentous matters before a situation has become too grave.

Here are some quotations from Humphrey's judgment of Khrushchev *before* the latter's American tour:

I think there is a basic psychological pattern behind many of his reactions, and many other observers agree that it is a key to the present-day political outlook of the Russian leaders.

That meeting of ours gave me an indelible impression—here is a man with an almost sentimental humility at times, who will switch over to an arrogance so extreme that it seems irresponsible. Thinking it over, I concluded that some of his cockiness and threatening manner comes directly from his feelings of inferiority. He and Russia are new arrivals in the great and grim business of twentieth-century power diplomacy. He has some of the same swagger which you may find in the "get rich quick boy" who has just muscled his way up in society.

Like all such comparisons, it is dangerous to take this too far. We cannot even compare Khrushchev's competitive spirit with the competition that a small firm, now become powerful, might have towards General Motors. He and Russia are engaged in trade competitions with us, by the way, but they are also engaged in far more serious conflict on the social, ideological, and weapons production fronts. This particular "new arrival," throwing his weight around, could blow up the whole town. But let me be clear, the Soviet Premier is sophisticated in his chosen profession, I am not implying ignorance when I say "new arrival"!

But neither he nor his people feel comfortable in their new position in the world. The Russian people admire us keenly, they almost worship such names as Ford, yet at the same time they distrust "capitalists." They want greatly to equal our production, to pass us, and triumph over us—and at the same time or at in-between times, they still feel inferior, they look up to us, and they want our help, but hate to admit it.

These are national attitudes reflected as a matter of policy in Khrushchev's statements—and on top of that he is *personally* competitive. He frequently makes startling competitive statements about other Soviet leaders. If you tell a joke, he wants to top it. When I told him that I expected the Democrats would soon be in power, and then our production and our ideas "will run you out of Gorki Park," he seemed to like it. At that point his mood was such that I am confident he felt rather pleased that the great American power might extend itself to compete with Russia—it flattered him. He laughed, although I meant this seriously, that there would soon be more exertion on our part. But he immediately set out to answer my comment.

If you know how a younger athlete may admire, and compete with, and be inspired by, and at the same time *resent* an older athlete, I think you have a basic clue to Mr. Khrushchev and to understanding the Russians. At the time when the younger athlete has finally developed and matured, the most inflammatory thing the older can do *is to be condescending*. Khrushchev personally and politically wants acceptance from the United States. I say this regardless of what arrogant remark he may make the same day you read this.

In my opinion we can expect trouble in communications at any time that people dealing with Mr. Khrushchev forget that Russia today is a great power and her First Minister is an able and resourceful man. A most likely error is to underestimate him, and often in the past, our leaders have underestimated the Russians.

CHAPTER XVI

To Live without Fear

Perhaps the most consistent theme in all of Senator Humphrey's activities has been his constant effort to understand modern weapons and therefore to work toward realistic negotiations for arms control and a better understanding with the Russians.

In July of 1955 he introduced the resolution that created a special Subcommittee on Disarmament, which reports to the larger Foreign Relations Committee. Ever since, he has been chairman of that subcommittee and has worked through it and by every other means available to alert the Senate, the Executive, and the public to the need for arms control and a peace based on the realities of the atomic age.

His fellow senators are explicit in their admiration of the knowledge and enthusiasm Humphrey has brought to this often unpopular issue. Informed persons who still believe that ways and means may be found to avert a world catastrophe agree that he has been the principal spokesman for new ideas. His leadership and his staff have made the Senate committee the information center for all organizations and experts— including many persons in the State Department—who seek practical ways and means to avoid a big-power stalemate and ultimately a war of hydrogen bombs dropped by intercontinental missiles.

Through thick and thin, when the cause of disarmament seemed most dreamy or most dangerous as an approach to the Russians, and when it has become popular and therefore likely to be a political football, the senator has been remarkably consistent in his main theses.

This task is in many ways uniquely suited to his talents. Idealism, a belief in the brotherhood of man, even a knowledge and appreciation of the hideous potential of weapons that could kill hundreds of millions, are not enough to make an effective "fighter for peace" in the world of today. Very few people realize it but it seems to be true that a hopeful technology of peace is growing up alongside the technology of war. Humphrey has emphasized again and again that armament and disarmament must be considered together, and that both defense and negotiation policies must be constantly re-examined in the light of the latest technological and scientific advances. You have to know your weapons in order to know how they might be controlled or abolished.

Just as a physician, no matter how idealistic and merciful, cannot cope with illness unless he understands specific symptoms, specific dangers, and specific remedies, the problem of the peacemaker in the modern world is in part a technical problem as are most twentieth-century problems. Humphrey has the idealism, the practical experience of the Senate, the eloquence, and the ability to push and nag and coax the Executive—and sometimes to square off in outright battle against the secrecy that smothers the facts. But his idealism and political effectiveness have been uniquely served by his unsurpassed ability to absorb new facts and new scientific developments. Like the late Senator Brien McMahon, he understands that science has given politics new dimensions in which to work, to wage war, or to wage peace.

Some other senators have been better at using the committee system to make headlines and reputations for themselves, but few if any have ever surpassed Humphrey in the way he leads a committee staff. He uses the congressional hearing system to produce report after report that would do credit to the most scholarly department of a university. This is why the reports of the Subcommittee on Disarmament have served as virtual handbooks for our negotiators at Geneva.

In 1952, when "massive retaliation" was the theme of the hour, both our military and our diplomatic postures were relying heavily on big bombs. Public statements by the highest officials, as well as countless advertisements of aircraft companies, echoed the boast that if war should come the massive might of the Strategic Air Command would obliterate the enemy within the hour. No one but a few fanatics, mystics, and enthusiasts of civil defense, plus a few hard-headed generals and a few people like Hubert Humphrey, worried about what would happen to the United States within that same hour. In 1953 and 1954—the latter year saw Senator Joe McCarthy reach his peak—it was considered somewhat ridiculous, if not in fact subversive, to worry too much about whether national goals or the life of humanity would truly be served by massive atomic wars.

But Humphrey was willing, characteristically, to think out loud about some of the things that troubled Quakers, apathetic neutrals, and quite a few military men who had begun to think about the first hour and the first month of massive retaliation.

Through 1954 Humphrey tested some of his ideas, and as usual tried to deal practically with certain problems within the Senate itself . . . where the Joint Committee on Atomic Energy more or less owned the atom, the Committee on Armed Services owned "armament," and the Foreign Relations Committee of course had jurisdiction over all matters of foreign policy. (This past year the senator has begun to think about and to urge the creation of a really good staff and a really comprehensive Senate committee that would do for the Senate roughly what the National Security Council should do for the executive side of the government.)

In 1955 that first Subcommittee on Disarmament was composed of six members from Foreign Relations, four from Armed Services, and two from the Atomic Energy Committee. It would be an understatement to say that some of these men were reluctant. What was there for the Senate to say about disarmament, except that on the record we were strong for it but in practice there was no hope of it? What was the committee to do? It might be an excellent thing to meet in silent prayer for disarmament—but one didn't need to go to a committee room to do that.

These objections were to recur even after the committee staff and an extraordinary group of distinguished witnesses in successive years had laid out a grim picture of the world as it was and as it would be . . . and also brought out some ingenious ideas as to how it could be. The committee's path has always been thorny.

In 1955, after Korea but before Sputnik, the basic theme of many persons was that we would never start a war, the Russians could not really threaten us for a long time, and our basic approach should be to see that all the neutrals of the world understood just how evil and poorly run the Russian system was, and just how peaceful and strong and well run our system was.

Into this atmosphere Humphrey plunged full tilt, and his critics thought that once again he had gotten too far ahead of the facts of political life.

Three years later Jerome H. Spingarn, a Washington

lawyer and a long-time student of arms control and international relations, wrote of Humphrey in the November 1958 issue of the *Bulletin of the Atomic Scientists:*

Back in 1955, when all the glory went to the investigator who could stage the roughest, toughest spectacle, followed by the largest number of contempt or perjury convictions, Senator Hubert Humphrey set up a series of hearings on disarmament that had all the "oomph" of a nine o'clock graduate seminar. Hearty and outgoing in manner, sometimes glib and vigorously partisan, Humphrey could easily have turned in a colorful performance. Instead, he announced, in a very humble way, that he had come to learn, and proceeded to call the best minds of the country to a series of quiet sessions at which problems of arms reduction and control were thoroughly and patiently explored and broken into component parts. Even when the administration left itself wide open after taunting him with occasional snubs, Humphrey refrained from counterpunching. The problem of controlling modern armaments was too serious for interparty warfare.

As a result, Humphrey performed a unique service in getting important segments of the national community to begin giving serious attention to the problem of controlling and reducing armaments. The hearings educated a group of senators and stimulated the interest of a large number of scholars, journalists, scientists, and community leaders, widely scattered throughout the country.

The subcommittee also helped to build a climate of public opinion in which actual progress became possible. During the committee's first year, when Governor Adlai Stevenson suggested a suspension of nuclear weapons tests, he was derided by the professional politicians and the editorial writers. Two years later, after the committee completed a series of hearings and staff studies, which thoroughly explored the subject, a substantially similar proposal has been advanced by the administration with the support of Capitol Hill leaders and with a fanfare of congratulatory editorials.

Through this activity Humphrey has won support for new ideas from both sides of the aisle, and pressure for new proposals therefore reaches the Administration from within the ranks of the Republican party.

Spingarn noted a fact that was then and still is true: all reports of the committee have been unanimous. No subject is more global and vague and subject to individual opinion than that of how to achieve world peace or even a measure of arms control. But Humphrey, as an inveterate teacher as well as politician, has been determined that his subcommittee reports should be so objective that all kinds of persons can read them and agree that this is the basic reality of the situation, as best expert opinion and political judgment can make it.

Each year the committee has held a series of hearings on one or more aspects of control and reduction of armaments. These have enabled some of the nation's most imaginative and informed persons to gain an audience for ideas that would otherwise have an uphill fight to be heard. If any scientist has an idea on how to make a more diabolical hell bomb, the doors of many government offices will swing open to him. But if he, or a student of political science, or a labor leader, has an idea on how to invent some machinery to promote arms control or peace, not many doors will open. As Senator Humphrey finally brought into the open, technical experts were supposed to be serving with Harold Stassen when he was head of a disarmament office and dubbed "Secretary for Peace." But in fact very little scholarly or imaginative work was initiated by the Stassen office.

The committee reports have discussed the need for special studies, the pros and cons of nuclear testing, and the means taken to present our position on arms control abroad.

Many people fear that tapering off our defense industries would cause major or minor depressions at home. Some prominent officials have said so, and the Communists are pleased to tell the world that we have to produce war goods, that capitalism cannot endure any other way. Many economists disagree, but opinions differ as to the result of such a cutback. What would be the results of arms control on the economy? If we are serious in peace proposals, we ought to know what they will mean.

The Humphrey subcommittee calls witnesses from the State Department, from Defense, the Atomic Energy Commission, and many other parts of the government. It has sometimes gone to such technical and university capitals as Boston to hear expert witnesses. In Boston a famous chemist, Charles D. Coryell, made the ingenious suggestions that may lead to a trial zone in which arms control ideas could be tried out.

Since then military and political strategists have elaborated on this basic idea, and it has been a major feature of many other contributions in the diplomatic field. The change in American opinion—which is still in progress—on the various issues concerned in nuclear tests owes a great deal to the information brought out by the subcommittee. To a great extent the basic contribution has been assembling information in an understandable form—but no one who does not battle with secrecy can realize just how much of a fight that has been.

Most newspaper readers will recall that Senator Humphrey and others had to use all their strength to pull out of Lewis L. Strauss' Atomic Energy Commission a correction of an important and totally wrong statement on nuclear tests. This is not the only such battle for the facts but it is an exceptionally clear illustration of some of the difficulties in this field.

If Russia and the United States were to agree to stop atomic tests, the first stage toward banishing atomic warfare, it would be important to have quite reliable means of knowing that the agreement was being kept. There has to be some system of "inspecting" the world for illegal tests.

Radiation detection systems can pick up radiation from most tests but have more trouble detecting underground tests and some small surface shots. However, seismographs, the instruments that detect earthquakes, can also detect nearly all ground explosions. Scientists differ somewhat as to whether systems could be worked out to detect satisfactorily all violations of any test ban. In the world today technical facts are irrevocably bound up with political situations. If a good inspection system could assure Russia that no U.S. bombs were being tested, and vice versa, both sides would be much more comfortable about the world situation. But if the inspection system were not tight enough—it might not have to be "perfect"—so that it was markedly unsatisfactory, then any test ban system would perhaps increase rather than decrease world tension.

The Russians are bitterly against any widespread system of inspection stations located in towns and cities of the U.S.S.R. If a system to detect at long range—by radiation, radar, aerial photos, or seismological instruments—can be devised, then we will be technically and psychologically much better prepared to work out an arms control system with the Russians.

Against this background, it was most important when on February 4, 1958, the Livermore Laboratory, an AEC center in the San Francisco Bay area, announced the Rainier bomb tests and declared that seismic stations had detected bombs 110 to 350 miles away. This would indicate that Russia or the U.S. *could* go 500 miles away from their outer borders and successfully test bombs without being detected. The facts seemed to indicate that ground shock detection would not work.

On February 28, Mr. Stassen was testifying before the Humphrey subcommittee and said that the Rainier test shot had been "recorded in every seismic instrument within a thousand miles."

This was quite a different figure, but W. F. Libby, a scientist and member of the AEC, testified on March 6 before the committee and again referred to a much smaller distance. That same day an AEC press release gave 250 miles as the "maximum distance."

Meanwhile Washington atomic circles were full of gossip as to which was the correct figure, and Humphrey resolved to get the truth into the open.

Four days later his pressure resulted in an AEC statement saying there had been an error, that the Rainier test had been detected at Fairbanks, Alaska, more than 2000 miles from the test site.

Experts are still discussing the precise technical uses of the seismograph in test detection, but the issue might have been absolutely dead if some powerful influences on Capitol Hill had not picked up their telephones to turn the heat on the AEC.

Humphrey made a brief statement—naturally well received on the Hill—to point out that it was his work and a Senate subcommittee that had brought about this public correction:

"To have the AEC come out publicly less than a week after Mr. Stassen spoke and say that the test was recorded no further than 250 is indeed confusing to the public . . . it gives the impression that scientific facts are being used by someone to prove a political point, a dangerous concept to perpetuate in our efforts to work out effective arms control agreements."

Other senators were well aware that Dr. Libby, Admiral

Strauss, and Dr. Teller, the key scientist of the Livermore Laboratory, were all opposed to stopping nuclear tests, so they appreciated the senatorial vigilance and Humphrey's statement, which had brought them up short.

Humphrey's basic conclusion about the incident was more profound: the facts on weapons and possible controls must be brought out if we are to have peace with security. If it is important to see that new facts on new weapons are put in the hands of the United States Government, it is also important to see that new facts and ideas on peace are brought home to the American public.

His great practical concern here was to see that the government gave serious and imaginative thought to devising better control systems, so that we could make better and more realistic offers to the Russians—and also have the facts and the intelligence to understand a good Russian offer when and if the Russians should make one.

Concerning the seismic incident, Humphrey told the Senate: "The matter of developing adequate inspection systems is one of the key questions in our search for a beginning step in halting the arms race. Therefore it is essential that the facts on test detection be made available. It is also imperative that the executive branch expend considerable effort to devise inspection systems that will work."

It is easy to make a speech full of bombs, blood, and thunder, in which the speaker emphasizes that we should never give the time of day to the Russians "until we have an airtight inspection system." It is far more difficult—and an arduous task for scientists and statesmen—to work out a system that might be called airtight. Few people understand the intricacies of such matters, but those who do feel that Humphrey is uniquely fitted to deal with such things. He has already achieved remarkable successes in bringing the Administration and the intellectual community to think realistically about practical means of making arms agreements with the Russians.

What is the truth about the so-called "clean bombs" that could be used in war but would create a "minimum amount" of radioactivity? Is testing needed to perfect such weapons? Would such tests really be a contribution to a more "humane" atomic bomb, to use Admiral Strauss' memorable word?

212

Could space satellites be used for reconnaissance, as part of an "open skies" arrangement, so some U.N. agencies would know immediately if a major power was mobilizing forces for a war?

All these questions may rightly involve some element of military security, yet our approach to other nations depends upon the American public knowing something about them.

The Subcommittee on Disarmament has often been asked by government witnesses to hold hearings in executive session, in which witnesses would testify in secret. The committee has never asked anyone to testify in secret, but it arranges for secret testimony when it seems necessary. Senator Humphrey soon found that the army, AEC, and State Department were censoring such testimony for the wrong reasons.

Therefore the committee started reviewing all such censored testimony, to force the department concerned to justify its reasons for leaving out this statement, covering up that fact, and suppressing this report.

Once the Central Intelligence Agency suppressed a statement by the world-famous physicist, Hans Bethe, the discoverer of the hydrogen-helium reaction that powers the sun. The CIA official's reason was that "he did not agree with the conclusion of the scientist and incorrect information should not be given out." The senator set him straight.

If "clean" bombs are practicable, one might assume it would be interesting to have the statement of the head of an AEC division that *there* was *no evidence the Russians were producing them.* But the AEC struck that out—and put it back in when the subcommittee objected.

Once the State Department struck out material it considered "irrelevant." The colleagues of Senator Humphrey enjoyed his making the point that the particular line had been brought out through the questions of the chairman. The Senate believes that if a senator wants to ask questions of the executive no one over there should plead that the subject is irrelevant; the Constitution created the legislative branch to ask questions as well as to pass appropriations and make laws.

Seismic information was held back for months but has eventually begun to trickle out, in response to pressure. In the case of testimony on new atomic weapons, many statements by the Army Chief of Staff, General Maxwell D. Taylor, were taken out by his own Department of the Army. But when the Humphrey team had finished with their excuses 90 per cent of the cuts were restored.

Approximately half of all congressional committee sessions are now closed and secret, and the testimony is never released or is cut to ribbons. Humphrey made a stirring speech to the Senate on "The Need to Know," and prepared a special report urging that Congress always review the cuts of the reviewers and make them justify every deletion. Humphrey believes that this is not "a deliberate effort to deceive the public" but "is due to a habit of being overcautious . . . to classify [i.e., mark "secret"] when in doubt."

But he believes that reviewing the reviewers would force the executive to do a better information job, so that the public—and Congress—would have the facts necessary if they are "to perform their Constitutional responsibilities."

This aspect of peace making appeals to the "district attorney" streak in Humphrey, which first showed itself when he went after gangsters and liquor law violators in Minneapolis. When the senator is cross-examining a witness who is covering up for an executive department, it is sometimes a little difficult to realize that it is all part of the quest for peace. But in the well-known words of Sergeant Friday, "In the interests of law and order you have to have the facts, ma'am."

And once in a while it is the interests of law to make the witness come clean with the full story.

If the reader were to go to Humphrey's office and ask for copies of one year's statements and reports relating to arms control, he would be justified in thinking that was not merely the dominant interest but the only pursuit of the senator. The reader would need a small suitcase to carry away the press releases, speeches, studies, letters, petitions, questioning of witnesses, and resolutions introduced into the legislative machinery.

Here is a Senate speech of the spring of 1959, on "The American Will for Peace," which says: "I fear that we have failed to direct our energies and attention as we should to our traditional works of peace. . . . We seem to be forgetting that it is only through unflagging vigilance and effort that we can attain well-being and peace . . . we appear to be shrinking from risks. . . ."

Humphrey was outlining his particular program of works

214

for peace: education . . . a great white fleet . . . food for peace . . . science for peace . . .

But he was mainly saying that, while there is some risk in stopping nuclear tests or negotiating with the Russians, there are risks in the other direction: "The risk of continuing the present state of mutual deterrence with the threat hanging over us of mass annihilation is, in my estimation . . . an unreasonable and unnecessary risk."

In April and May he was writing detailed letters to the Secretary of State and reports to the Senate on the question of seismic stations, supplemented by on-the-spot inspections, and possible ways of approaching the Russians with a proposal to limit the number of on-the-spot inspections.

On June 4 he made a major Senate speech on defense and disarmament, which ranged over the pros and cons of limited war, tactical weapons, and the problems the major powers will face when many countries have nuclear bombs.

In June he appeared as a witness himself—he went to the Senate Appropriations Committee to plead for more funds for the State Department for a set of "Special Foreign Policy Studies." His own committee had recommended such studies, plus an additional use of non-governmental experts to supplement the work of six or seven staff people there who study disarmament policy. The committee report had said it was "struck by the disparity in the effort the world is putting into thought and action for controlling and reducing armaments and the effort going into the development, fabrication and buildup of armaments."

In July, Senator Humphrey and thirteen other senators wrote the President about the agreement to share atomic weapons and equipment with NATO countries that the United States was putting into effect.

In part, the letter said: "A number of people in this country and abroad . . . question the necessity and wisdom of these agreements on sharing nuclear weapons materials and data. In view of this concern here and abroad, we respectfully suggest, Mr. President, that serious consideration be given to the issuance of a declaration of policy by you on behalf of the United States. We have in mind a declaration which would clearly show that the dictates of military policy do not take precedence over United States political and diplomatic policies. It could reassure our people that the agreements in no way preclude the United States from entering into agreements in the future with the Soviet Union and

other nations concerning the control and reduction of armaments, that they in no way prejudice the reunification of
Germany, and that they in no way bind the United States
to continue to supply the recipient governments with nuclear
information and materials if this action should be prohibited
by international agreements. . . ."

This letter showed that a sizable body of senators, and presumably American opinion, was unhappy with the idea of
achieving security through placing atomic weapons in European countries, including a rearmed Germany.

In July the senator appeared again as a contributor to the
Foreign Affairs Quarterly, an authoritative journal on international affairs. In this article he discussed the Senate and
foreign policy and proposed two new agencies for studying
national policy.

He suggested the executive branch should "consider seriously the creation of a permanent research and policy-analyz-
ing agency charged with the responsibility of thinking about
comprehensive national strategy, embracing in that term all
essential factors of domestic and foreign policy. . . ."

Then before Congress he discussed the proposal he had
made for a national strategy committee.

He said: "Perhaps the Congress could prompt the Executive to put its house in order by itself creating a Joint Committee on National Strategy, to include the chairmen and
ranking minority members of the major committees of the
House and the Senate. . . . Its purpose would be to look at
our total national strategy—military, political, economic and
ideological. This Committee, a counterpart in the Congress
of what I have proposed for the Executive Branch, would not
usurp the functions of any of the present Committees, but
supplement them by endowing their work with a larger
frame of reference. The Chairmen of the Committees represented would come away from the meetings of the new Joint
Committee with a greater appreciation, for instance, of the
relationship between fiscal policy and national productivity
and how both factors relate to our defense posture and our
negotiating position. Responsible statesmanship consists precisely in the capacity to see complex relationships in a perspective as broad as the national purpose itself.

"No amount of structural manipulation can make up for
a lack of leadership that is politically wise and morally responsible. But if the essential idea underlying these twin proposals were adopted, I believe it would make a modest con-

tribution toward creating a more integrated national policy; and in the face of the Communist challenge, even a modest contribution toward better strategic planning is not to be brushed aside."

Behind this seemingly abstract proposal is a long history of hot discussions with administration officials—including a fruitless effort to get the real facts on the so-called "technical task forces" that were supposed to be helping Mr. Stassen. Similar road blocks were thrown up when it was contended that the State Department could learn a great deal through the studies of RAND corporation—the "brains agency" that advises the Defense Department—but did not need anything like RAND studies for itself. Humphrey contended that there would not be much overlap between RAND studies and similar but separate studies done for the State Department on foreign policy instead of defense policy.

This description does not do justice to the Humphrey thinking along these lines. In fact very few present-day foreign policy issues can be briefly dealt with, and *that* point itself was discussed by Humphrey in another full-dress Senate speech on July 17, 1959.

Humphrey abhors "briefings" and "digests"; he believes they are the curse of modern government. And this speech on "The Path of Peace" he concluded with a plea for fuller debate in the Senate . . . for more "knowledge and debate."

He said, in part: "There is a habit forming in this body that when a senator wishes to discuss foreign policy, he rises and makes a brief statement and then takes his seat, hoping to hit the headlines.

"This is a deliberative body, a body for discussion and debate. If not, why do we not change the rules, and have a five-minute limitation? That would surely expedite business. It seems to me that instead of having discussions behind the closed doors of the Foreign Relations Committee, they should be conducted in this Chamber, where representatives of the free American press, the radio, the television, and the press of the world, as well as the citizens of America and our visitors and guests in the gallery, would have an opportunity to hear at least what Members of the Senate feel and say and think.

"This would compel us to do a little more thinking, too. It would compel us to do a little more homework. If there is anything this country is short of today, it is knowledge and debate.

"We have a sickness in the nation. We want everything on one page. I regret to say that there are some problems in life that are not susceptible to a one-page settlement. I know that the Gettysburg Address was brief and to the point, but I doubt that we could discuss all the atomic agreements or all the agreements between this nation, the Soviet Union, and other countries, in the brief confines of one page, no matter how wise and prudent we might be.

"I appeal for a resurgent spirit in this country, and for debate and discussion in this body. The Senator from Idaho comes from a state which gave to this body years ago a great Senator named Borah. Whether one agreed with his position or not, at least positions were hammered out on the anvil of public discussion, and not behind the 'patsy' of closed doors.

"When we get censored testimony, it is pretty flat stuff. We might just as well buy a paperbacked, 'two-bit,' less than interesting book. What we need is the testimony, alive, filled with the political vitamins and minerals that indicate some virility in this society of ours."

In mid-August he made another major speech on nuclear tests, and the question of whether or not the United States should resume testing. His verdict, a direct contrast to the opinions of others was: ". . . our security would in no way be prejudiced by the continuation of the suspension of nuclear tests. I say this because the experts in our Government, both military and scientific, have told us in the Congress that we are ahead of the Soviets in nuclear research, that we are ahead of the Soviets in nuclear weaponry, and that we are ahead of the Soviets in tactical strategic weapons. If that is the case, it is surely not to our disadvantage to continue a cessation of nuclear testing, because it is only through nuclear testing that the technological gap can be filled by the Soviet Union. Every time there is new testing the Soviets come that much closer to our position of strength. So relatively speaking, testing has been advantageous to the Soviet Union.

"This is not the testimony of Senator Humphrey. It is the testimony of experts before our committee. . . ."

In the latter part of August he spoke for a much larger civil defense program and a reassessment of the "problem of survival in the thermonuclear age."

In pleading for a shelter program he said:

"There is little or no realistic defense against the direct impact of a multi-megaton weapon. But the gravest danger to the United States from a nuclear attack, according to our foremost authorities on nuclear weapons, would not be from the *blast* effects of hydrogen explosions over targets, but from massive radiation which would blanket much of the country, kill or incapacitate the majority of the people exposed to it, and which could seriously cripple our national capacity to recover.

"It is important to distinguish between a 'fallout shelter' program and the enormously more expensive program to provide not only protection against radioactive fallout, but also against heat and blast. While even the fallout shelter program would require a major investment, the return from such an investment would be so fantastically large—perhaps twenty-five million American lives saved in the case of a medium-sized nuclear attack—that it must be given the most serious consideration."

In an October speech in Pontiac, Michigan, Humphrey summarized his basic positions on disarmament and possible peace with Russia.

First he sketched the atomic potential for catastrophe and the basic importance of the inspection problem:

"The large nations of the world have just about given up the old concepts of strategy—soldier against soldier, ship against ship, army against army. Now our military calculations involve the bombing of cities, the destruction of population centers, the elimination of production facilities. These measures mean death to millions of people at a time.

"And the most frightening thing is that we have almost grown accustomed to it.

"But it does no good to express horror, or to display moral indignation. The problem is also a practical one, and we must solve it practically. We must insist on a fair solution even as the loaded guns are pointed.

"In his speech at the U.N., Mr. Khrushchev stated that the Russians want to reduce arms at the present time. This is encouraging. But up to now, they have shown little willingness to allow international officials to inspect the Soviet Union to ascertain whether they are performing according to agreement.

"The job of American diplomats is twofold; first, to persuade the Russians to accept inspection, and second, to be sure that our inspection demands are reasonable and necessary to police an agreement effectively. We must not yield

219

on any essential, because an agreement without real inspection would be worthless. But we must recognize that the Russians have a historic passion for secrecy, and that the thought of foreign inspectors traveling freely around their country is repugnant to them. We must make sure that our demands entail the maximum in control and the minimum in complexity."

Then he made a particular proposal for a system of a few inspections and a prohibition on tests only above a certain size. The first atomic bombs had approximately the power of fifteen or twenty thousand tons of TNT—and bombs since then have been measured in "kilotons" of TNT equivalent. The Humphrey proposals would ban all bomb tests above five kilotons.

Those who characterize Humphrey as glib or superficial had better not seek to debate disarmament issues with him, and one suspects they have never read the disarmament studies or the introductions Humphrey writes for them. Those who have read them may have other reservations about Humphrey, but they do not believe he fails to understand the issues. Nor do they doubt his sincerity. In the same Pontiac speech he closed with a plea for America to regain her world reputation, not as the maker of the atomic bomb but as a peace-loving country. He made it clear that he was not implying that America has become a military-minded country, but that it certainly has let the world believe that Russia is the great seeker of peace in the world today.

Perhaps the most comprehensive review of the peace issues Humphrey has ever made was in a spectacular four-hour Senate discussion on February 4, 1958, almost exactly ten years after he had come to the Senate. It is interesting to compare the reaction to his eloquence and documentation of today's senators with senatorial reaction when he attacked Senator Byrd's committee and the old buffalo gave him a calculated snub.

Time after time he was interrupted by his fellow senators.

Lyndon Johnson: "The distinguished senator . . . has rendered many great services to the people of this nation . . . has never rendered a greater one than in taking the floor today and in making the speech on the subject he has selected. . . ."

Clinton Anderson: "I am grateful to the senator from Minnesota, who has performed many tasks with which I have been happy to associate myself. I am glad he continues to stress the need for abandoning the use of frightful nuclear weapons—for the benefit of the people of the world."

Mike Mansfield: "If anyone knows this subject it is the senator who is now addressing this body. . . . There is no one inside or outside the government who is more capable of talking on disarmament and foreign policy. . . ."

Stuart Symington: "The senator from Minnesota has done at least as much in recent months and years for peace through disarmament as anyone else. I ask the senator if I am not correct in saying that he warned all last year, long before Sputnik was launched by the Soviets, about the grave dangers of this country attempting to negotiate disarmament at the same time it was unilaterally disarming."

This speech was made months before Humphrey went to the Kremlin and had his eight-hour conversation, and many months before Vice-President Nixon had the "row in the kitchen," and before Mr. Khrushchev came to the United States. Thus it was a full-scale review long before millions began to talk of ways and means to live with the Russians and without nuclear tests, and perhaps without fear of atomic catastrophe.

Today many more persons are examining the facts and the ideas that Humphrey and his committee members and staff have gone over and over—with and without co-operation from the government agencies that control so much of the information.

But in this marathon speech the Senate accepted Hubert Humphrey as one of the leaders of this generation of senators, on the basis of his knowledge and skill in debate. The verdict of the Senate is already in, and since the issues are the greatest before mankind, his contemporaries in the Upper Chamber know that the verdict of history may be that here has been one of the outstanding senators of American history.

The next few years will hold other prospects for Humphrey. The next generation—if there is a next generation—may remember other names. But if the next ten years can even equal his record so far, Senator Humphrey will deserve study as an American conscience seeking to understand American purposes in the age of the hydrogen bomb.

He has worked, not to make America feared, but to make

her a real leader, respected for strength and compassion. Between Hiroshima and Sputnik Hubert H. Humphrey labored unceasingly to blend the new evils and new promises of science with the old traditions of the American dream, as he understands that dream.

CHAPTER XVII

Food for Peace

In 1959, when Humphrey introduced a Food for Peace bill, he was getting down to cases on one of his favorite themes —the need to relate American foreign policy to the underlying areas of strength in our society. A real examination of his work on this bill would show the persistence of the man and illuminate the methods he has developed for getting action by the Senate.

The 1959 Food for Peace bill was only the latest in Humphrey's attempts (frequently successful) since 1954 to strengthen the famous Public Law 480 legislation authorizing a program of disposal overseas of surplus food and fiber.

In 1951 Humphrey was the chief congressional proponent of emergency grain shipments to India, which were finally authorized after considerable delay. Two years later he was a strong supporter of an administration proposal to use Commodity Credit Corporation stocks for famine relief in Pakistan. In fact on this occasion he somewhat scooped the Republican Administration by introducing authorizing legislation before the Administration did.

P.L. 480, the Agricultural Trade Development and Assistance Act, was passed by Congress in 1954 through the efforts of a strange coalition that included Humphrey, the Dixiecrats, and the highly conservative Farm Bureau Federation, as well as other farm organizations more closely allied with Humphrey's views on farm policy—and the Republican White House. The conservatives saw in it, apparently, a temporary program to dump overseas some of the stocks of wheat, cotton, and other commodities acquired by the Commodity Credit Corporation under the farm price support program.

And in 1953 the Farm Bureau had begun to back the use of these stocks in the United States foreign aid program either through direct famine relief or through sales for foreign currency.

Many such proposals were put forward as amendments to the Mutual Security Act, by Senator Humphrey, by Senator Andrew Schoeppel of Kansas, and by Senator John McClellan of Arkansas.

The one that was finally passed was an amendment offered by Senator Dirksen, which authorized up to $25,000,000 for the purchase of surplus agricultural commodities, including peanut oil, soybean oil, wheat, cotton, et cetera, for use in foreign aid programs in Asia and the Pacific.

More sweeping amendments were defeated. Humphrey had wanted to make surplus stocks available to "any nation friendly to the United States to meet famine or other critical requirements upon such terms and conditions, appropriate to promote the foreign policy and security of the United States." His amendment would have authorized a cancellation of notes of the Commodity Credit Corporation in an amount equal to the domestic market value of the commodities furnished. The proposal actually was based on consultation among several government departments.

But after Republican spokesmen had made their protests to the Foreign Relations Committee the proposal was shelved. Humphrey brought it up again on the floor and introduced it there; this led to an acrimonious debate but it was defeated. More limiting amendments were acceptable to the Senate, and although he did not think they were perfect, Humphrey voted for them. Most of the Senate's liberals voted against them.

In more recent years the conservatives have been trying to "turn off the P.L. 480 faucet" and have battled to hold the legislation to one-year extensions, keeping it on a "temporary" basis. Farm leaders critical of the Farm Bureau position and of Secretary of Agriculture Benson can be heard to say that this conservative position may lead to such surpluses and taxpayer costs that public opinion will demand a "free market" for agriculture—meaning no federal assistance to the farmer. Foes of "conservative" farm policy think the conservatives really want this to happen.

Humphrey's idea that P.L. 480 could be more than a temporary palliative for the farm surplus problem was steadily reinforced by his travels in Europe in 1957, particularly when he observed the startling effects of the use of American food in southern Europe and the Middle East. He began a regular correspondence and series of discussions with the voluntary relief agencies that utilized the surplus food in their activities overseas.

In the next two years he put through a number of strengthening amendments—such as the ocean-freight amendment permitting the United States Government to pay the cost of shipping P.L. 480 stocks for these relief activities, rather than forcing the voluntary agencies to bear the cost.

Over the five years following passage of the basic act Humphrey built up a heavy file of information from discussions with the State Department, the International Cooperation Administration, and Department of Agriculture officials—some official, and some entirely unofficial, by subordinates risking the wrath of their superiors. His year as an American delegate to the United Nations in 1956, in which he established very close communications with scores of delegates from Asia, Africa, and Latin America, gave him new insight into the ways in which American food and fiber could be more broadly and intelligently used in "have-not" areas.

Humphrey consistently refers to the American agricultural surplus production as "America's food and fiber abundance," and frequently points out that if the Russians had this blessing they would not curse it but put it to dynamic use in their overseas political and economic operations. He tried to captivate the public imagination by coining various phrases such as "food for freedom" and "using America's farm abundance" and in 1959 he put forth various projects as part of a Food for Peace program.

Humphrey thinks fundamentally that we *should* keep on producing more than we can use; the world needs it. The Department of Agriculture spokesmen would like to see no surpluses produced. They are in favor of producing less food and they say that the ten-year feature of the Humphrey plan "will tend to create the unfortunate impression that surpluses will be with us for at least that period."

Humphrey's attitude is that "surplus" in itself is a negative word, whereas "abundance" is positive—plenty of food is a positive, says Humphrey, and he makes his audience agree with him. He plans to continue fighting for food production and for using our abundance with imagination and humanity.

He feels that a sound policy on American abundance is essential to a sound foreign economic policy, and could be a vital part of our national security. To him it represents a new application of American resources to peace, security, and progress throughout the world. And he has done a lot more than make speeches about it, as his staff warmly explains to critics.

In the first place, he has always known this would be an uphill fight in the Senate and would involve some "jurisdictional problems" between committees. In discussions of the Senate Committee on Agriculture, of which he is no longer a member, it became clear to Humphrey that many of the members did not want to look at the foreign policy implications of this legislation.

For this reason certain provisions that Senator Humphrey considered important and necessary failed to find firm committee support; among them were a longer-term extension of the act, additional appropriations, and expanded uses of local currencies for economic development, education, and health services in the recipient countries. Any conversation along these lines was inevitably met with a declaration on the part of the chairman or some other committee member that the jurisdiction of the Committee on Agriculture was confined to agricultural matters, that the Foreign Relations Committee had jurisdiction over matters touching foreign policy.

Therefore, in drafting S. 1711 in 1958-59, the senator risked the wrath of the chairman of the Senate Committee on Agriculture—and committee chairmen are notoriously sensitive to any threat to their jurisdiction—by boldly asserting in the preamble and title of the bill the change in emphasis that he considered imperative: "A bill to promote the foreign policy of the United States and help to build essential world conditions of peace, by the more effective use of United States agricultural commodities for the relief of human hunger. . . ."

The Agriculture chairman is Allen Ellender, Democrat of Louisiana. Senator Ellender undoubtedly has forgotten it, but many years ago the mayor of Minneapolis came to Washington to testify before a Senate committee. The young mayor, even then becoming known for his fight for civil rights, was hotly—but not in a personally hostile manner—questioned by Senator Ellender. Now the veteran senator had troubles again with the man from Louisiana.

Upon introduction, the bill was referred to the Senate Foreign Relations Committee instead of to Ellender's Committee on Agriculture and Forestry. The name—"International Food for Peace Act of 1959"—became quite important.

There was a strong public response in favor of this proposal, strengthened somewhat by President Eisenhower when he said in his farm message in January that he "would explore anew the possibility of making broader use of farm surpluses as instruments of peace." Senator Humphrey had been using this approach in public addresses and private remarks for some years, at least back to 1954.

Public hearings on the Food for Peace proposal were held on July 7, 8, and 10 of 1959 before the Senate Foreign Relations Committee. The Departments of State and Agriculture submitted testimony as did the Export-Import Bank, Senators Wayne Morse and Stuart Symington, and Representative Chester Bowles (D., Connecticut) and representatives of some thirty private and voluntary organizations.

The general position of the executive branch was one of opposition, as expressed in testimony and letters of the Departments of State and Agriculture, although there were several key aspects of the bill on which no comments were received.

All of the members of Congress who testified, the governor of Wisconsin, and the representatives of private organizations and individuals with only one exception (American Farm Bureau Federation) *strongly supported the bill.*

Upon the completion of these hearings, the Foreign Relations Committee studied the proposals made in the bill, the specific changes suggested by witnesses, and in due time approved the Food for Peace proposal, incorporating many of the new suggestions and some suggestions offered by the executive agencies. These changes in no way changed the heart of the matter—the declaration that surplus food and fiber are vital parts of the struggle for world peace.

The Foreign Relations Committee-approved version of S. 1711 was reported to the United States Senate on August 10 by Senator Humphrey. In the report Senator Humphrey made it clear that he realized that a delicate legislative situation existed. He stated: "In recommending Senate passage of this legislation, which consists of amendments to Public Law 480 of the 83rd Congress, the committee recognizes that it does not have primary jurisdiction over one of the main aspects of Public Law 480, namely the sale of U.S. surplus agricultural commodities. The Committee on Agriculture has had and undoubtedly will continue to have primary jurisdiction over this matter. The Foreign Relations Committee, nevertheless, believes that S. 1711 represents an example of concurrent jurisdiction. Much of the foreign currencies collected as a result of the sale of food and fiber are spent for projects over which the Foreign Relations Committee has primary jurisdiction and interest. To name a few of these uses: exchange of persons, international economic development, promotion of binational educational and cultural centers and foundations, loans by the Export-Import Bank, loans and grants by the International Cooperation Administration, and the publication, translation, and distribution abroad of textbooks and books covering science and technology.

"Thus, in reporting out S. 1711 favorably and urging its passage, the committee emphasizes that it in no way seeks to compete with the Committee on Agriculture in connection with jurisdiction on this subject. If the Committee on Agriculture requests opportunity to inquire into this legislation before full Senate consideration, the Committee on Foreign Relations would not object."

Senator Humphrey had good reason to realize the extent of the opposition of Senator Ellender to the "grand design." In an Agriculture Committee meeting on July 14, the chairman had requested that the committee report favorably the bill *he had introduced* to extend the operation of P.L. 480 for only one year. He claimed that any amendments to the law, including the minor ones suggested by the Department of Agriculture, were controversial. He suggested that *this bill* be reported, with the understanding that if changes were proposed the Agriculture Committee should hold open hearings. At this point Senator Humphrey discussed the Food for Peace bill, described the full hearings that had been held, and urged that it be given consideration by both committees. The chairman countered by suggesting that Senator Humphrey request that S. 1711 be transferred from Foreign Relations to Agriculture. After lengthy and sometimes heated discussion it was agreed that the Agriculture Committee would report the simple one-year extension, S. 1748, as introduced, but that it would consider the recommendations of the Foreign Relations Committee and other amendments later.

These recommendations were taken up at a meeting on August 25, at which Senator Humphrey stated that it would be desirable for both committees to agree jointly to the amendments to the act. Repeatedly he moved that S. 1711 as approved by the other committee should be adopted as a complete substitute for S. 1748. Repeatedly this was turned down. Instead, the bill was discussed, item by item, often sentence by sentence, with strong objections raised to many minor points. Four representatives of the Department of Agriculture had been invited to attend the meeting, and their opinions, already known through testimony and letters from the Secretary of Agriculture, were put into the discussion as "expert testimony."

In spite of the oft-repeated objections of the chairman, the majority of the committee, which favored most of the amendments as written in S. 1711, were able to express their will. Reluctantly, and because the delaying tactics threatened the entire proposal, Senator Humphrey agreed to the deletion of some proposals, such as the preamble and certain uses of local currencies, and the section dealing with improved administration under a Food for Peace Administrator.

In spite of the difficulties and opposition encountered, Humphrey was designated to present to the full Senate the Food for Peace amendments to S. 1748, as approved by the Senate Agriculture Committee.

Because of the difficult history of the legislation up to this time, Senator Humphrey agreed that the Ellender bill should be brought to the floor of the Senate for consideration in lieu of his own S. 1711, which was, of course, also on the calendar.

In theory Senator Humphrey brought the Food for Peace amendments to the attention of the Senate in a strong position, for these proposals and recommendations had gone through a tough winnowing process of three days of public hearings and the deliberations of *two* full Senate committees. On paper, the prospects seemed quite good, but the Senate is full of independent minds and at this time they all had many other things to consider. Among topics undoubtedly uppermost were the forthcoming Khrushchev visit—and the chances of adjournment.

This did not turn out to be the case. In his presentation of the bill and his remarks on the amendments Senator Ellender again expressed his heated opposition. As Senate members expect the chairman of a committee to support measures that have been reported favorably, the hostility of Chairman Ellender was confusing.

Further to compound confusion, the parliamentary situation was frequently obscure, calling for frequent rulings from the chair.

Floor debate opened on Friday, September 4, late in the day and continued until 10:42 P.M., when the Senate stood in recess without having achieved any positive result except to bring to the attention of the full Senate the controversy over the true value and the actual potential of using America's abundance as part of foreign policy.

When the Senate gets into this hot a negative mood on Friday, the atmosphere is likely to produce *no votes* anyway. Humphrey was furious, tired and frustrated, but over the weekend he cooled off quickly and bounced back. *He didn't quit.*

On Labor Day the struggle was again joined, but the time lapse had provided Senator Humphrey the opportunity to rally to his support the senators, both Democrats and Republicans, whose views and beliefs paralleled his own on these matters. He had also talked personally with many of the senators who stood in opposition, in order to reach some mutual understanding as to the procedures to be followed. The atmosphere was somewhat cleared and the wind and weather changed in the Senate.

Therefore the principal Humphrey amendments—provision for non-food relief assistance in disasters, authorization for donations of animal fats and edible oils to charitable institutions, use of foreign currencies to assist binational foundations, projects dealing with education, health, and public welfare—were approved, along with a domestic program for the use of food surpluses: a demonstration food stamp and food allotment program to be set up in six communities of greatest need. These were in addition to the three-year extension and other uses that had the approval of both committees involved.

Other improving amendments were passed; and some amendments that were not improving were defeated; and some amendments that had nothing whatever to do with surplus commodities or P.L. 480 were approved and disapproved.

Agriculture Committee staff members, who have watched Humphrey operate since he came to the committee, are constantly amazed at the way Humphrey amendments, defeated one week, keep turning up in the following week, only slightly rewritten. Humphrey, smiling like the cat that swallowed the canary, also turns up with new "proxy" votes handed him by unavoidably absent committee members. And the amendment passes. "We never consider a Humphrey amendment dead," they will tell you. "Humphrey keeps turning up like a bad penny—so we hang onto the files like grim death. You never know when he'll have the amendment back on the table!"

After final approval of the bill by the Senate—and the final vote was 68 to 14—the House-Senate conference still had to be held before the extension of P.L. 480, with its expanded uses and food stamp proposal, could go to the White House, for the House of Representatives had passed a bill quite dissimilar to the Senate version. In the spirit of negotiated compromise essential to a conference committee, the time extension was set at two years—a compromise between the Senate's three years and the House's one year. A modified version of the House-passed permissive food stamp program was accepted, and a section establishing long-term supply contracts—a proposal that had been part of the original Humphrey bill as introduced—was also approved.

After months of preparatory work, many conferences, drafts and redrafts of the legislation, days of hearings, hard-fought committee meetings, and many hours of floor debate, the bill was approved and sent to the White House for signature. It was signed by the President on September 21, 1959.

Humphrey was particularly pleased to have won a two-year extension of P.L. 480, which would carry the program forward through 1961. A new, perhaps Democratic, President would have on the books a "going" program which under aggressive and enthusiastic administration could immediately become a genuine "Food for Peace" adjunct to American foreign policy.

An interesting sidelight on the legislation was the about-face made by the Republican President over the use of the slogan. Late in the 1959 session of Congress, the White House succeeded in deleting the words "food for peace" from the title of the act which extended P.L. 480—over Humphrey's bitter opposition. Several weeks later, Eisenhower suddenly made a resounding speech in New Delhi, India, calling for —yes, a new "food for peace" program.

This legislative action is cited by his staff members as almost a prototype of the manner in which Humphrey has been able to achieve substantial legislation in the face of almost overpowering opposition from the executive branch, and often from within his own party. He usually knows exactly what are the goals he hopes to win, and he knows the intricate ways of politics and parliamentary procedure—further, he knows pretty well what to expect of various people. As an assistant says, "Don't forget that on all his speaking occasions he meets new people—he knows as many kinds of people as anyone in the U.S." In this case Humphrey had secured, as he often does, the best advice, the best recommendations he could find. He had held detailed and thoughtful hearings. He was aware of all the circuitous devices that may be used for and against legislation, and here, as often, he had steered his chosen piece of legislation by a perceptive political skill past dangerous waters—it would not be utterly inappropriate to say shark-infested waters.

Humphrey has never been afraid of a fight but he would always rather be for something than against something, he would always rather seek out grounds of common agreement than search out and pinpoint areas of disagreement. He does not expect to "win 'em all." But he does expect to come back again and again to a piece of legislation until it grows and expands into the best form possible.

They may not be plainly visible to the public, but to associates in the Senate and to those who have worked with him in campaigns there is no question that Humphrey has more than his share of patience and persistence. He does not like to lose, he does not consider his job is accomplished by taking a stand for a noble ideal and going down in glorious defeat. His attitude is to see if part of the idea can be gotten through, by fighting again and again, and then to see if the next part can be won. Similar accounts could be given to tell the story behind other of Humphrey's main legislative concerns.

CHAPTER XVIII

The "Spark of Greatness"

What is Hubert Humphrey really like?

It is, of course, much harder than it at first appears, to say what a man is really like. It is even more difficult to say what any man would be like in high elective office. After election many candidates have grown in capacity and changed beyond their friends' belief. This point deserves more attention than it usually gets, for few people ever think coolly about how great a man must be to be a good leader. The capacity for growth is the vital factor.

American folklore assumes that men who were great leaders were great men before they took office. Perhaps there is something in this belief that "there is a spark of greatness" in all men who get very close to a nomination by a major party. But that greatness may not have been visible until they got the job.

Some rather conservative historians (such as Winston Churchill) have acclaimed the administration of Harry S. Truman as outstanding in American history. Yet it is hard to find anybody who predicted before Truman was President anything like the tribute that Churchill now pays him: that he will be remembered in history as one of the great American Presidents. When Truman was in the Senate few persons would have compared him—in "stature"—with Taft. But historians now and in the future may judge that Mr. Truman had more capacity to understand our twentieth century than the "brilliant" Mr. Taft.

There was a time when Franklin D. Roosevelt was considered a kind of a rich playboy in politics, a brilliant smiler, a man with a lot of charm, excessive intellectual agility, and a certain ability to hypnotize audiences. One can even go back to what his critics, and to some extent his friends, thought of that country lawyer from Illinois, Abraham Lincoln, who to many contemporaries seemed to be a rural politician.

How are we to judge the ability of any man to cope with the responsibilities of leading a great country today? How can we read the future? Roosevelt was elected to deal with a depression, then fought a war—and started the atomic project. Surely the capacity to adapt and to learn, through new responsibilities and new experiences, must be crucial.

It seems to his admirers and to the writer that Mr. Humphrey has shown this capacity for growth and a surprising ability to understand and surmount new events, new phases of his own life, and new conditions in the world. This is the more extraordinary because to many persons he seems to be unusually unself-conscious and nonintrospective. There is no question that each of his close advisers has spent much more time trying to figure out how Humphrey got to be that way than the senator ever has.

Also there is, it would seem, a hard core of integrity and consistency that has remained constant for decades, so that he has rather more old friends around him than the average political figure has. His personality and character do not change with every political wind. Certainly every political leader is in touch with old allies, managers and captains, but numerous men are still in touch with Humphrey, on a daily and weekly basis, whose political alliance and personal friendship go back to his college days. He has grown but he has not swollen or inflated.

However, his old friends do not appear certain as to what kind of program he would have or how he would develop it if he were in the White House. Since most of his long-time associates are students of history, they are well aware that it is extremely difficult to predict such things. One can assume with safety that Humphrey would provide firm leadership on civil rights. Certainly he would press vigorously for fresh approaches to disarmament and negotiation with Russia. He would also work hard to compete with Russia. But he would do many different unforeseeable things, in a more active and positive way. He feels deeply that we have to re-establish American leadership of our allies and the world.

But precisely what would some of his steps be? Not even his friends can say with certainty whether he might become more conservative or more confidently liberal in the White House. Some of our best Presidents have been our biggest surprises because of the very fact that they were capable of growth and therefore of changing their outlook upon society and public issues. Can anyone remember F.D.R.'s first campaign and how he hammered for economy in government? This can be said with certainty: we could expect many new ideas and we could expect to be surprised by a stream of new programs.

Humphrey is brilliant and has an extremely agile mind. He has never been doctrinaire or rigid. He has a paradoxically conciliatory and flexible attitude toward those with whom he disagrees. He has been determined for years to be practical, and it is rather difficult, as it was with F.D.R., to try to blueprint at what point he will be pragmatic and at what point he will be idealistic. Which of the two is liable to be uppermost next Thursday? Very likely Humphrey does not know. This trait is not infrequent in successful political spokesmen and the voters often find it extremely attractive.

Does he talk too much?

This is the most common criticism made of Humphrey by friends and foes, by people who do not know him, and by some who have known him for years. Today he thinks more, perhaps pauses a moment in interviews, before he answers a question, and his closest associates are pleased.

On most of the subjects Humphrey talks about, he knows a great deal. The Senate press reporters and many others have learned that when one sits down to examine a Humphrey speech it turns out to be full of facts and logically organized. And perhaps it is not too long, either, considering the complexity of the subject it is covering.

It was Humphrey's speaking ability that put the civil rights plank into the platform in 1948. Humphrey's speeches and his debating ability in the Senate have won many a victory for his goals. There is no question that his speaking ability enabled him to win the office of mayor and to win and keep the office of senator.

It was his quick thinking and his quick tongue that so interested Nikita Khrushchev that their interview in the Kremlin lasted more than eight hours. It is true that Khrushchev has now had conversations with other Americans, but it remains significant that Khrushchev was profoundly impressed by this man, even though Humphrey made no bones about the fact that he had been a foe of the Communists for many years.

Even speaking through the interpreter Troyanovsky, Humphrey was able to convey his ideas and his concepts in a lucid and interesting way and perhaps—we do not know—in a persuasive way. He really could be a voice for America, as Roosevelt—and Wilson—were in their day.

Yes, the critics will say, his speeches and his debating are legitimate instruments of a political figure, and he uses them well, but doesn't he often use them too much, and doesn't he sometimes say things he shouldn't?

There seems to be no doubt that some of his speeches are too long and that he speaks out on too many issues. Sometimes, though rarely, he gives information he has not verified or makes a hasty conclusion when swept along by oratory. Sometimes, either through a desire to talk or through a desire to get attention for his ideas, the senator in the old-fashioned phrase "wears out his welcome."

On his way home from Moscow, it is said, reporters asked him questions at every stop and the net result of his answers seems to be that some of his talk with Khrushchev oozed out a little more at each press conference. But the press that says that he shouldn't have dribbled the story out this way was the very same press that besieged him at every airport and tried to pull additional information out of him. In any case the senator did have material from the interview that he could talk about, and he did have other more restricted messages that he delivered to the President. Some of this material in due course became public knowledge, but not through leaks from Humphrey.

Comb through his record and you can find phrases, hyperbole, or oratorical flourishes that he or his friends would like to be forgotten. But actually this is true of anyone who has been in public life for decades, meeting the press and the public and constituents every day. In view of his thousands of speeches and press releases, not to mention countless hours of Senate debate and questioning of witnesses at hearings, it is rather surprising that there has been no really major episode and no major blooper as a result of talking too much or saying the wrong thing at the wrong time.

Is he an intellectual?

Would the voters elect a scholarly President?

When asked this question his friends shrug their shoulders. What is an intellectual?

He is a Phi Beta Kappa. He is constantly in touch with experts of all kinds in the government and on university cam-

236

puses and in research laboratories. There is no doubt that he loves to learn what's what about a new subject, in terms that are useful for public affairs. By his own statements, a politician should be curious about everything. Yet he would never call himself an intellectual.

Humphrey sometimes speaks of "those intellectuals" as if they were separate beings. Others say that perhaps his friends squirm a little over this question because the idea is hard to define. Or because they think it would absolutely kill him with the voters if he were thought to be an intellectual. But would it? This country is supposed to be anti-intellectual, but it once elected a political science professor, Woodrow Wilson, to the presidency.

Perhaps it is a little hard to define Humphrey as anything but a politician who may be on his way to becoming a statesman. He is certainly not an abstract theoretical student of government, although he is keenly interested in methods of organization. He reads quite a bit, but swiftly and in a fragmentary, journalistic way, reports, magazines, and sometimes a topical book of the hour. He does not read long books for work or for play—few senators ever do—but it does not seem as if his schedule is all that keeps him from books. He likes action. He loves the on-the-spot extemporaneous play of ideas, when lively people are having a discussion, but he would not enjoy that same play of ideas so much in a book. In general he never seems to enjoy being alone, he never says he is looking forward to a quiet time in which to read and think over some report.

Yet Humphrey remains something of an anomaly. He might someday be an excellent university president, as other important candidates have been. He does in fact know a tremendous amount about a lot of things—ranging from the development of the Middle East to civil defense, nuclear fallout, the farm economy, the management of scientific research. But his knowledge always seems to be tied in with what people are *doing*. He is not interested in painting, fiction, or drama. He knows quite a bit of history but is not hungry to read more about the Romans or the Middle Ages or the American Revolution. He does not seem to be interested in constructing a philosophy of government. His references to American history tend to be rather standard. He has not, at least recently, done the reading in past American politics that was done by Harry Truman and Franklin Roosevelt.

Does this mean, then, that Humphrey has no sense of history, as the phrase goes? Does this mean that he is too much centered on the present and the pragmatic approach, always seeking a solution for right now?

There are critics who say yes. There are even friends and Democrats who would like to be friends of Humphrey, who admit that he has great virtues but say that he is just too quick to make up his mind. Or they say he is too flexible and adaptable, moving from one thing to another without a basic program. They don't see what his friends see—that he has a basic set of beliefs rooted in the way he looks at history and at the potentialities of this nation.

His critics say that his press releases and speeches are too frequent and too concentrated on phrase making and headlines—that they do not add up to a carefully considered point of view on the various events of the day. In other words, they consider him brilliant but still superficial—precisely what people used to say of young Franklin Roosevelt —and sometimes of the older Roosevelt.

There is a feeling that the glibness and superficiality that his critics believe to be characteristic of Humphrey's views are also related to opportunism and to a basic political drive to take advantage of first one thing and then another.

To some extent these criticisms are leveled at all politicians, and they are often directed at Lyndon Johnson, Nixon, and Kefauver. In the past, F.D.R. was often called an "opportunist." Friends of Humphrey have been known to use the word about Senator John F. Kennedy.

Nonetheless, for good or ill, an element of agility and an unceasing drive to learn more—to advance his causes and himself—distinguish Humphrey.

Is Humphrey "self-seeking" or too "ambitious"?

All politicians and perhaps all successful men are ambitious, but this is still a good question to ask about any candidate.

It is true that Humphrey is always running. When he was mayor, he was always thinking of his re-election, the same is true of him as a senator, and in both positions he has quite often seemed to be thinking about some higher job.

One way to answer this would be to say that of course he is ambitious, and many admirers are ambitious for him, and it is for the voters to decide whether he is too much so. One (partisan) observer has said, "He is not coldly ambitious like Nixon or Tom Dewey, he is warmly ambitious."

William Jennings Bryan, once the idol of the Humphrey family, candidly observed, "Certainly from the time I was fifteen years old I had but one ambition in life, and that was to come to Congress. I studied for it. I worked for it, and everything I did had that object in view." Humphrey was not in a position to do this but obviously would have managed his young life that way if he could.

It should never be overlooked that an experienced senator like Humphrey may have many logical ambitions, many ways to serve his country. He is running very hard this minute—to be re-elected senator from Minnesota—and in the front and the back of his head there must be other destinies that the reader may not have in mind.

Humphrey's friends would like to see him as President. They would like him to lead a more lively or liberal Democratic party. Some can see him as Majority Leader of the Senate. He might become "Mr. Congress," or the indispensable man to a Democratic President, as Taft was to Eisenhower in the early months in the White House. Senators have also done well as representatives at the United Nations, which in some ways is a super Senate. There is reason to believe Humphrey could make a unique contribution in some capacity there, a record quite different from that of Henry Cabot Lodge. This role would not be far from the dreams Dad Humphrey had when Wilson fought for a parliament of man.

Although commentators and others have assumed he is first and last running for President, Humphrey is not *blindly* ambitious: he would not continue to campaign for the nomination without a major portion of the Democratic party on his side. His ambition does not cloud his vision of his strength. Few public figures are more accurate in judging their place in their party or in other councils.

Humphrey has a great quality that helps him keep his balance—he has a well-developed sense of humor.

William E. Bohn, a veteran journalist of the *New Leader* magazine, was amazed by three things in a recent interview with Humphrey: his candor, his *silences*, and his sense of humor. Bohn asked Humphrey what he thought when Mrs. Roosevelt made that remark about a "spark of greatness." Humphrey replied, "I felt deeply flattered, humble." And Bohn writes, "Then he subsided into silence as if embarrassed."

Bohn then stirred him up with a sentence from the article in the *Saturday Evening Post* in which Walter Ridder said, "He just doesn't look like a President."

"Humphrey's silence ended immediately," said Bohn. " 'What can a guy mean by a statement like that? What a man does and what he thinks is more important than how he looks. The one who looked most like a President was Harding. And the man who looked least like one was Lincoln. Truman may not have had the presidential look, but he had the ability. Someone ought to tell Ridder that this isn't a beauty contest.' "

Today Senator Humphrey would be voted among the most popular senators by the Washington press corps. Where they formerly thought he was overserious, they now feel that he is almost too playful. They are not easy to please. Most would say, however, that he puts out too many press releases.

One reporter has written that after surveying the candidates the most complete and candid answers came from Humphrey. Another has said that his mental faculties are "awesome." Another heard him make a speech that ran quite a bit overtime and said to him after the meeting, "Of course if you are ever in the big white house it would be quite a thing if you spoke twenty minutes more than you were supposed to." Humphrey smiled and said, "Boy, wouldn't that be murder?" The reporter now pronounces himself a confirmed Humphrey man.

Recently newsmen have noticed that Humphrey is not so quick as formerly to speak on every subject under the sun. They now think that he is probably wise in slowing down, they do not seem to resent a "no comment" from the man who used to be inclined to give them too much comment. Television viewers have seen that he now gives more time to his answers.

In off-the-record discussion Humphrey is considered to be not only frank and accurate but an amazingly good appraiser of just what part he played in any given set of proceedings. If he says that such and such was his idea or that it wasn't his idea but his was the key voice that turned the tide for a particular project, then checking with others corroborates what Humphrey has said. He does not overestimate—or play down—what his work and influence have done. This is a rare quality in Washington.

Today he is not quite so given to broad and corny jokes but he still permits jokes on himself that others in the public eye consider beneath their dignity. Mrs. Humphrey has always taken such things in stride and says that "living with Hubert isn't just colorful—it's in Technicolor."

Some who would never deny Humphrey's brilliance and knowledge or question his genius as a politician still wonder about his "courage" in fighting for unpopular causes. Is he a real leader or just a person who can gauge when the time is ripe? Does he lead or follow?

Of course some very serious students of leadership believe that timing is of the essence in leadership. When you have said—and many have—that Humphrey has an acute sense of timing, that he has a "sixth sense" as to when a project can go through, you are granting that he possesses a basic leadership quality.

But the question is whether Humphrey can fight for causes that are *not* ripe—that can be furthered only if political leaders and supporters will *risk* something to bring them about.

Many would say that Humphrey has often shown political courage, as witness his candor with Khrushchev, his continued interest in disarmament and in nuclear fallout. Most American leaders have not dared to question the absolute necessity of continued atomic bomb testing. Few laymen were prepared to battle the Atomic Energy Commission on its secrecy and half-truths. And of course, year in and year out, Humphrey has battled for civil rights. Humphrey has often said that this government should appoint more Negroes and other members of minority groups to the diplomatic service. Their understanding of cultural differences and minority problems would be useful to the State Department, and their appointment would of course be concrete evidence of advancement toward the ideals we preach. Such statements involve great political risk in a party that counts heavily on a bloc of support below the Mason-Dixon line.

Another example of leadership cited by his friends was his determination in the campaign of 1954 to help the Middle West understand the issues of foreign aid and foreign policy. He knew that farm policy was the burning issue, but he carried through a resolve to mention the crucial issues of foreign affairs in every single speech. He was told this would be unpopular but felt this was part of his job as a leader.

Another example often cited is his appointment, in his first month in office, of a Negro to a staff position in the Senate. Cyril King, who is now a respected and experienced staff member, well known on Capitol Hill for his personal abilities, was the first Negro staff man in history. Since then, Senators Douglas, Lehman and others have followed Humphrey's pioneering step in this matter.

The day after the campaign announcement of his friends, Humphrey went to New York City, where he spoke to the National Association for the Advancement of Colored People. His topic: "Civil Rights: A Moral Issue."

Several columnists noted that it was "just like Humphrey" to start off his campaign with a speech on an issue that could only cause him trouble with future convention delegates in the South. Some thought that either he showed rare political courage or was shrewdly making a bid for the Rooseveltian mantle and the solid liberal vote.

He told his audience that he had grown up with the NAACP: ". . . your lifetime just about spans my own . . . your goal of absolute equality for all people is my goal." In discussing the segregation picture in the United States, he noted that there were about two hundred cases involving desegregation in federal and state courts. He said, "It is not enough to say that the Supreme Court's desegregation decisions, whether we like them or not, must be obeyed simply because they are the supreme law of the land. More than a question of law enforcement is involved. At stake is a basic moral issue which underlies our very conception of democracy."

Humphrey also referred that day to the kind of leadership Americans should expect from the presidency. He said: "This was a function of the presidency which Franklin Roosevelt understood so well. 'I want to be a *preaching* President—like my cousin,' he once said.

"We could use a little *preaching* from the White House right now—preaching the gospel of desegregation because it is right and moral. I am saddened that in the more than five years since the historic desegregation decisions we have yet to hear from the White House one simple declaration that these decisions were correct and moral. Indeed, anyone studying the statements coming out of the Administration today would think that the only thing that mattered was balancing the financial budget. I suggest that once in a while this Administration consider the importance of balancing our moral budget.

"And I regret to report that the record of Congress is little better.

"In 1947 President Truman's Civil Rights Committee said, 'The time for action is now.' It is twelve years later and except for the Civil Rights Act of 1957, pared down under threat of Senate filibuster to avoid any support whatever for the desegregation decision, the Congress has done nothing to balance the moral budget."

Humphrey also got in a word for his own Douglas-Humphrey bill, which he said would, if passed, "put the full force of the federal government behind the processes of desegregation; it will be a signal to all the world that this is indeed the land of equality and of opportunity for all. There are few things that would do more to raise the prestige of our nation throughout the world and thus contribute to the cause of peace."

Believers in the Humphrey ideals and methods say that if their leader had been in the White House he would have led for the whole country the kind of citizen-participation program in human rights that he launched in Minneapolis. They say he would never have permitted the conditions on which "massive resistance" feeds—he would have seen to it that citizens' channels of education and voluntary cooperation were brought into play. Naturally their attitude implies criticism of what they consider lack of leadership from the Republican Administration, and perhaps their view is partisan.

Where did Humphrey get his rock-bottom convictions on civil rights? He himself believes he learned them from his father, who taught him absolute acceptance—not just *tolerance* of "different" people. He also says that as a young man who had to fight for his education he knew there were "high and mighty people who looked down on country boys."

It is possible that Humphrey sympathizes so much with the feelings of minorities because in his youth and adolescence in Huron, where his father was a Democrat and the proprietor of a business not popular with the rest of the business community, the Humphreys were "different" people, in a way allied with the minority or the underprivileged. Certainly small-town Chambers of Commerce and socialites often look down on the "apple knockers," "clodhoppers," and "dirt farmers" who came into the Humphrey drugstore. At the same time young Hubert knew that he could run rings around the young merchants' sons in the pursuit of knowledge if he had the chance to get an education, and with his brain and tongue it was obvious he could compete in politics.

But one should never conclude that he did not also enjoy *business* competition.

Quite early in his Senate career Humphrey learned to take care of what he considers "reasonable requests" from businessmen. Many conservative lifelong Republicans in his home state think of him mainly as a man who works hard and gets things done for Minnesota. He gets them Washington information promptly when they ask for it. He has drive and knows how to push things through the federal bureaucracy. He does not take the attitude that a big or little businessman (certainly not one from Minnesota) is bound to be a "force of evil." He takes businessmen's requests and inquiries under consideration as he would inquiries from any other constituents. Many such men would rather have a "live wire" Democrat in Washington than a less capable Republican. This isn't unique; a capable senator frequently becomes an institution.

Humphrey considers himself a small businessman and through the years has had extraordinary success in negotiating with businessmen on public problems and in giving them rousing speeches. He was an all-time hit at the convention of the National Food Brokers Association in Chicago. Many of these men are conservative Republicans who were not at first "particularly enthusiastic" to learn that Humphrey was to be their speaker, but the speech saved the situation. The program chairman wrote him: "When 2500 independent businessmen . . . give a speaker . . . the standing ovation which made it necessary for you to come back to the platform three times to acknowledge applause, believe me, it is worthy of special mention . . . your talk was right straight from the shoulder, forward-thinking, but just as solid as it could possibly be . . . many of our members said that frankly they had been misinformed and had formed erroneous impressions of Senator Humphrey."

Of course it is one of a politician's problems that to succeed like this at one end of the scale may merely unsettle admirers at the other end. What would liberals think of

Humphrey if they felt his philosophy was, as this chairman put it, "the kind of sound, but progressive, philosophy under which businessmen must march forward together"?

It is difficult for the all-out liberal to understand some of the things Humphrey is for, as supports to help business. Franklin Roosevelt often disappointed liberals because he never saw himself as a social reformer out to make over the economic system. Like F.D.R., Humphrey has an unshakable faith in the free enterprise system—he has worked merely to patch it up, to guide it, to see that government steps in promptly when the system has in whole or in part failed to work for the greatest good of the greatest number. Humphrey, like F.D.R., admires organizations that get things done. He is enthusiastic about a great variety of agencies—TVA, REA, port authorities, hybrid organizations like RAND Corporation, which is both public and private—and he is strong for private business and the enterprising, profit-seeking businessman.

Public opinion polls have proved that a majority of small businessmen voted for F.D.R. in most of his elections. The small businessman admires an enterprising operator.

Humphrey has an honest liking for the kind of temperament that can hit the road, get up early, think up new ideas, and beat the competition. There is something of the salesman and the entrepreneur in his personality too. This statement may very likely alienate some of the hard-core intellectual liberals, but there is little doubt that it is true. Humphrey likes to see every project pay a political profit, he likes to offer a diversified line, and he likes to meet the real needs of the community. His "line" now carries some unprofitable items that he is stubbornly convinced the customers need.

Does this "businesslike approach" extend to his political views? Does it color his outlook on free enterprise?

In the view of many observers, including this writer, it does indeed. He devoutly believes in and personally practices the principles of free enterprise. He has met a payroll, he has met competition, he has even been involved in manufacturing in a small way, and he understands the American free economy from the grass roots up.

Yes, but hasn't he expressed bitterness against "the system" —attacked bankers and all that?

To this day Humphrey can get emotional about Wall Street bankers and "bankers' bankers"—people who make money by speculating or by abstract understanding of the fiscal system, "without producing anything." Many small businessmen agree with him, and they could all be wrong or right. But no one has ever credited Humphrey with really radical opinions, except perhaps the extreme rightists, who would also class Eisenhower and Nixon and others as "radicals."

Humphrey has been a staunch supporter of Social Security expansion, the Rural Electrification Administration, and so on, but it would be impossible to identify him with even the most moderate of socialists. He was brought up in a business which was the life of his family. He enjoys the company of businessmen—no doubt today he is more at home with them than they are with him. He also has a personal though not inordinate interest in money. He really appreciates the fact that he is able to earn money by lecturing and prides himself on his business ability in driving a bargain. He has not amassed any fortune and his family lives, as someone says, "like a professor's family at the University of Minnesota."

In Humphrey's own mind he sees himself as belonging still to the small-town business or proprietor class. His father used to talk to him concerning the migrant workers and depression-driven transients who sometimes drifted down the main street of Huron or came to the back door of the drugstore for a handout. When the conversation turned to talk of social unrest and what might have happened in this country if the New Deal had not worked, Dad Humphrey would say, "Son, to those folks we are rich people. If they ever start throwing stones, we'll be the ones they throw them at."

Even at the height of his youthful pure idealism, when he wrote his master's thesis, Humphrey believed in the free enterprise system. But he was and is willing to think up new ways for it to surpass its past records. He knows that there is no practical political use in trying to re-establish the past. There is only hope in trying to adapt the good of the present to the onrushing forces of the future.

In spite of his experience at four national conventions, the senator has never before been so involved with convention maneuvers and politics on a national scale as he is today. From every part of the country come suggestions and pressures of various kinds to support this measure or to fight such and such a program. He has never had so much professional and amateur advice, because he is recognized to have a real chance for the nomination, although the odds are against him.

The responsibility of being executive head of a city was a great learning experience for Humphrey. Entering upon the national stage, through the civil rights fight at Philadelphia, and being elected senator, were different kinds of experience. In the Senate he learned from his hazing experience and from other setbacks, battles, and Senate victories. The scramble for the vice-presidential nomination was a tough classroom. His U.N. experience and his travels abroad have also changed the man whose position for years was that he was a country boy who had not seen much of the world. He has the responsibility of knowledge, and world issues seldom become simpler as one learns more about them.

Today Humphrey is a seasoned political leader—but no one who knows him considers him to be crystallized and fixed in his goals or his methods. The intense pressures of election year, added to the steady burdens of foreign and domestic issues that national leaders carry, are changing him in ways not yet entirely clear. The senator is young enough to be a serious contender in the conventions of 1964 or 1968.

Meanwhile, all the trouble spots of the world remain threatening, and there is lively discussion of issues in which Humphrey has experience and keen interest: dealing with the Russians, disarmament, nuclear testing, farm policy, labor legislation, civil rights, progress in science, expanding our economy. . . .

Under these increasing pressures Humphrey is seeking to change some of his methods. He is trying to delegate more, and to give various fields some sort of priorities, so they are not all considered equally important. This kind of thing is hard for him, however, as his success has been built upon his astonishing ability to give personal attention and response to persons and to situations. Of course he relies on experts—within his circle are experts on foreign affairs, disarmament, domestic political strategy, et cetera—but he doesn't believe large subjects can be covered briefly. One has to know quite a bit about them.

In any case his advisors through the years have found it difficult to change him, for the basic reason that he enjoys himself as he is. Egotistical or not, his theme might be the song from *Porgy and Bess*, "I Still Suits Me." One friend said, "The trouble is that he is practically Mr. Mental Health—he likes everybody, they like him, he isn't troubled by the way people are, he isn't troubled by the way he is!"

So it would be wrong to speak of a "new Humphrey."

Governor Orville Freeman, who has been for two decades as close as anyone to Humphrey says that "the amazing thing is that Hubert has changed so little." This conclusion is echoed by many other people. In fact old Minnesota friends find it vastly amusing that the young Humphrey was so much like the mature Humphrey who is a famous and powerful figure, respected in the Senate, the U.N., and the Kremlin. People who know him often begin to smile as they speak of "Hubert"—they find his energy and high spirits impressive, and there is also an element in him of exuberance that brings a twinkle to their eyes.

The senator himself listens with surprising patience to frank criticism from friends or staff. Sometimes it seems merely to roll off like water off the well-known duck's back. He has even stood still for impromptu psychological sessions at which friends try to tell him *why* he does what he does. At such amateur psychoanalysis sessions—conducted by political scientists with no license to practice as psychiatrists—Humphrey listens usually with amused tolerance. He is like a jazz musician listening to a critic explain where his riffs come from. Humphrey is interested in effects and not how or where they come from.

He thinks temperament and character traits are rather hard to explain. No matter how clean his office desk looks when he comes in in the morning he likes to take his handkerchief and dust it off himself. Several times a week he takes a dustcloth and goes over the kitchen cabinets at home while talking with Muriel, or perhaps while talking Democratic politics or the future of Israel. His friends speak glibly of a "compulsion" to make things clean and tidy, "a need to keep busy." Humphrey says this habit is a hangover from the endless battle against dust in the drugstore of the thirties. Muriel says correctly that lots of other people lived through dust storms in the Dakotas, not to mention Kansas and Oklahoma, and very few of them are still dusting off their table tops.

Meanwhile, Humphrey seems to learn about new subjects and to invent new ideas and new political arrangements and to sponsor new approaches in foreign policy as often at the age of fifty as he did at the age of thirty. So when one says

248

that he hasn't changed at all it doesn't mean that he has the same methods, the same ideas, the same education, and the same political goals that he had some years ago. This is not the same as undergoing major changes in philosophy or political views.

For better and for worse, this Humphrey of today is as he is and intends to stay that way.

CHAPTER XIX

Postscript:
Near the President

Washington
Autumn, 1964

Today the accidents and tides of history have entirely changed the future outlook for Hubert H. Humphrey. Surprising turns of fate—some cruel, some kind—have given him a far larger prominence in the national spotlight. Even before Mr. Johnson tapped Mr. Humphrey, the Democratic vice-presidential candidacy of 1964 had become the most discussed second place in American history.

Now it is the intention of President Johnson to give Mr. Humphrey more power than any Vice President has ever had. Mr. Nixon was steadily given more and more information as Vice President, and Mr. Johnson himself when he was Vice President was given a handsome office in the White House. But if fortune continues to smile on Mr. Humphrey, it appears that tomorrow he will have more Vice-Presidential power than either of them ever had. He will have a great deal to do as he works just one heartbeat away from the Presidency.

Today Senator Humphrey is 53 years old, so if Mr. Johnson should stay in office for two terms, Mr. Humphrey would still be, at 61, young enough to be a Presidential candidate. His earliest assignments from Mr. Johnson indicate, however, that even if that should never come to pass, his unique position will enable him to exert a decisive influence upon the conduct of the nation's affairs, most particularly in the area towards which his father guided him, "the quest for peace."

Mr. Humphrey's Recent Record. This biography, originally published in 1960, was edited and revised to provide useful information for readers in time for the 1964 campaign, and it is not possible to review in detail the numerous interests and achievements of the Senator in recent years.

But the main facts are that after his defeats in the 1960 Wisconsin and West Virginia primaries, and the nomination of John F. Kennedy, Mr. Humphrey did not become merely a Senator from Minnesota. He became a close advisor and close personal friend of the late President Kennedy. He became the Majority Whip for the Democrats in the Senate. And he went on to achieve many legislative triumphs. Since the assassination of Mr. Kennedy, he has become an intimate advisor to the new President.

In recent years, Senator Humphrey's reputation has continued to grow nationally, mainly because of his successful management and achievement of the nuclear test-ban treaty which stopped Russia and the U.S. from testing atomic bombs in the atmosphere, and his remarkable handling with Senator Everett Dirksen (R., Illinois) of the difficult Senate consideration of the Civil Rights Act. However, Humphrey's speaking ability, his parliamentary ability and his liaison between the White House and the Congress have covered dozens of other subjects, first under Mr. Kennedy and then with Mr. Johnson.

Many years ago, the first bill the young Humphrey introduced in the Senate was the forerunner of a medical aid bill which can truly be considered a predecessor to Medicare. He is still one of the best-informed men in the Senate on health problems. He was the author of the National Defense Education Act. He was the principal architect of the Arms Control and Disarmament Agency. As discussed elsewhere in the book, he was the person who thought up the Peace Corps, an idea which John Kennedy borrowed from him and developed. He has been a key advisor in the development of the Youth Corps and the "attack on poverty."

As Chairman of the Senate Government Operations Subcommittee on Reorganization, he has recently completed a far-reaching investigation of Food and Drug Administration handling of prescription drugs.

Senator Humphrey remains a firm supporter of fair-trade legislation which is of great importance to the small retailer. As a matter of fact, Mr. Humphrey is a businessman himself. He still retains his interest in the family drugstore and is still its unsalaried president.

It has become apparent in the last two or three years that

while he retains his deep convictions on certain matters such as disarmament and civil rights, he is more willing than he was as a young man to listen to the views of others and to seek some accommodation or compromise. It is this spirit of conciliation that lay behind his victory after the weeks-long filibuster against the Civil Rights Act of 1964.

This was the most far-reaching Act to assist minorities passed by the Congress in many generations. Senator Humphrey established a close and friendly relationship with the man whom he personally likes although they often disagree politically—namely, the Republican leader, Senator Dirksen. Day-by-day and hour-by-hour Humphrey labored until he was sure where every man in the Senate stood on every shading of opinion relating to every clause in the law. It was Senator Humphrey who long before the "long hot summer" of 1964 had sold President Kennedy on the absolute necessity of including in this national legislation strong provisions relating to equal employment opportunity and public accommodations.

As 1964 started, Senator Humphrey prepared himself mentally and physically for the civil rights battle. One afternoon the writer of this book visited him just as the civil rights debate and filibuster got under way. He found the Senator in what one Washington editor calls "Humphrey's high good humor." Senator Humphrey had taken a rest—one of the few he ever took. He had reduced in weight, and was entering upon this contest not only as a politician but as an athlete who knew that it would be an enormous drain upon his physical stamina and nervous system. There is no record, in spite of the sometimes intense nature of the struggle, that the Senator ever lost his temper in the hundreds of encounters with others who were necessary to get this bill through.

As a result, he became the logical choice at the Democratic Convention to work out the compromise regarding the controversial seating of delegates from Mississippi and Alabama. For a time this contest appeared to be a serious split which might result in a walk-out similar to the walk-out which Senator Humphrey had provoked with his fiery speech in 1948. In the year 1964, Senator Humphrey, seeking a common ground, was able to work out a compromise which averted a walk-out. Thus his work was vital in keeping the Democratic Party together in a year when its leaders were working desperately for unity.

Senator Humphrey has long been accepted by those businessmen who have had some contact with him. The businessmen of Minnesota look upon him as the best kind of representative they could have in Washington. The Senator has often made outstanding successes in speeches and conferences with business groups.

To some this raises a question of whether the Senator is still to be classed as a liberal. Sometimes today the Senator, like many other people, says that he is tired of the label of liberal and that he finds it vague. Recently he has said he would rather be called "a moderate progressive," a name which, of course, is a close echo of what President Johnson has said about himself, namely that LBJ is a "prudent progressive."

In 1964 there were three books published under Senator Humphrey's name. They are *Moral Crisis*, on the subject of civil rights, a book called *War on Poverty*, and one called *The Cause Is Mankind*. The latter book is subtitled, "A Liberal Program for Modern America."

Meanwhile, few liberals would doubt that Hubert Humphrey remains their main representative in national life. Although Senator Eugene McCarthy had nominated Adlai Stevenson for President at the Los Angeles Convention in 1960, Senator McCarthy's voting record and philosophy are not so liberal as Senator Humphrey's, and therefore President Johnson's choice was seen to be in the direction of liberalism. Political observers in Washington felt that the President's selection of Humphrey for the ticket would help to keep up the spirits and hold together the liberal wing of the Democratic Party. Strangely enough, considering the bitter primary campaigns which John F. Kennedy and Humphrey had waged in 1960, it was felt that Hubert Humphrey would help to keep many Kennedy supporters actively interested in the Democratic Party as Johnson and Humphrey called for their help in carrying forth the ideals for which John F. Kennedy had been such an eloquent spokesman.

To some extent, the changes in the Senator are partly changes of style—not that he has changed even his style very much—but he does have a greater willingness to listen, and he has learned many of the procedures by which things are best done in Washington. Recently he said, "In the Senate you learn manners . . . you learn to have manners without sacrificing convictions."

The Race for the Vice-Presidency. Senator Humphrey's new patience was sorely tried in the early months of 1964 in the curious drama which developed around the question of who would be the Number Two man on the Democratic ticket in 1964.

When Washington recovered from the shock of the assassination of President Kennedy, political interest in the Democratic Party centered on who would be the running-mate of Mr. Johnson. It was a situation unprecedented in American history for several reasons. One was that the Kennedy family had occupied unique positions of power. Many considered them a kind of "American royal family," with a member in the White House, a young brother, Edward Kennedy, in the Senate, and another brother in a position almost comparable to that of a Crown Prince, Attorney General Robert F. Kennedy. John Kennedy had done something unprecedented in nominating his brother to the Cabinet. Many Washington insiders before the assassination expected Robert F. Kennedy to do something still more unprecedented, namely, to run for President when John F. Kennedy had finished the two terms to which he would be limited by the Constitution. After the assassination, many Kennedy supporters wanted Johnson to choose Robert Kennedy as his Vice-President.

Although many different Democrats were considered by the President and by politicians as possible Vice-Presidential material, to many insiders the choice always seemed to lie between Robert F. Kennedy and Senator Humphrey.

On the side of Mr. Kennedy was the fact that no man in history had ever been closer to a President than Robert Kennedy was to his brother. Mr. Kennedy was intimately familiar not only with domestic affairs, and with the business of managing Democratic campaigns, but also in the field of security affairs. And of course, he had the magic of the Kennedy name. In early 1964 there was a special poignancy about the name of Kennedy, and after the tragedy there was tremendous feeling that JFK's program simply must go forward. There was a strong emotion, not often expressed but still very deep, that there should be a Kennedy in the White House, and therefore Robert Kennedy deserved it almost by right. Except for a madman's bullet, there would have been a Kennedy in the White House and here in the person of Robert Kennedy was a man who was accustomed to being an assistant to the President.

Against Mr. Kennedy there were several factors in the minds of politicians. One was the fact that he was young, another that he had never held elective office, i.e., he had not campaigned for himself, and another, perhaps the one most mentioned, was that it had fallen to him as Attorney General to take the steps in support of civil rights which had made him unpopular in the South.

According to White House assistants, however, and in the insight of many politicians, a more telling argument against Mr. Kennedy was that he and Mr. Johnson did not get along well. They did not see situations and issues in the same way, although they were essentially in agreement as to the major policies of the country. Robert Kennedy had been opposed to the selection of Lyndon Johnson as Vice-President, and even in the first hours when his brother had selected Johnson to be the nominee for number two man on the ticket, Robert Kennedy had still spoken out against Johnson. Thus, in the White House in the winter and spring of 1963 and 1964, there sometimes seemed to be two camps of persons; those who had been devoted to John Kennedy and were now closely connected with Robert, and those who had followed the career and the star of Lyndon B. Johnson. In American history there have been a few cases where the President and Vice-President did not like each other and hardly spoke to each other. In the present day, when the Vice-Presidency is seen to be so much more important than it had been in the past, it was considered essential that the President of the United States have a man close to him in the role of Vice-President with whom he would be largely in agreement. It is said by some that actually Senator Eugene McCarthy of Minnesota and Mr. Johnson are closer personal friends than Senator Humphrey and Johnson. But as a matter of fact, as mentioned earlier in this book, the warm friendship between Mr. Johnson and Mr. Humphrey goes back many years.

Early in 1964 the country saw something it had never before seen, namely, the spectacle of people actively campaigning for the Vice-Presidency and trying hard not to appear to be campaigning. As William V. Shannon, astute Washington correspondent for the New York *Post*, described it, men were campaigning for Vice-President in much the same way as candidates ran for President 100 years ago. The candidates made no major public statements about their ambitions, but they were very careful in their speeches generally. They wrote many letters. They took foreign tours. They encouraged friends to speak at the White House in their behalf. They gave many interviews. They received many visitors and they kept themselves informed and ready to help the White House at any time.

Literally dozens of people were mentioned by the President or in the press as possible candidates for Vice-President. The situation was such a subject of gossip and of jockeying for position that at times it really became somewhat comical. Hubert Humphrey's keen sense of humor led him to say, "Just look at what's happened. The President sent Bobby Kennedy to the Far East. He sent Sargent Shriver to deliver a message to the Pope. Adlai Stevenson got to escort Mrs. Johnson when she went to the theatre in New York, so I asked the President, 'Who is going to enroll Lynda Bird in George Washington University? I'll volunteer.'"

No President could be more aware of the importance of the office of Vice-President than is Mr. Johnson. He had seen what happened in Washington when Mr. Harry Truman had to take over and start out unprepared, without any inside information, because in those days the Vice-President was not briefed on important affairs. Mr. Johnson, when he was Majority Leader, had seen the illnesses of Mr. Eisenhower and how Mr. Nixon on three different occasions had thought that he might have to take over the Presidency at any time.

Then in Dallas on November 22, 1963, Mr. Johnson himself had to take over the reins of power without a moment's notice. Mr. Johnson had been the first Vice-President ever to be given an office in the White House itself—in the Executive Office Building just across the way from the President's own office on the White House grounds. It is Mr. Johnson's stated intention to give his Vice-President even more inside information, and an office that will actually be closer to the President's famous Oval Office.

The President took until mid-summer to make an announcement that among the persons he was considering for the Vice-Presidency he had ruled out all Cabinet level officials. There were many reasons given for ruling out the Cabinet. They included the fact that Cabinet Officers generally do not have elective experience and that being in the Cabinet they could not take an active part in the election campaign if nominated. Washington insiders felt certain that

Mr. Johnson had ruled out all consideration of Sargent Shriver, Secretary Rusk, Secretary McNamara, and Attorney General Kennedy solely for the purpose of getting a whole group of persons to be dropped out at the time he ruled out one above all, namely, Robert Kennedy. He did not wish to single out Robert Kennedy.

This announcement, while it narrowed the field, did not absolutely end the suspense as to who might become the Vice-Presidential nominee. Mr. Johnson still kept talking about other names. He still kept asking visitors to his office what they thought of this one or that one. He would ask visitors to suggest men who might make a good Vice-President.

It was not until the day before the Atlantic City Democratic Convention closed that Mr. Johnson made the announcement in Washington that he had picked Hubert Humphrey to be his running-mate. The President added drama to the announcement by deciding to fly to Atlantic City a day early. Thus he personally gave the convention his announcement that he had picked Senator Humphrey.

When President Johnson spoke to the convention on August 27 to announce his decision of Humphrey for Vice-President, he said, "I have reached it after discussions with outstanding Americans in every area of our national life. I have reached it after long and prayerful thought, consulting my own experience of that office and the burdens that it brings. All of this has had a single guide, to find a man best qualified to assume the office of President of the United States, should that day come. I have found such a man." The President added:

"The qualities that he brings to office will help make the Vice-Presidency an important instrument of the executive branch. From that office he can help connect Congress to the White House and he can help carry America around the world. And I want to say to you that I feel strengthened knowing that he is at my side at all times in the great work of your country and your government.

"Nothing has given me greater support in the past nine months than my knowledge of President Kennedy's confidence that I could continue the task that he began.

"I have found a man that I can trust in the same way . . ."

257

The Polls and the VP. Aside from the question of whether a Vice-President is capable of being President, and the question of whether he is a man who gets along with the man who is President, there is, of course, another tremendous consideration in our form of Government. That is the question, "How many votes will the VP nominee bring to the ticket?"

In December, 1963, after President Kennedy was assassinated, a poll by the Associated Press showed that throughout the country Democratic county chairmen thought that Humphrey was the Party's best choice for Vice-President. Robert Kennedy was a close second. In this poll Humphrey received 185 votes and Kennedy 166. The other candidates were far behind. For example, Mr. Stevenson, 75, Mr. Wagner, 47, and Sargent Shriver, 63.

In polls conducted by Louis Harris in April, in early July and in late July, the surveyors did not ask Democratic leaders but asked *voters* and found that Robert Kennedy was more popular with voters than was Senator Humphrey. For example, the voters went for Robert Kennedy in April to the tune of 44% whereas only 11% went for Senator Humphrey. The interesting thing about these three polls was, however, that in each poll Senator Humphrey got increasingly more votes and Robert Kennedy in each poll got fewer votes as the emotional impact of the assassination died down. During this period, of course, Robert Kennedy was not nearly so much in the public eye as he had been under the Presidency of his brother. Senator Humphrey was even more in the public eye than ever as he was leading the fight for the civil rights act. Since they were not actually matched against each other in an open campaign, there is no real way of telling which of them would have gained the most votes for the ticket. That may never be known for certain. In any case, it is not just a question of total votes, but of the states in which the votes would be gained in order to tip the balance of electoral votes. Perhaps even more influential were a poll taken by Public Opinion Surveys and polls taken of newspaper editors and members of Congress. The Public Opinion Survey study, made during the last two weeks of May, compared the performance of a hypothetical Johnson-Humphrey ticket with a Johnson-Robert Kennedy lineup, as against a Goldwater-Scranton ticket. The results showed Johnson-Humphrey drawing 2.1% more of the total vote than Johnson-Kennedy. The polls of editors and

Congressmen, taken in early June, indicated that the largest percentage of both these important groups believed that pairing Johnson with Hubert Humphrey would give Democrats "the strongest possible ticket."

Very possibly, one factor weighed more in Lyndon Johnson's mind than any pollster's figures: the fact that it was in the Midwest that the most states were in the "contested" category—where the contest between the Johnson and Goldwater tickets could swing either way. It is, of course, in the Midwest that Hubert Humphrey draws unequaled strength.

The question of Humphrey against a Kennedy may be interesting again in the future as it has been in the past. It may well be that in the future turn of events there will be a struggle in the Democratic Party for the Presidential nomination between Robert Kennedy and Hubert Humphrey, just as there was in the primary campaign of 1960 when Mr. Humphrey and Mr. John F. Kennedy battled it out in Wisconsin and West Virginia and Humphrey went down to defeat. Nor is this competition with Robert Kennedy the only possibility. Edward Kennedy, a much younger man, will in eight years be old enough to be considered Presidential timber and, if his popular following develops, it might be that Hubert Humphrey would by fate have had a career in which he had to face the Kennedys four times. He contested with John F. Kennedy for Vice President in 1956, then for President in the primaries of 1960. Then in 1964 he was paired against Robert Kennedy in the strange Vice-Presidential sweepstakes. Possibly he will meet either Robert or Edward Kennedy in the Presidential politics of 1968.

As of now there have been three Humphrey-Kennedy contests and the score is two to one in favor of the Kennedys, but Mr. Humphrey has won the current round. In politics it is always today.

Following the elimination of the Cabinet, President Johnson let it be known that he would not discourage expressions of sentiment concerning Vice-Presidential possibilities from the 50 states, provided that such expressions also included the proviso that the President's choice would be accepted, whomever he might be. At that time the Senator's supporters launched a quiet drive which resulted, among other things, in public endorsements of support from 30 state delegations to the national convention and from 40 Senators. Beyond this, many governors, Congressmen and state chairmen *pri-*

vately made known their sentiments to President Johnson, as did labor and farm leaders. By the time the convention began, a national consensus had been formed. (A majority of the Democratic governors present at the White House meeting preceding the convention were also on record for HH, and so expressed themselves.) There was also a flood of mail to the White House from business leaders, ordinary citizens, and political leaders—uninspired by HH supporters —in support of Humphrey for the nomination. In addition, major national columnists and newspapers had added their endorsements before the convention. By the time of the convention, President Johnson would have sawed many Democrats off limbs had he chosen anyone but Humphrey.

Among those most active in bringing about this national consensus were William Connell, the Senator's administrative assistant; Max Kampelman, a Humphrey adviser and former staff member; Ronald Stinnett, 1960 chairman of the Kennedy campaign in Minnesota; Pat O'Connor, Minneapolis attorney; Marvin Rosenberg of New York, a longtime Humphrey supporter; and Ted Van Dyk, on leave from his job as Washington lobbyist for the European Common Market. These efforts were noted in newspapers following the nominating convention in Atlantic City, but were unreported previously.

Washington observers felt that LBJ had held off the decision to the last to add suspense to the convention, to give all possible thought to the matter, and to show the country that a great deal of consideration had gone into the selection. There was one additional purpose. By leaving it open in that fashion, the friends of Hubert Humphrey were able, before and at the convention, to build up more and more sentiment for the man they admired. So, after the President announced his selection, the convention nominated Humphrey by acclamation. Some other course of action might not have been so long-drawn-out a procedure, but it would not have produced such an unusual consensus. The President himself made the selection and at the same time the convention itself *also made the selection*. The delegates enthusiastically supported the one-time controversial figure of Hubert Humphrey. In the larger context, this became a part of the drive for unity which Mr. Johnson had been pursuing.

In the story of Hubert Humphrey's life, it was his most triumphant hour. In spite of the many last-ditch battles and hard-fought bitter struggles in which he had been engaged, he received a tremendous ovation by an audience representing all shades of opinion. As this book indicates, there have been many defeats and victories in Mr. Humphrey's life. No triumph could have been sweeter than that moment at Atlantic City when the delegates gave the remarks of President Johnson a standing ovation, and Mr. Humphrey was applauded by delegates from all over the nation.

In his acceptance speech the next night, Senator Humphrey devoted most of his time to a discussion of the presidency, to words of praise for the record of President Johnson, and to an attack upon the opposition and "the temporary spokesman of the Republican Party."

In this speech Humphrey spoke earnestly of the great responsibilities of the presidency in the thermonuclear age and said:

"There is no margin for error. The leader of the free world, the leader of American democracy, holds in his hands the destinies not only of his own people but holds in his hands the destinies of all mankind.

"Yes, yes, the President of the United States must be a man of calm and deep assurance who knows his country and who knows his people."

In praising Lyndon Johnson he said, "Above all, he must be a man of clear mind and of sound judgment and a man who can lead, a man who can decide, a man of purpose and conviction . . ."

In his first appearances on the national stage in 1948, Mr. Humphrey had spoken out in a way as a spokesman for one section of the country and as a spokesman for one viewpoint. But in his acceptance speech at Atlantic City he sought to represent himself and his party as a ticket which appealed to all Americans. He specifically invited Republicans to join in with the Democratic campaign.

Taking an indirect attack at what he called "the Goldwater Party" he said:

"While others may appeal to passions and prejudice, and appeal to fear and bitterness, we of the Democratic Party call upon all Americans to join us in making our country a land of opportunity for our young, a home of security and dignity for our elderly, and a place of compassion and care for our afflicted."

Making a direct appeal to the Republicans, Mr. Humphrey said:

"I say to those responsible and forward-looking Republicans who put our country above their party—and there are thousands of them—we welcome you to the banner of Lyndon B. Johnson; we welcome your support.

"Yes, we extend the hand of fellowship. We ask you to join us tonight, for this President, my fellow Americans, is the President of all of the American people."

Mr. Humphrey (and Mr. Johnson in his own speech) made clear that the Democratic Party was out to capture all the voters in the middle whether they were Democrats, Independents, or Republicans. The Democrats were also determined to be a party which did not recognize a division of the country into west and east or north and south. In part this was a response to the San Francisco meeting of the Republicans which had laid such emphasis upon the revolt of Western political leaders against the East Coast and of Southern political leaders against progress in integration and civil rights.

Senator Humphrey, in his acceptance speech, said that Mr. Johnson was "the President in the great American tradition—for labor and for business; no class conflicts; for the farm family that will receive the unending attention and care of this President and for the city worker; for North and for the South; for East and for the West. This is our President! President Lyndon Johnson represents—in fact he is the embodiment—of the spirit of national unity, the embodiment of national purpose, the man in whose hands we place our lives, our fortunes and our sacred honor."

In conclusion Mr. Humphrey said:

"I am proud to be the friend of this great President, and I am very proud that he has asked this convention to select me as his running mate.

"And I ask you, my fellow Americans, I ask you to walk with us, to work with us, to march forward with us, to help President Johnson build a great society for America of the future."

The Team of Johnson and Humphrey. How well will these

two men, both full of energy, both generating ideas and action, work together?

The answer is that they have worked together for years and have had a closer relationship since Mr. Johnson entered the White House. Some think they will work like twins because they are really very much alike. Others think it would have been better if Mr. Johnson had picked someone quite different from him. Yet, after all, they come from different parts of the nation, have had different political philosophies, and have rather different interests in public issues. They have different tastes in reading and speechmaking, and many different friends as well as many friends in common.

Washington observers thought they were different enough to provide a contrast and to insure that many different persons had an open door at the top. At the same time, Washington had long noted that both loved politics, loved crowds, and loved to talk. Mr. Humphrey has more of a reputation for being a non-stop talker, but many newspapermen had noted that Mr. Johnson also hates to say goodbye to a listening group or even to an individual listener.

Against Humphrey in 1964, people still mentioned that he talked too much or that his speeches were too long. His admirers thought he was articulate; his detractors thought he was glib. Some commentators thought that both Mr. Johnson and Mr. Humphrey had a certain down-to-earth manner and others said that in certain ways they were both "rather corny." To some persons "folksy" is a favorable adjective, and to others, it seems to mean "common."

The fact that Senator Humphrey likes to talk was referred to by President Johnson on the day after their acceptance speeches, as they left Atlantic City for a week-end political conference in Texas.

As they were leaving a committee room in an Atlantic City hotel, the President left first and went with aides towards a waiting limousine. Senator Humphrey for a moment lingered behind with members of the committee. Suddenly, Jack J. Valenti, the President's first assistant, noticed that the Vice Presidential nominee was missing. He exclaimed. "My God, he's making a speech! Get Hubert!" he told a Secret Service agent.

The President smiled and said, "You know Hubert. That's one of the problems I took into consideration when I picked him."

A few moments later, Mr. Humphrey turned up and

jumped into the limousine with the President, and they were on their way out of Atlantic City toward Texas.

Walter Lippmann was the foremost of many commentators who now have pointed out that Humphrey and Johnson are "the same breed of public men." To him it was clear that these two men do not complement each other; "these two men duplicate each other." Lippmann explained that though Humphrey "is a brilliant controversialist, [he] is by instinct a peacemaker, conciliator, and harmonizer." Lippmann wrote: "Both men have proved that they know how to make our difficult system of Government work."

There are certain to be many lengthy conversations in the White House as long as Mr. Johnson and Mr. Humphrey are partners in deciding what would be the very best way to work.

New Importance of the Vice-President. Ever since Harry Truman took over the Presidency, there has been a steady growth of the duties of the Vice-President.

Every President who has succeeded to the White House through the death of another has served some period without a Vice-President, and Mr. Johnson felt that absence very much in the months after the assassination of Mr. Kennedy. Starting immediately after the Democratic Convention, he began to give special assignments in the campaign and in other areas to Mr. Humphrey. When Mr. Johnson gave his unprecedented nomination speech he gave an importance to the Vice-Presidency which it had never had before.

He also made public the fact that he was going to take several additional steps to give Mr. Humphrey special responsibilities in looking after foreign affairs, disarmament, the general policies relating to what he calls the "Quest for Peace," and to use him as a roving ambassador to, in the President's words, "Carry America around the world." He also announced his intention to have Mr. Humphrey look after problems of legislation and executive action relating to farm problems.

Moreover, President Johnson has revived discussion which had appeared at times in the past about the need to provide an official residence for the number-two man of the executive branch. In other days, it has been noted that the Vice-President, who frequently greets foreign visitors and frequently takes trips abroad, has no special arrangement for formal receptions and dinner parties which he might hold in the national capitol for domestic and foreign visitors. There is no suggestion now of providing a "second White House," but merely of giving the V-P a home which would have a capacious dining-room and reception room where the Vice-President could better fulfill his social obligations. Much of the business of state is conducted in an informal manner at such affairs. Both the New York *Times* and the Washington *Post* led the newspaper response of approval to this idea. In the time of President Eisenhower, this was frequently proposed for Richard M. Nixon, but at that time the Congress was generally Democratic and it refused to make such a provision for a Republican. It is considered likely that this will be given more thorough consideration in the near future.

Hubert Humphrey Is Unique. Today Hubert Humphrey is a unique figure in American politics.

None of the other major candidates in the 1964 election has behind him such a record of liberalism, such a reputation for knowledge of foreign affairs, such an ability to charm an audience with his eloquence, nor such a well-deserved reputation for scholarship and intellectual ability.

To practical politicians, however, there is something still more amazing about Hubert Humphrey. That is the simple fact that he has never had money—not from inheritance, not from business, and not even from backers of his political campaigns. No other national political figure has had so little funds to spend on his campaigns. Like the traditional "log-cabin candidate," Hubert Humphrey has risen from obscurity and has had first-hand observation of poverty. Today, he is a relatively poor man compared with other leading political figures on the American scene. The fact is that nearly all presidential candidates of the last few elections have been millionaires. Mr. Kennedy and Mr. Rockefeller, of course, represented great fortunes. Mr. Goldwater and Mr. Johnson are both millionaires, not through inheritance, but through their own business abilities. Hubert Humphrey stands almost alone in national politics as a man who made it the hard way. It is also interesting that he has done this in less than 20 years. Just twenty years ago he was, in his own expression, "pushing bowls of chili across the drugstore counter in Huron."

In understanding what is going on in the world today, both Mr. Johnson and Mr. Humphrey have knowledge from the inside of some of the sentiments which motivate people in the new countries—people who are struggling to arrive at prosperity, at recognition of their talents, and at an understanding of human dignity. Most countries in the world are not ruled by men of inherited wealth and a background of cultivated education. Their rulers do not have the tradition of the Old School Tie. As a matter of fact, one-fourth of the countries of the world have governments which came into power through revolution or violence. This is a turbulent world in which the *have-nots* greatly outnumber the *haves*, and governments are faced with the rising expectations of people who want a better break than their grandfathers had.

Today, as these new countries look toward America for help and leadership, they wonder whether we Americans have settled down and forgotten our tradition of revolution for human liberty. They wonder if we are now self-satisfied or whether we are still intent upon a program of evolution for human advancement and human welfare. It may turn out to be a fortunate turn of events for America that Lyndon Johnson and Hubert Humphrey alike have a first-hand knowledge of what it is like to be at the bottom of the heap.

Mr. Humphrey, in particular, in the days of the dust storms in South Dakota, and of the radical and sometimes desperate policies of farmer and labor voters in Minnesota, saw with his own eyes the time in America when we were closest to domestic revolution. In South Dakota he saw the dust and despair of the Thirties. In Louisiana he saw how poverty and unrest had supported the Huey P. Long regime. And in Minnesota, Humphrey—alone of all of the major American figures of our day—had recognized and battled face-to-face, American voters who were led by American Communists. These were not imaginary names and lists, and Humphrey and his associates did not defeat them by smears and secret police, but in hard-fought debates and political combat.

Mr. Humphrey's understanding of the human needs and the revolutionary forces of our day has served his country well. At present it appears the main contributions of Hubert H. Humphrey are just beginning.

The safe progress of mankind now depends upon the mutual human understanding of men. Many emerging world leaders are traveling in a few years from simple villages to the age of thermonuclear power. The best debater of Doland,

South Dakota, now has the chance to make his voice heard around the world. And Hubert H. Humphrey is one of the best Americans we could send to speak—and to listen—to the other leaders from the other villages.

Acknowledgments

The author is greatly indebted to Mrs. Evelyn Metzger, Washington editor of Doubleday & Co., who conceived the original idea for this book. Our purpose was to produce a reasonable introduction to a man many people will be thinking about in 1960 and perhaps in 1964 and 1968. None of us working on the book has thought expressly of furthering a candidacy or a program, but we hoped that it would appear in time to be of interest in the 1960 political campaigns.

Senator Humphrey, Mrs. Humphrey, and their friends have been outstandingly co-operative, although somewhat nervous since they knew this was not to be an "authorized biography."

Many associates of the senator gave freely of their time and their references and files. Future reporters and biographers will have a wealth of documentation available to them. The senator has taught, written, and practiced in the field of political science. So have many of his friends. There is more material available on this man than on many other American public figures, simply because political scientists around Humphrey have been more aware of the function and needs of the record-keeper and historian.

By and large the senator seems more willing than most politicians to operate in a goldfish bowl. He suggested to his associates that they turn over files and let me go through them. I have seen much of his personal correspondence, a great help in seeing a person as he really is. Such material was not all grist for this book, although some might be for *Time* or for *Confidential* magazine. But the fact that such things were freely shown to me was quite disarming, and to me indicative of an astonishing willingness to say, "I am as I am; judge me by that. I have decided to work and win, or lose, as I am."

Among the Humphrey political associates who have been

of major help were Evron M. Kirkpatrick, who is now executive secretary of the American Political Science Association; William Simms, businessman in Springfield, Virginia; Max N. Kampelman, attorney in Washington, D.C.; and Arthur J. Naftalin, now Commissioner of Public Administration for Governor Freeman.

Governor Orville Freeman, Mrs. Eugenie Anderson, Mr. and Mrs. George Jacobson, Fred Gates, and Herb McClosky, professor at the University of Minnesota, were the principal persons to whom I spoke in Minnesota. I am also indebted to various staff members of the Minneapolis *Star* and *Tribune* for their co-operation in letting me read through files and in selecting outstanding photographs. I am particularly indebted to Charles W. Bailey, who has observed the senator for years, and written a short biography of Humphrey, for the book *Candidates, 1960*.

The few brief days I could spend in Huron and Doland were rare and memorable to me, and retaught me some things about America and Americans that I have tried to put in this book and will return to more than once in the future. I cannot describe the direct quality of Dewey and Hazel Van Dyke, but there is an immediate contact they make with human beings, a contact one sees sometimes in mystics, in great physicians—and in children.

Others in Huron who gave interviews or sent material to me were Carl Bahmeier, Hubert's schoolmate; Bob Lusk, editor of the *Plainsman;* the Rev. Hubert Kitelle, of the First Presbyterian Church; and Rep. George McGovern.

In Doland I found everyone I met was proud of an acquaintance with the Humphrey family and eager to help an outsider understand their world. Mrs. Leslie Coats has acted as my "Doland editor," helping me locate items and get the dates straightened out. But I am also indebted to Al Paine, for many years postmaster of Doland, to Willard Doty, and to Michael Twiss, who today has given banking in Doland a new and better name than it used to have.

Back in Washington, D.C., the member of the senator's staff who has spent many hours assisting the writer of this book is Mr. William Connell.

Of course I am indebted to the interpretations and reporting of many Washington reporters, particularly Douglass Cater in *The Reporter*. Rufus Jarman and Walter Ridder in the *Saturday Evening Post* have each done a sketch. I drew heavily upon articles by and about Humphrey in *The Progressive*, the liberal monthly.

The source I went to most often, however, was the work of Charles E. Gilbert, a doctoral thesis in political science at Northwestern University. Gilbert observed Humphrey for a year and then worked on his staff a year to write "Problems of a Senator; A Study in Legislative Behavior." This writer had not read Gilbert until well along in writing this book, but then found Gilbert's observations and conclusions highly similar to his own. Dr. Gilbert and his work speak for themselves, however, and in future years scholars will find the time to appreciate his contribution to the understanding of Humphrey and the understanding of legislative behavior. Such scholars will also find that I have taken many facts from his 400-page thesis, and owe him a great deal.

In this revision I am indebted more than I can say to Emma Harrison, who volunteered her keen editorial eyes and ideas.